Exam
June 7 4 p.m.
in Knitting Class Room

THE COMPLETE BOOK

OF PROGRESSIVE KNITTING

"Progress is the law of life."

—ROBERT BROWNING

THE COMPLETE BOOK OF

PROGRESSIVE KNITTING

By
IDA RILEY DUNCAN

Instructor Adult Homemaking Classes,
Wayne University, Detroit

WITH FOREWORD BY

JULIA P. GRANT

Supervisor of Home Economics

and

GERTRUDE S. CAPPS

Supervisor of Adult Homemaking,
Detroit Public Schools

LIVERIGHT PUBLISHING CORPORATION

NEW YORK

FOREWORD

by JULIA P. GRANT and
GERTRUDE S. CAPPS

"IN this work, the author has set forth a truly comprehensive word picture of her vast knowledge of knitting. It should prove an invaluable guide to beginners and experienced knitters alike. The method of formulas which she uses, carries the knitter, step by step, from the casting on of the first stitch to the binding off of the finished garment. It removes the uncertainty which has been the bane of knitters for centuries past, and assures a perfect fit of the article she would create."

(signed) Julia P. Grant, Supervisor of
Home Economics, Detroit Public Schools

"For the last four years Mrs. Duncan has been successfully teaching the art of knitting to women in the metropolitan area of Detroit. More than three thousand mothers and homemakers have completed from 12 to 24 intensive weeks of study under her guidance. These adults have participated in classes sponsored by the Adult Homemaking non-credit unit operating out of the College of Education, Wayne University, and the homemaking program in the Detroit Public Evening Schools.

"The constant demand on the part of lay-groups for classes in knitting, new groups as well as those previously contacted, is indicative of the author's ability as a teacher. Techniques which she uses in her teaching are presented here in book form. The printing of this handbook for knitters should be well received."

(signed) Gertrude S. Capps, Supervisor of
Adult Homemaking, Detroit Public Schools

v

ACKNOWLEDGMENTS

THE author wishes to express her grateful appreciation to the many persons who have aided her in the preparation of this book.

Special thanks are due to William Cattell for his untiring efforts in taking the many photographs, and also to my daughter, Peggy, for her assistance with the numerous diagrams, and for her illustrations, without which the book would have little meaning.

To The United States Department of Agriculture, through its various departments, I am greatly indebted for much information and scientific research regarding wool; also to The Royal Society, Agents for Paton and Baldwin's Wools, who furnished me with considerable information on hand-knitting yarns; to The Botany Worsted Mills, manufacturers of Botany top-dyed yarns; to The Associated Wool Industries for their untiring effort in aiding me to obtain special information; and to Fleming Reid and Co., The Worsted Mills, Greenock, Scotland, for their samples showing the processes in manufacturing worsted knitting yarns.

I acknowledge with thanks the generosity of Mrs. A. C. Weibel, Curator of Textiles, Detroit Institute of Arts, in lending me photographs of knitting.

CONTENTS

THE COMPLETE BOOK

OF PROGRESSIVE KNITTING

CHAPTER I

THE HISTORY OF KNITTING

IT IS generally thought that knitting was not one of the early arts. As a matter of fact it is older than history and covers every class and degree from princess to peasant, and takes its place with basketry, braiding, weaving and netting, the earliest forms of textural work. There is no country in the world where some form of knitting is not known and practiced.

The ornamental band of humming birds in Plate I is Peruvian and belongs to the Prato-Nasca Culture dating

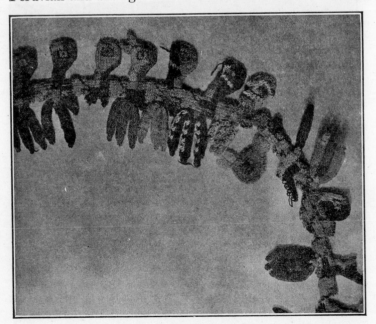

PLATE I. Knitted ornamental band (Peruvian).

1

before 200 A.D. The intricacy of design, the fineness of detail, the craftsmanship and coloring show the degree of efficiency knitting must have reached at this period. The

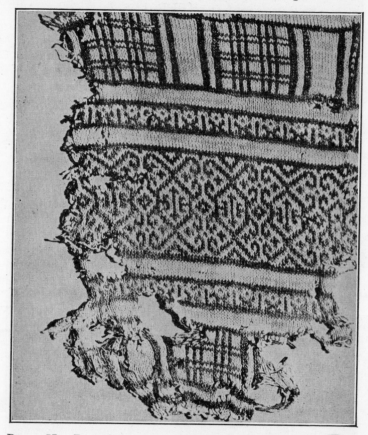

PLATE II.   Burned fragment of blue and white silk (Egyptian).

original band is on display in the Textile Gallery of the Detroit Institute of Arts.

Plate II is a photograph of a burned fragment of knitted blue and white silk that was unearthed from the ruins in Egypt and belongs to the Islamic period of the

12th century. It may have been a shawl of great beauty. The exquisite design and detail may readily be seen here.

The hand-knitted insertions and laces knitted by the women of the ancient city of Syrmia, which is adjacent to Belgrade in Jugoslavia, were the inspirations for some of the openwork lace patterns of today, while many other countries of Europe supplied ideas for a different type of openwork design and different combinations of stitches.

In Germany and Switzerland, the women knit as they sit beside their wares in the market place and even as they walk to and from church, while the women of Iceland and the far countries of the North knit while the old songs are sung and stories are told around the hearth.

In Canada, the British Isles and many countries of Europe and Asia, knitting is learned at a very early age; but in the United States, except for our forebears who settled in this country, little interest in knitting has been shown.

Until recently, any mention of knitting brought a mental picture of Grandmother or Great-grandmother seated comfortably in her rocking chair, a half-knitted sock or mitten growing upon the needles she manipulated with her fingers, and in her lap a ball of yarn fashioned on her spinning wheel. This quaint picture is as progressively correct as would be a picture of a prospective buyer entering a present-day automobile salon to find Elwood T. Haines or R. E. Olds waiting to sell a car of the vintage of his first mechanical brainstorm.

Throughout the centuries, great consideration has been given in some countries to color and design in knitting, and in others to the need for supplying adequate clothing; the actual construction of garments and accessories has received but little consideration and during the World War the same principles were employed for sweaters, mittens and helmets for soldiers and sailors as had been used in the olden days. The result was that hand-knitted articles were perfect in craftsmanship, but only in a few instances were they of the correct shape, hence knitted garments were not generally conceded to be "things of beauty."

During the last few years new interest in knitting has been developed, chiefly by the manufacturers of hand-knitting yarns. Unfortunately, too many knitters relied upon stereotyped directions and designs which left no scope for originality and gave no thought to individual

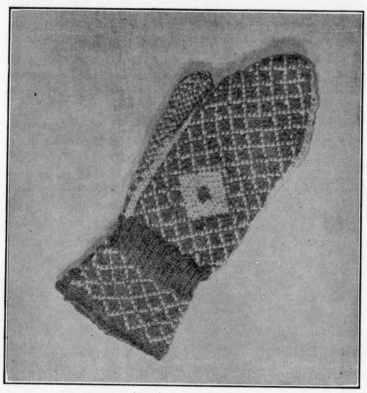

PLATE III.   Decorative mitten.

needs and to differences in material. As a result, the article was often either too big or too small, and was generally unsatisfactory.

Knitting is rich in artistic and constructive possibilities, and in these respects no other craft is more adaptable. Although in "art" there should be no formulas, yet for

PLATE IV. Decorative socks.

knitted garments and accessories—just as in the construction of a beautiful building—there must be principles by which to shape them. When once these are understood, the true joy of knitting follows.

The decorative mitten in Plate III was constructed according to the same formula as is used for all mittens, whatever may be the size, or the material and needles used. (See Chapter on Mittens.)

The above illustration of socks is interesting. The absence of long strands at the back of the cuff on which to catch the fingers is an innovation.

The mitten and the socks were made simply from a stitch gauge and measurements, thus blending aesthetic design with constructive principles.

CHAPTER II

WOOL

HISTORY OF WOOL

To DELVE into the history of wool is to delve into the history of man. One dates back with the other almost to the beginning of time. Earliest recorded history is full of references to shepherds and flocks. Most of us are sufficiently acquainted with the Bible to know that Abel was designated "a keeper of sheep," and we have all heard of Benjamin's coat of many colors.

Exactly how long ago manufactured or processed wool came into use, we do not know. We do know, however, that it dates back many centuries. The early Swiss Lake Dwellers of the Neolithic age, ten to twenty thousand years ago made fabrics from wool. Some of these have been unearthed in the ruins of the villages they inhabited. Alexander of Greece on a crusade to India found wool shawls of exquisite design. It was the Egyptians who gave many processes of wool manufacture to the Greeks. The Greeks gave them to the Romans and from the Romans these processes found their way into the occidental world.

The history of wool in America might well be called a history that repeats itself. The first sheep to arrive in this country were brought to Jamestown in 1609. Necessity demanded protection from the elements, but Americans were not able to follow the artistic manipulation of wool that certain parts of the Old World had achieved. The women of the family spun wool into yarn, made coarse homespuns and knitted heavy sweaters, caps and stockings to keep their families warm.

In 1776 George Washington imported into this country

the best grade of sheep, and he also tried to encourage the American woolen industry by bringing experienced spinners and weavers. In 1800 the first Merino sheep were smuggled from Spain.

Since that period the raising of sheep has grown tremendously, and now there are approximately 50,000,000 head of sheep in the United States which are owned by 600,000 farmers.

MATERIALS FOR HAND-KNITTING

There is a large variety of hand-knitting or "fingering" yarns and threads. Some are made of wool, silk, cotton, linen, rayon, other synthetic materials, rabbit wool, or a mixture of any or several of these, and all have a place in the knitting world.

Yarn is a continuous strand of any kind of twisted material, but is less tightly twisted than thread, which is smooth-finished and consists of several twisted strands of cotton, silk or linen. The threads, therefore, are smooth and uniform in size, and never rough, uneven, fuzzy and nubby as is sometimes the case with yarns.

The quality and appearance of a finished product depends upon the yarn and the thread from which it is made, and each has its individuality and purpose, so before commencing any project, no matter how small, consider the suitability of the material.

As wool is the fiber which is most used for hand-knitting, it is to be studied in greater detail than any other fiber.

WOOL

Wool is a natural animal fiber and is the soft fleecy covering of sheep. Fibers and hairs from other animals are also used. These differ somewhat from wool in structure.

Cashmere is named after the little Cashmere goat which lives among the Himalaya Mountains of India and China. Angora is obtained from the silk hairs of the small Angora rabbit, and the fine, soft hair of the camel is used for fine knitted garments.

Wool is the most important of the animal fibers because of its variety of uses, and is an ideal fiber for the construction of clothing.

CHARACTERISTICS OF WOOL

1. *Wool Is Elastic*

Wool is elastic because of the wonderful structure of its fibers, which vary in length from one to twelve inches. Each individual fiber consists of distinct layers of cells.

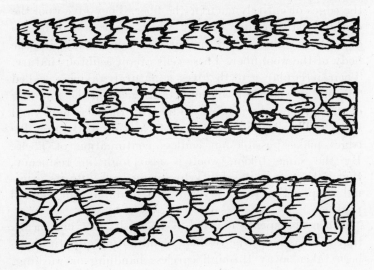

Serrations or Scales

ILLUSTRATION 1. Wool fibers highly magnified.

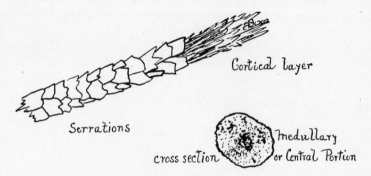

ILLUSTRATION 2. Construction of wool fibers.

The outer layer is made up of flattened, scale-like cells, varying in shape and size, according to the different breeds of sheep. These scales, called serrations, may overlap at the edges or entirely encircle the fiber. They give wool the characteristic felting quality which is possessed by no other fiber. The second, or cortical, layer makes up the body of the wool fiber. These cells are of a fibrous nature. Their irregular growth gives a natural waviness, called "crimp" in wool. It is an important factor in the spinning of fine yarns, because it influences the elasticity and stretch. The elasticity and the interlocking of the saw-like edges make possible an endless continuation of fibers. By the same token, wool is also high in resiliency, that is to say, in its ability to spring back into its original shape. The third layer is the medullary or central portion.

When one speaks of wool as losing its life, one means that the elasticity, the resiliency and felting qualities have been taken away through careless handling or washing. One should remember that wool, like a living thing, should be treated carefully. It is this "life" and elasticity that allow wool clothing to resist wrinkling and, when unduly stretched after hard wear, to return to its original shape.

2. *Wool Absorbs Moisture without Feeling "Clammy"*

All textile fibers absorb some moisture. Wool, however, is capable of holding as much as 30 per cent of its own weight without feeling wet to the touch. That is the reason why it is sometimes heard that "woolen articles have to be dried twice."

3. *Wool Is Exceedingly Strong and Durable*

Yarn specifications state the amount of strain a yarn can endure without breaking. Comparing the tensile strength of metal wires of the same diameter, one can say wool is as strong as metal. Wool is, therefore, most desirable for apparel which is to have hard wear.

4. *Wool Is Thermostatic*

Wool maintains a more even temperature than any other fiber. It therefore gives greater protection against extremes of heat and cold as well as against sudden changes of temperature. It will be seen, then, that wool is an important asset to health in general.

5. *Wool Is Light in Weight*

Wool may be knitted or woven into fabrics of delicate sheerness, unsurpassed by any other fiber, and lightness is one of the essentials of modern attire.

6. *Wool Is Fire Resistant*

Garments of pure wool yarns are hard to ignite even with an open flame, because wool is slow to oxidize. This is a great protection in the home, especially where there are young children.

7. *Wool Means Long Wear*

Throughout the ages wool has been noted for its lasting wearing qualities.

SHEEP

The temperate zone is the natural home of sheep, but they also thrive to a certain extent in the mountainous regions of the torrid zone. Australia and New Zealand have vast areas of grazing lands and for years these countries supplied about two-thirds of the world's wool supply. Southern parts of South America and Africa possess almost similar conditions and now produce large quantities of wool.

The United States ranks third as a wool producing country, with every state in the Union producing wool. The most productive wool growing states are those in the mountains and on the west coast; Texas is the largest producer, with Montana second. It is generally considered that the finest wools come from Ohio—which is neither in the mountains nor on the west coast—because the "farm" method is used. The flocks are small, generally fenced in, and carefully guarded against the weather.

There are numerous breeds of sheep, some of which have been developed for the growing of wool and others for the production of meat. Also different types of sheep yield different types of wool fiber, and different parts of an animal give different grades of fineness. The wool from the shoulders of the sheep is best for strength, quality and length, and the quality decreases backwards over the animal to the thighs and belly, while the wool on the legs is torn and ragged.

FACTORS THAT DETERMINE THE GRADE OF WOOL

It is possible to grade the breeds of sheep into three classes, according to the length of the fibers which they produce. A general classification may be made for fineness and length of fiber, since the fiber wools are generally shorter and the coarser wools longer.

Merino and Rambouillet are producers of fine wool. Cheviot, Dorset, Southdown, Shropshire, Suffolk, Oxford, Hampshire, Tunis and Corriedale are producers of medium wool, and Cotswold, Leicester, Lincoln and Romney Marsh produce fibers which are uniformly long and lustrous.

Fine Wool Breeds

Merino sheep were first smuggled from Spain during the year 1800. All fine wool sheep are descendants of earlier Spanish stock. The length of the Merino wool varies, less than one third of the fleeces being long enough for combing. The fleeces of fine wool sheep are also heavy in oil, sometimes losing over 70 per cent in scouring. Rambouillet fleeces vary in fineness and length, but are usually quite dense. They carry less oil than the American Merinos.

Medium Wool Breeds

The Southdown, Shropshire, Hampshire, Oxford and Suffolk breeds are collectively referred to as "down" breeds because of the nature of the country in which they were developed. Southern England is characterized by ranges of hills or "downs." The fleece of these breeds occupies a middle position between the length and coarseness of the long wools and the extreme fineness and density of the fine wools.

Coarse Wool Breeds

The long wool breeds, the Cotswold, Leicester, Lincoln and Romney Marsh are the largest breeds of sheep. Their fleeces are open or loose as compared with the fine wools and middle wools, and are coarser and very long.

Whatever the breed of sheep there are certain conditions which affect the grade of the wool fiber, notably the nature of the pasture and climatic conditions; in the case of farm sheep which are fenced in, the fiber depends upon how they are stabled during the bad weather. In the open range method, which is largely used in the west, the sheep graze on the open range sheltering on the lee side of a hill, and the character and quantity of foreign matter in the raw wool vary considerably. How the sheep are sheared and the way in which the fleeces are handled and packed are factors influencing the quality of the wool.

To a great extent the traditional hand shears have been superseded by electrical equipment for machine shearing. In the case of farm sheep the farmers pen the herds into their barns to await the arrival of the shearers; their sole business is sheep shearing, which they perform with their motor-driven clippers. The average sheep yields its entire coat in one piece with very little protest. A good shearer is able to shear from 175 to 200 sheep in one day. The United States does most of its shearing in the spring. It is done twice a year in Texas, New Mexico, Arizona and Southern California, owing to the favorable climatic conditions.

After the shearing, the fleece is shipped. Most fleeces go to Boston, Chicago, or Philadelphia. Boston is the largest wool center. The wool dealers serve as distributors for the growers. In recent years growers have formed co-operatives with organizations of their own, having central warehouses and offices in Boston.

After being sold, the wool, in the form of tightly rolled fleeces, must be opened and separated according to diameter, length and quality of fiber.

SORTING

In a large, light, airy room arranged with rows of tables which have wire-meshed tops, the wool is sorted. The sorter removes the dirtiest parts and the largest burrs, and at the same time the coarse dirt falls through the wires. He next separates the different qualities, placing each in distinctive piles. The finer wools of even quality require little sorting, but the coarser wools vary greatly in fineness and length. Modern improvements in machinery have, however, decreased the necessity for close sorting.

SCOURING

Wool in its natural state is called grease wool or "wool in the grease." It contains substances of two types, fatty and foreign. Each wool fiber is surrounded by sebaceous glands which secrete wool grease, and sweat glands which secrete sweat. This grease prevents the matting or the felting of the fibers when in the fleece, and it is sold for making soap and axle grease and is used as a base for lanolin. The foreign substances which have to be removed are the dirt and vegetable matter, and the impurities have to be removed without injury to the fibers. Large wooden or metallic bowls or troughs are used for this purpose. Usually there are four troughs altogether; of these, three contain cleansing baths of water in which is dissolved soda potash or other dirt-removing chemicals, while a fourth contains vegetable oil to preserve the elasticity, lubricate the fibers, and reduce breakage. Big iron forks slowly move the wool forward and immerse it in the scouring liquid from one trough to another until it finally drops like soft white flakes of snow into a funnel. It is then blown by fans through a drier called a hydroextractor to the card room.

During the scouring process the wool loses in weight. This is known as shrinkage.

CARDING

All wool fibers, no matter what their length, must be untangled in order to be spun with any degree of evenness. Carding is the name given to the process of straightening out textile fibers. This was formerly done by hand. Two cards or boards were covered with little wire teeth and the raw material placed upon one of them. One card was raked over the other and the process repeated many times until the wool came out a soft ball with no tangles remaining, and ready to be drawn out and twisted into yarn.

The same principle is now employed in factories. In the card room the "scoured" wool is fed into carding machines. These machines consist of a series of great rollers covered with sheets of rubber, over which wire teeth are set closely together. The raw wool is licked from one roller to another, the wires picking the fibers apart and at the same time throwing off waste material, such as burrs. The wool emerges from the last of the wire-covered rollers in a soft light roll about two inches in diameter, and is then wound into a ball known as a card-ball.

COMBING

The principle of "worsted" spinning consists in having the fibers parallel and of a uniform length. The "combing" machine throws out all fibers below a given length, therefore the criss-crossed fibers of the card ball are first straightened and the short fibers separated, while the long fibers are made into a soft, smooth strand. This operation is known as combing.

Fibers 2½ inches or more are usually required for successful combing. These fibers are used in making worsted yarn. "Combing" wool requires strength as well as length in order to stand the combing process.

The combing machine consists of double circles of steel pins through which the carded wool is drawn. The long fibers are drawn out and balled and are then known as "tops." The short, tangled fibers that have been separated lie in a shapeless mass and these are spoken of as "noils." These cannot be used for worsted yarns, but are sold to woolen mills for woolen yarns. The "tops" are sent to the drawing room.

DRAWING AND DOUBLING

In the drawing room the thickness of the "tops," or untwisted slivers as they are called, has to be reduced. This is accomplished by passing them through drawing frames which decrease their size and increase their length. In this process, which is known as "slubbing," several strands enter the drawing machine separately and are united into one strand. This may be continued until the doublings are formed of fibers from hundreds of thousands of original fibers. One manufacturer of hand-knitting yarns says that it is sometimes necessary to have as many as a million doublings for some of the finer yarns. And yarn can be so carefully drawn out that a pound of the finest wool can be spun out to a length of sixteen miles.

During the final stages of the drawing and doubling process, a slight twist is put into the strand of yarn to hold the fibers together. This process is called "roving." The yarn is then sent to the spinning department where it is ready for the spinning frame to put in the final twist.

SPINNING

With the exception of a small percentage of wool fibers used in the manufacture of felt, it is necessary to convert the loose fibers into yarn before they can be knitted or woven into fabric.

All primitive people knew the art of spinning, that is, creating a continuous twisted strand from fibers. The discovery that wool fibers could be drawn and twisted into a continuous strand was used early in the construction of fabrics, but there are no means of determining the exact date of the discovery of spinning. Primitive people first found that by twisting the short fibers with the fingers, a long strand could be made. The clean, straightened fibers were held in the left hand and given a continuous twist with the right. Crude instruments were gradually introduced by spinners to assist in the process. First a stick was used on which to wind the yarn, so as to prevent it from tangling as it was spun. During this process the discovery was made that the stick was assisting in the spinning; hence the spindle was introduced, and for hundreds of years yarns were spun by this simple method.

The spinning wheel was next invented. In the early Colonial days the women spun and knitted and weaved clothing while the men hunted and tilled the ground. It has taken years of experiment and research to achieve the marvelous success of our modern textile machines; and, strange to say, most of the large spinning frames are tended by women.

Compare the present-day spinning machines with the spinning wheels of our ancestors. It was necessary for them to work hard all day to produce a few pounds of poor, uneven yarn. Now it is possible to spin yarn so accurately that a certain number of yards must weigh a given number of grains.

HAND-KNITTING YARNS

There are three different methods of spinning yarn from wool:

1. The Woolen System
2. The Bradford Worsted System
3. The French Dry Spun System

The Woolen System is the oldest and has been developed industrially according to the original principles of hand-spinning; it can be employed for wool of short and irregular lengths of staple, and gives an especially full but a rougher and very much more irregular yarn, which can be sold at a price considerably cheaper than a worsted yarn.

The Bradford Worsted System was developed to give a yarn of lighter weight, that would still maintain and improve the warmth and hard-wearing qualities. As has been previously stated, it required wool of longer and more even staple; for this purpose the raw material is first "combed" to remove the short fibers, then the remainder of the fibers lay parallel for the purpose of subsequent drawing and spinning processes. The great advances in the Bradford Worsted System are made possible by the careful breeding of the sheep, and it is today the most common system of spinning in America and England.

WORSTED YARN IN DIFFERENT
STAGES OF MANUFACTURE

1. RAW WOOL (unwashed) as used in the manufacture of hand-knitting yarns.
2. RAW WOOL (washed).
3. CARDED WOOL. The wool has now gone through the process of Carding, and is known as the "Carded Ball."
4. COMBED WOOL. The "CARDED BALL" has gone through a further process. The "Noil" has been combed

out and the wool is now known as "Top." The wool is now formed into a thick, rope-like length which is called a "Sliver," in which the fibers are lying parallel.

5. NOIL. This is the short wool which is combed out of the "Carded Ball"' and is used for the production of woolen yarns.

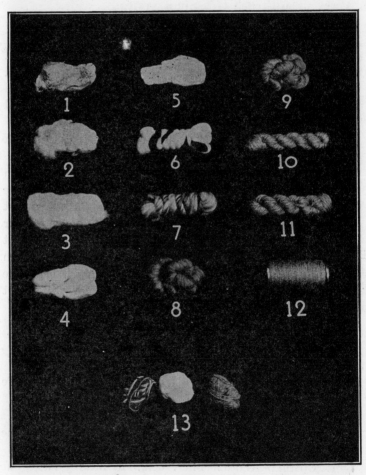

PLATE V.   Worsted yarn in different stages of manufacture.

6. SLIVER after first GILLING.

7. SLIVER after second GILLING. After combing, a blend of dyed or undyed Tops is gilled together ready for the drawing process.

8. SLIVER after first process of drawing.

9. SLIVER after further process of drawing.

10. SLIVER after further process of drawing.

11. ROVING. This is the final process of drawing before spinning.

12. SPUN YARN. The Spinning process consists of reducing "roving" to the required thickness of yarn and putting in twist suitable to the purpose for which the yarn is going to be used. After this the single yarn is twisted into 2, 3, 4 or 5 ply to give the variety of thicknesses used in hand-knitting.

13. BALLS OF FINISHED YARN.

The French Dry Spun Method can make use of shorter stapled wool than the Worsted System, and technically it is composed of that and of the older Woolen System; thus it is intended to produce in the one yarn the primary advantages of each system—the fulness of the woolen, and the greater evenness and added strength of the worsted.

Many yarns now produced use dry combed tops, and are processed on the French or Continental System of drawing, with mule or ring spinning. By hand-knitting yarns that are French combed and French spun, are meant yarns dry combed and dry spun without the use of oil.

The essentials of a good hand-knitting yarn are:

1. Soft handle
2. Fullness
3. Wearing properties

Each can be obtained individually in one or the other of the systems mentioned, but to secure them all it is necessary to blend various classes of raw wool, giving attention to the merits of each when used in the particular production method being employed. For this reason, since it has now been developed to such an extent that very fine and short staple wool can be produced on it, the Worsted System is proving the most likely to give a combination of the requirements. Moreover, expert sheep breeding has resulted in the securing of fine quality wool of greater length—normally the longer the wool the lower and harsher the quality—and there can be secured innumerable types and qualities of wool of more than the minimum staple length required for the satisfactory working of the Worsted System.

"Zephyr" Yarn

What is known as zephyr yarn was originally that which was spun on the French principle, though the special soft and full properties which were thereby secured have lately been produced equally well on the Worsted System, and many qualities now sold as zephyr are not actually French Dry Spun.

"Worsted" Yarn

Worsted yarn is technically that spun on the Worsted System, and therefore from wool of longer fiber than the woolen and the zephyr. The knowledge that, as a rule, a longer fiber means a coarser quality, led people to believe that worsted was a long, coarse yarn. But this is incorrect, because, for example, yarns spun from a very fine Australian wool, Zephyr, and other types of high grade hand-knitting yarns are often spun on the Worsted System, and are also worsteds.

The Significance of Fineness of Fiber

The factor of the fineness of the wool fiber is the basis of the English System of grading, known as the Bradford

Spinning Count System, which classifies wool according to the number of hanks of yarn it will spin to the pound of clean wool, a hank being 560 yards. From a pound of the finest wool approximately 80 hanks can be spun, while 36 hanks can be obtained from a pound of the coarsest.

The Twist of the Yarn

From the spinning room the yarn is taken to the twisting department, where it is made into two, three, four or whatever fold or ply may be desired. The yarn is then reeled into small skeins or large hanks, carefully examined for any imperfections and sent to the dyer.

Yarn Counts

One strand of twisted fibers is called single, while yarn made from twisting two, three, or more strands is called two ply or two fold, three ply or three fold and so on.

DYEING

Until approximately seventy years ago people used natural dyes from berries, roots, branches and a limitless number of barks and flowers, which contained the coloring matter they required. They were highly skilled in this process of dyeing—as may be seen from the old oriental rugs of Persia and Turkey, the ancient Mohammedan prayer rugs, and the exquisite shawls from India and Egypt, which retain their original coloring. This form of dyeing still is used by the natives in many countries. Our Colonial grandmothers knew no other, while the dyes from branches, berries or roots of their native soil still are used to dye the yarns for the famous Scotch Harris Tweed.

In 1856 Sir William Henry Perkin, an English chemist, revolutionized the coloring of cloth. Artificial dyes are now manufactured from aniline, or coal tar, which is a by-product obtained in making coke from coal.

The dyeing of yarn is one of the most exacting processes. It means the complete immersion in a color bath so that every part is thoroughly permeated with the coloring matter. The yarn is looped on poles and submerged in the dye vats. Each pole is handled by two men, one on each side of the vat. These men keep the poles moving constantly to and fro. In a well-dyed yarn each individual strand is evenly colored. After the yarn has attained the desired shade, it is carefully rinsed and taken to the drying room where it is once more examined, matched for color and tested for fastness. To be satisfactorily dyed, the color should be clear and of a tone that will stay unchanged after long usage.

Top-Dyeing

Wool is the only fiber that is ever dyed before the fibers are spun. This is called "Top-dyeing." The wool tops are dyed so that every individual fiber of raw material is thoroughly penetrated by the dyestuffs.

No matter how much wool "top" is to be dyed, the original amount is divided into batches for individual dyeings. Each batch is then dyed with the same standard color dye formula. The dyed batches are then blended together by doubling, and whatever change is necessary in the color is obtained by the addition of small portions of dyed tops. This eliminates the need for dye lot numbers because the colors match perfectly. A final test of each successive dyeing is generally made by knitting the newly-dyed yarn into a piece of fabric of the previous blendings. Where there is the slightest variation in color, it is corrected by further blending.

Other Methods of Dyeing Yarns

Yarns which consist of mixtures are dyed in top form and are either recombed or blended in the drawing or doubling. Two-color effects may be obtained in a variety of ways. They may be simple twists of two or more yarns of solid shades, or they may be blended like mixtures, or be yarn spun from two rovings of different colors. There may be also cross-dyeing effects, that is, blended yarns, the components of which do not take the same type of dye stuff—for example, wool and rayon, wool and cotton, wool and silk, and others.

Novelty Yarns

There is also a great number of novelty yarns on the market, yarns whose source of attraction depends as much on the structure as on their color and handle, although in many cases the color is made to accentuate the yarn structure.

The following are a few examples of this type of yarn:

1. Spot or Nub yarns, in which one thread is excessed around another at given intervals of time, thus giving nubs at equal distances along the yarns. The nubs are usually a different color from the ground and binding threads. These yarns necessitate the use of a fancy twisting frame and the nubs may be made with any given spacing.

2. Slub yarns, which may have either random or mechanical slubs. (Slubs are thick pieces in the yarn.) For the production of mechanical slubs a fancy twister must be used. The slubs are usually made from cotton and placed in a wool yarn.

3. Loop yarns, where small loops are formed along the yarn at frequent intervals, the loops often being a different color from the rest of the yarn.

4. Gimps. These are yarns which have a tight core or center thread, with a thicker yarn forming a gimp effect around it. These can be produced on an ordinary twisting machine.

5. Many other types of fancy yarns are employed, for example bouclé, imitation chenille, cord yarns and others. These are used either singly or sometimes two or more types are combined in one yarn.

GENERAL QUALITIES OF THE MORE COMMON TYPES OF YARN THEIR USES AND SUITABLE NEEDLES

As the correct choice of yarn depends upon the purpose for which it is to be used and the nature of the stitch employed, the general qualities of the more common yarns is given to aid in the selection.

1. *Knitting Worsted*

Knitting worsted is a sturdy 4 ply yarn, moderate in price. It is an excellent yarn for rough usage and is suitable for any of the following: Heavier sweaters of all types for men, women and children. Heavier socks, caps, scarfs, mittens and gloves. Sportswear of all kinds for men, women and children. Heavier afghans.

Needles: Aluminum or steel, American standard #4 to #6 or a set of #10 or #11 steel needles, depending upon the article to be knitted.

2. *Zephyr Germantown*

Zephyr Germantown is a very soft, heavy 4 ply Zephyr yarn, nearly always spun from pure Australian wool or from stock of the same type. It has a smooth texture achieved by long staple wool, and is light in weight but warm. It is one of the finest yarns for blankets, robes, afghans and baby garments.

Needles: The same as for knitting worsted.

3. *Sport Yarn*

Sport Yarn is a tightly twisted 4 ply worsted yarn of fine quality. Its rather firm twist makes it excellent for garments and accessories that will have hard wear. It does not, however, give a finished product the appearance of being as coarse or as heavy as one made of knitting worsted.

Its uses are almost endless. These include sportswear for men, women and children, also socks, stockings, mittens and gloves. Women's suits and coats, and children's coats, dresses and sweaters.

Suitable needles are steel or aluminum, American standard, #3 to #5, and a set of #12 or #13 for mittens, gloves, stockings, etc.

4. *Shetland Floss*

Shetland Floss was originally the name of the yarn obtained from the sheep in the Shetland Islands. It is distinguished for its hairy nature and fine but strong fiber.

It is a fine 2 ply weight worsted, loosely spun, and makes a good all around material. It is not suitable, however, for garments with a lace stitch. Because of its loose twist it fluffs up after it is worn and spoils the lace pattern. Nor is it suitable for men's and children's sweaters requiring hard wear. It is, however, suitable for lighter wearing apparel for women and children, as well as for infants' wear of all kinds, shawls, scarfs, etc.

Needles of steel, aluminum or composition depending upon the purpose, ranging from #2 to #5, American standard.

5. *Crêpe Bouclé*

This is a wool and rayon bouclé which is heavily crinkled. It is especially suitable for women's dresses and suits, and girls' light-weight coats and dresses.

It is better to knit it fairly tight on needles #2 or #3, American standard.

6. Spanish Stocking Yarn

Spanish stocking yarn is ideal for sweaters and mittens, and, as its name implies, it is excellent for stockings and any article which will receive good hard wear.

Needles of steel or aluminum, American standard, #3 or #4, and a set of needles #12 or #13 for stockings, mittens, or gloves.

7. Saxony

Saxony yarn was originally made of wool from Saxony, Germany. It is an outstanding material for infants' and all children's wear, as it is spun from the finest quality wool stock and is uniform in texture. It may be bought in 2, 3 or 4 ply to suit requirements.

Needles of bone or composition, but not too flexible, American standard, sizes ranging from #1 to #4 and sets of needles from #11 to #14.

8. Bathing Suit Yarn

All good bathing suit yarn should be guaranteed fast color, that is, it should be immune to both sun and salt water when correctly dried. Bathing suits should always be knitted very tight on small needles or else they will stretch when in the water.

Needles, American standard, #2 or #3.

9. Angora

Hair from Angora rabbits is used for a very soft and fluffy yarn. A genuine rabbit's hair yarn may be made of 2 or 3 ply thicknesses. More often it is made with a combination of other fibers. Generally soft wool forms the foundation of the yarn and especially fine stock makes the yarn practical, for it loses little of its furry quality even after many washings.

Needles. Real Angora yarn knitted on needles, American standard, #4 and up. Mixtures to be knitted on needles varying in size from #2, depending upon the weight of the yarn.

10. *Other Yarns*

It is difficult for the inexperienced to understand the difference in yarns, because types of yarn with identical qualities have been given different names by the various manufacturers, and, as there are hundreds of different yarns with as many names, it is quite a task to attempt even partially to describe some of them.

There are on the market many beautiful softer yarns. Although they possess the same qualities and are produced from the same type of stock, each manufacturer names them differently. One is a pure Cashmere yarn blended with the finest Australian wool. It is delightful to work with because of its round, soft, downy qualities. It is an excellent yarn for light weight sweaters, scarfs, gloves, etc., but too soft to knit into skirts.

It requires needles, American standard, #1 to #3, or #12 or #13 if using a set.

Another beautiful yarn is comprised of a mixture of zephyr wool and synthetic silk. Its frosty surface is achieved by twisting the rayon with the wool yarn. Garments made of this yarn remain exquisite even after long wear and repeated washings. One might rightly say of this yarn, "A thing of beauty is a joy forever." It may be used for formal costumes or simple daytime suits.

It is impossible in this chapter to discuss all yarns in

detail. A great deal of information may be gained by visiting reputable stores where yarns are sold. Most of them are glad to show different types of yarn and explain the purposes for which they are used.

NOTE. That certain sizes of needles are recommended for a certain kind of yarn does not imply that no other sizes may be used with that particular yarn. The numbers given are for general purposes. Larger or smaller needles may be used according to the purpose for which the finished garment or accessory is intended.

As a general rule one knits looser with a composition needle than with either a steel or aluminum needle. In my opinion it is better to use bone needles, etc. for small garments or accessories knitted from soft yarn and in cases where no weight will tend either to break or bend the needle.

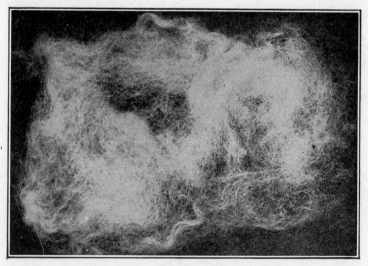

PLATE VI. Wool carded by hand.

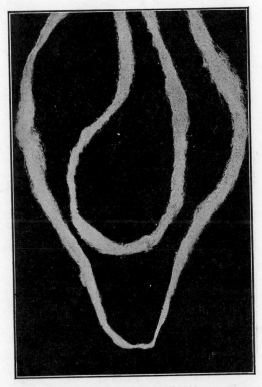

Plate VII. Yarn spun by hand using a spinning wheel.

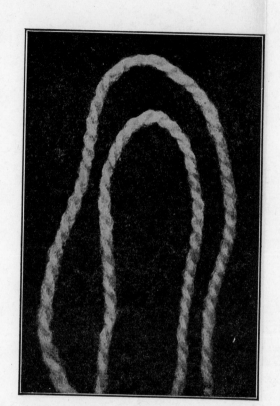

PLATE VIII.   4 ply worsted yarn.

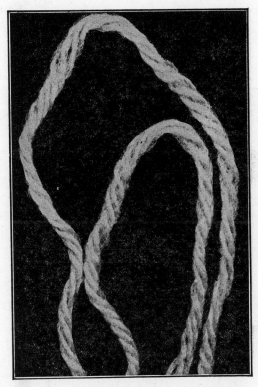

PLATE IX.   2 ply Shetland Floss.

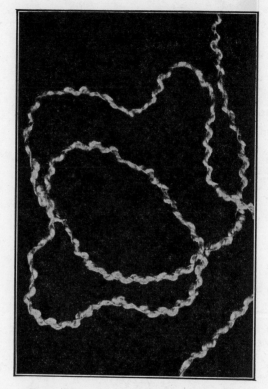

PLATE X.   Wool and Rayon Bouclé.

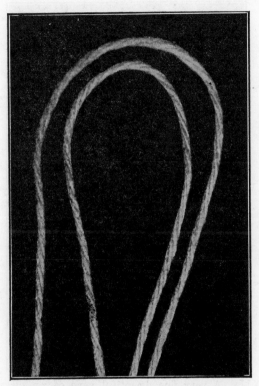

PLATE XI. 4 ply Germantown.

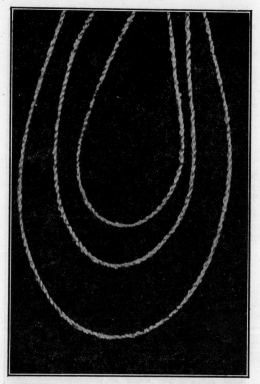

PLATE XII.   A very fine, beautiful yarn of zephyr wool and rayon.

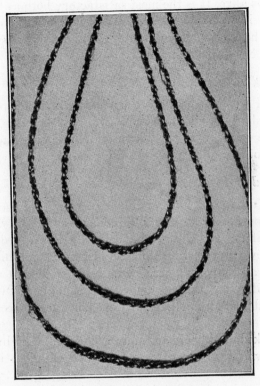

PLATE XIII. A nubby yarn.

Virgin Wool

Virgin wool is new wool which is shorn from the sheep when it is alive. It is the most satisfactory both as to looks and service; its fibers are stronger, longer and more crimpy, hence it posseses greater elasticity, more resiliency and higher tensile strength.

Pulled Wool

Pulled wool is the wool chemically removed from the pelts of slaughtered animals. Naturally it does not possess the same qualities as the Virgin or "live" wool, moreover it does not dye so effectively as fleece wool.

Reworked or Reclaimed Wool

The United States uses millions of pounds of reclaimed wool. Thousands of bales of old rags, discarded suits, worn-out sweaters, socks and underwear are shipped from Europe every year. In 1936, the last year for which figures are available, the woolen industry used 220 million pounds of clean new wool, generally known as "virgin" wool, and more than half of this amount of reclaimed wool.

Reworked wool fibers are more or less weakened by:

1. Garnetting, the process by which old cloth is torn apart.

2. Removing by chemical treatment the cotton and other foreign matter. This further damages the fibers, which have already deteriorated from wear.

3. The "stripping" of the original color.

SCIENCE OF WOOL

Shrinking

Many of the hand-knitting yarns made from wool and wool blends are subjected to one of many processes for rendering them unshrinkable. Either wet or dry chlorination is the most commonly used.

Moth Proofing

Moth proofing, through the treatment of wool fibers, protects the yarn from moth damage. There are many chemicals and processes which make the fibers repellent and poisonous to moth larvae.

SCIENTIFIC RESEARCH REGARDING WOOL
WOOL FROM MILK

Chemically, wool is a mixture of carbon, hydrogen, nitrogen, oxygen and sulphur. A synthetic wool fiber made from casein, a milk by-product, has recently been devised by scientists of the Bureau of the Dairy Industry. The chemical composition of casein fiber and natural wool fiber is almost identical. The synthetic fiber contains somewhat less sulphur.

The first step in the manufacture of artificial wool from milk is the separation of the butter fat. The casein content or curd matter is then coagulated and the whey, the sweet, watery part of the milk, is removed. This is used for lactic acid, or made into soap, or fed to the pigs.

The casein masses are washed, dried and ground. Then they are dissolved with chemical reagents and sent to the maturing and filtering tanks to take out all impurities. The casein is again in liquid form and is forced through a spinning machine where it is transformed into filaments which emerge as fine white wool threads.

It is interesting to note that artificial wool can be obtained from either sheep or goat's milk.

The artificial wool is non-shrinkable, water resistant, and soft to the touch.

Fibers made from casein will take "wool" dyes. Different dyes are required for coloring animal fibers from plant fibers because of different chemical compositions. Dyes which are used in coloring animal fibers are known as "wool" dyes, and those for plant fibers, "cotton" dyes, because they are the most common animal and plant fibers.

Blending a plant fiber with wool has been a problem to manufacturers because of the different dyes required. Generally, "stock" dyeing was resorted to, that is, the raw material was dyed before it was spun. Some rayons— synthetic plant fibers—will take wool dyes, but the color is always a different shade, therefore they are not so desirable for blending with wool as fibers from animal products.

Synthetic wool fiber made from casein, a milk by-product, is of animal origin and therefore takes wool dyes. The fact that the synthetic fibers contain less sulphur than wool, does not effect the wool dyes in any way, because the sulphur has no effect upon the dyeing.

The casein fiber also has the characteristic fine kink or crimp of natural wool and may be blended with it to make a product that has the elasticity and resiliency of pure wool.

THE CONSUMER'S POINT OF VIEW WHEN BUYING YARNS

"No garment is better than the material from which it is made."

From the previous pages it will be realized there is an infinite variety of hand-knitting yarns, running the gamut from coarse to fine. Naturally, the purpose for which the finished garment or accessory is being made is an important item when one considers the yarn. The price element is another important factor, because it greatly influences the choice. The kind of service that is expected from the finished article in terms of hard, general or light wear, as well as the length of service, are all very important when making a selection.

In comparison with cotton, wool is a high priced fiber. Also many kinds of deception are possible in its production. As in all other commodities, the appearance is not always the indication of true worth. There might be foreign fibers among the wool, or some reclaimed wool in the yarn. There is much reclaimed wool used in the construction of cloth. The yarn might also be made from "pulled" wool, which contains the roots of the fiber and lacks elasticity, life and luster.

If it is possible, when buying yarn, pull it to test its strength, unravel a little of it, test its elasticity and resiliency, examine the amount of twist and the length of the fibers, feel for any harsh, foreign materials, see if it is very fuzzy or rough. If the yarn is well-twisted and the fibers are long, the finished product will be durable. If the fibers are short and loosely twisted, making a rougher and much more irregular yarn, it may not prove serviceable; besides, it should be sold at a price considerably cheaper than a "worsted" yarn. Feel the yarn for softness. Rub it against your cheek. Naturally, soft yarn is not always desirable, but softness is a test of quality. Lastly, there is the very important point of "fast" dyeing.

I remember a woman who bought yarn from a manufacturer of whom she knew nothing, except that the price appeared very reasonable. She was very proud of her finished product, a sweater for her small son. Her disappointment came after the first washing. The color ran terribly, leaving a streaked and ruined garment and a much wiser knitter.

Unfortunately it is rather difficult for the average person to detect differences in the quality of yarn, and, of course, it is impossible to know about the dye, unless one tests the yarn before using it. Simply place a small portion, several strands in a bunch, in lukewarm water and leave it there for about fifteen minutes. If the water remains clear, the dye is fast.

One best realizes whether value has been received, after the garment is completed and worn, and has had its first washing or dry cleaning. (I might say here that all yarn to be serviceable should be washable.) It is here that the imperfections appear in the yarn and the weakness in the dyeing is evident. Threads split and break and the garment is altogether unsatisfactory.

There are today manufacturers and dealers in the yarn business who sell inferior grades because they have no standard to keep and no service to offer. They sell any yarn they can obtain, imperfect yarns, job lots, and what not, and entice customers into their stores to buy, through their advertising, at what one considers extraordinarily cheap prices.

When buying yarn at any store where circumstances warrant inspection, look at the labels on the boxes. How many different manufacturers are represented here? Have you heard the names of the manufacturers before? If job lots are carried, be sure you do not buy too little to complete your project, simply because the dealer says it is sufficient; the truth is he has no more, and no means of obtaining any.

"Those who seek the cheap things of life are the prey of those who seek to supply them," said Carlyle.

Buy yarn from a reliable store whose yarns come from a reputable manufacturer. A reasonable price will have to be paid, but one is assured of good quality, long wear, uniformity of dye and satisfaction in every way. The initial investment, or the actual cost of the yarn, is small when one considers the hours that are necessary in the construction of a sweater or even a scarf. When one makes an

article by hand, time, patience and skill are required, and
one wants to be proud of one's achievement.

Another thing to remember is the "good neighbor" pol-
icy. Does it seem the correct thing to send away for yarn
simply because the prices appear cheaper—observe, I did
not say because the value was better—while a little neigh-
borhood store is striving for existence? What would hap-
pen in large cities if most of the people sent away for
commodities because they thought the prices were lower?
The fact that one's earnings are not affected, or appear
not to be affected by these sales, should not mean that it is
no part of one's job to realize what such buying does to
others. One of the big problems of life is to learn to live
together, in the truest sense, with our family, our neigh-
bors, our community.

Here is a consumer story a woman told me. Her husband
is a butcher with a little store of his own. One of his customers, a dentist, hadn't been in the store for some time.
The butcher met the dentist on the street and questioned
him about his not having appeared at the store. The dentist
explained, "I can buy porterhouse steak in such and such
a town for eight cents cheaper than I pay you." "Too bad
I didn't know that three weeks ago," answered the butcher.
"I could have bought my new teeth at Dr. So and So's for
ten dollars less than I paid you!"

Another important thing to remember is to buy sufficient yarn at one time, or have sufficient yarn laid away,
to complete whatever you are going to knit. I am referring
now to yarns that are not "top-dyed." Many yarns have
a color and dye lot number. It is impossible to guarantee
that the color will absolutely match unless the dye lot
number is the same, and the slightest difference in tint or
shade shows perceptibly. It is safer to purchase a ball or
two extra. A good reliable store will always refund the

money. In the case of "top-dyed" yarns, the same color number always matches, so keep a label for reference.

It is advisable to collect from time to time different types and brands of yarns. Notice the length of fibers, the evenness and roughness of thread; pull to test the strength —this does not apply to angora—put into water to test fastness. Are you able to distinguish one type of yarn from another? What are the good qualities of this yarn? For what purpose would this yarn be used?

Boiling-Out Chemical Test

Wool fibers are often mixed with rayon or cotton. The boiling chemical test will advise one if this is the case.

METHOD. Boil a sample of the yarn in a cup of water containing a teaspoonful of lye. This should be done in an enamel vessel. Boil for five minutes and the wool will disappear, leaving the rayon or cotton.

CHAPTER III

KNITTING—FUNDAMENTALS

KNITTING is the manufacture of a fabric with yarn or thread on two or more needles. A number of loops are first made on one needle and then the fabric increased by drawing other loops through them as they are passed backwards and forwards along the needles from row to row.

Casting On

This is the formation of the first row of loops on the needle and is the foundation of the work.

There are two principal ways to "cast on" stitches.

1. This gives a firm edge and has no loose loops at the bottom, therefore it is much better for garments or accessories that start with ribbing or in which the edge is conspicuous. This method requires only one needle.

NOTE. If fine yarn is used, make a slip loop one yard from the end of the yarn for 100 stitches; the heavier the yarn the greater the length required.

METHOD. Make a slip loop about ¾ of a yard from the end of the yarn, then slip this loop on the needle and hold the needle in the right hand. Separate the yarn with the index finger and thumb of the left hand, placing the needle between the thumb and index finger and the yarn over the thumb and index finger, the short end of the yarn over the thumb, and the strands of yarn held by the other fingers, as in Plate XIV.

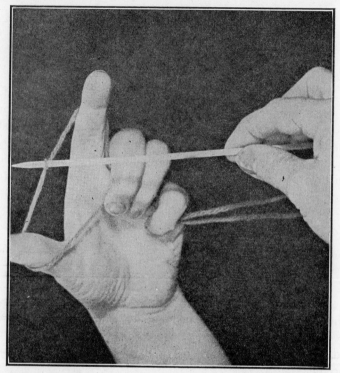

PLATE XIV.

*With the point of the needle, draw in the yarn which is on the outside of the thumb, then pass the point of the needle from left to right over the yarn which is on the index finger. It is this loop which becomes the stitch. A loop is now formed on the thumb through which the stitch passes, as in Plate XV.

Now draw the thumb from the loop and pull the thread with the thumb, returning to the original position and ready to form another stitch.* Continue forming the stitches as described between the *s until the necessary number of stitches is formed.

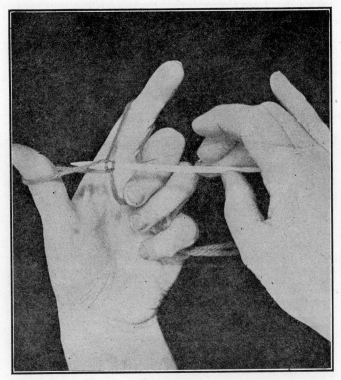

PLATE XV.

NOTE. Do not have the yarn held too loosely on the fingers.

2. The stitches are knitted on to the needle and two needles are required. This method has to be used when adding stitches for buttonholes, pockets, mittens, etc.

METHOD. Place a slip loop, which is made near the end of the yarn on the left hand needle, or have a piece of material already knitted. * Pass the point of the right hand needle from left to right through the loop. Pass the yarn under and around the point of the right hand needle and make a new loop through the slip loop, which will be on the right hand needle. Turn the stitch on the right hand needle so it slopes the correct way, that is, toward the right shoulder—this also gives distance between the stitches—and place the loop on the left hand needle. Repeat from * until the necessary number of stitches is cast on.

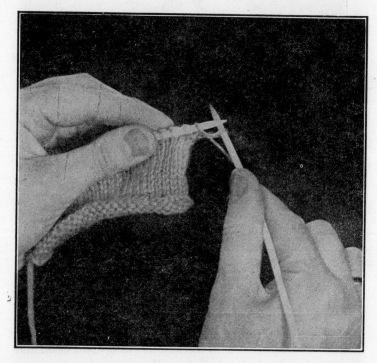

PLATE XVI.

NOTE. Casting on and binding off should never be done tightly. The stitches should have the same elasticity as the rest of the fabric.

Knit Stitch

The knit stitch is the foundation of all knitted fabrics.

Position of the Hands. The needle containing the loops to be knitted is held in the left hand with the needle underneath the hand as in Plate XVI. The other needle is held in the right hand as one would hold a pen or a pencil. There are many ways of holding the yarn to be worked over the fingers, but whatever way is used there should be no tensed muscles and no stiff fingers. Knitting for relaxation requires no tension. It is preferable that the yarn be fed over the fingers of the right hand. This is the only way different colored yarns may be worked in a pattern

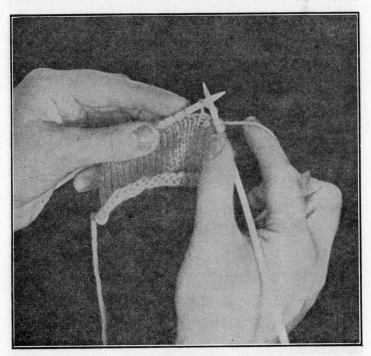

Plate XVII.

without having a long loop at the back of the work.

In Plate XVII the yarn passes over the index finger of the right hand, around the middle finger and is held by the other fingers. It is the way in which the yarn is held that makes the tension of the stitch. There should be absolutely no gripping of either the yarn or needles. The knitting should be worked with ease and the yarn drawn smoothly through the fingers.

METHOD. Hold the needle containing the cast on stitches in the left hand and the other needle and the yarn in the right hand. * Pass the point of the right hand needle through the first loop from left to right. Pass the yarn under and around the point of the right hand needle,

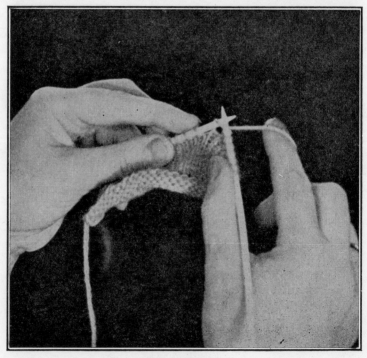

PLATE XVIII.

drawing the loop thus made through the loop on the left hand needle, forming a new loop on the right hand needle as in Plate XVIII. Now slip the used loop off the left hand needle. Repeat from * until all the stitches on the left hand needle have been worked. Change needles into opposite hands and start a new row.

Note.

1. The yarn is held at the back of the work when a knit stitch is being made.

2. A knitted stitch is smooth and like a chain in appearance at the front of the work.

3. Garter Stitch is the name given to the fabric when both sides are worked with the knit stitch. It is ridged from edge to edge, one ridge making two rows.

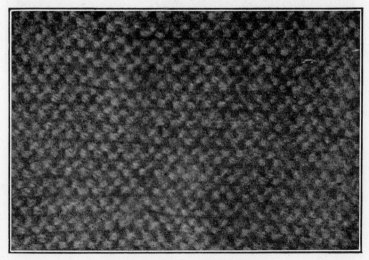

Plate XIX.   Garter stitch.

Purl Stitch

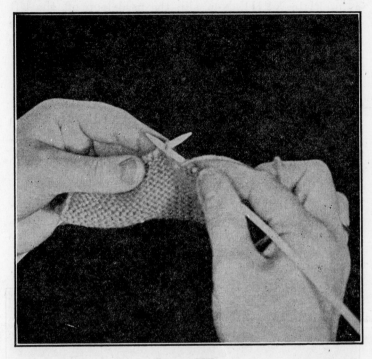

PLATE XX.

METHOD. Hold the needle containing the stitches in the left hand with the yarn in front of the work as in Plate XX. * Pass the point of the right hand needle from the back to the front through the first loop from right to left. Pass the yarn up and around the point of the right hand needle as in Plate XXI, drawing the new loop backwards through the one on the left hand needle to the right hand needle. Slip the used loop off the left hand needle. Repeat from * until all the stitches have been worked.

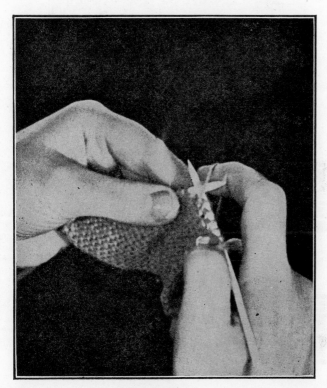

PLATE XXI.

NOTE.

1. A purl stitch looks like a bar or horizontal bump in front of the work.

2. A knit stitch in front of the work is a purl stitch at the back and vice versa.

Stockinette Stitch

PLATE XXII.

Stockinette stitch is made by knitting one row and purling the next for the desired length when straight needles are used. When worked on a set of needles or a circular needle, stockinette stitch is made by knitting around and around for the desired length.

NOTE.

1. Stockinette stitch is smooth on the right side and rough on the wrong.

2. It is lighter in weight than garter stitch, therefore it is not so cumbersome and requires less yarn to make the same garment.

Ribbing

PLATE XXIII.

Ribbing is the alternation of knitting and purling and gives a fabric that is very elastic widthways. With the same amount of stitches it gives a narrower piece of fabric than the garter or stockinette stitch.

Knit 1, Purl 1 is the narrowest ribbing and appears the same on both sides. To make a ribbing of K.1, P.1, cast on an even number of stitches and repeat this row until the ribbing is the desired length.

NOTE. When changing from knit to purl the yarn must be brought forward under the right hand needle for the purl stitch, and back again under the needle for the knit stitch. Many beginners do this too loosely, thus spoiling the widthways stretch of ribbing.

Knit 2, Purl 2.

To make a ribbing of K.2, P.2, as in Plate XXIII, the number of stitches must be divisible by four. The rows then always begin with K.2.

NOTE. It is hard to calculate the necessary number of stitches for a desired width of ribbing. From experience it has been found that ribbing is generally knitted looser than stockinette stitch, and therefore

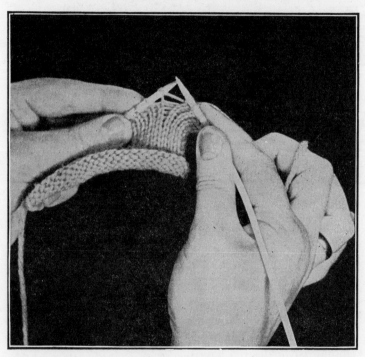

PLATE XXIV.

the number of stitches that would be necessary if stockinette stitch were employed will be satisfactory for the ribbing and allow for the necessary stretch.

Increasing and Decreasing

Increasing and decreasing are required to shape a knitted fabric so it conforms to the shape of the body.

Increasing

1. Knit a stitch but do not slip the stitch off the left hand needle but knit again in the back of the same stitch, then slip the loop from the left hand needle.

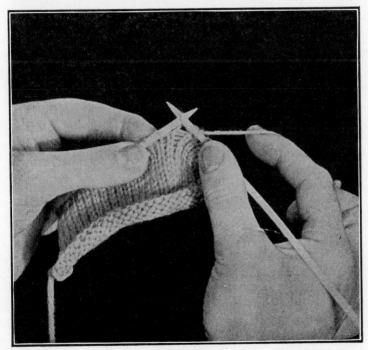

PLATE XXV.

NOTE.

a. The increased stitch is clearly seen from its likeness to a purl stitch.

b. When increasing to shape a garment increase on the first stitch, not on the second, as was previously considered better. The increasing is then hidden when the seams are sewn together.

2. Knit a stitch through the loop of the row below. This method should be used when the purl increase stitch would be conspicuous, as in collars, etc.

If the yarn between the loops is picked up instead of the actual loop of the stitch it will cause a hole in the work.

If one increases by either of the two previous methods, a stitch is added without leaving a hole in the work. There is still another way of increasing a stitch.

Yarn Over

This is the foundation of all openwork patterns. It is formed, when knitting, by bringing the yarn in front of the needle as if to purl, then knitting the next stitch as usual. When purling, it is made by passing the yarn around the front of the needle to the back and to the front again, then purling the next stitch as usual.

Decreasing

Decreasing a stitch may be accomplished in three ways.

1. Knit two stitches together, passing the needle through the front of the stitches as in Plate XXVI. That is, with the right hand needle pass the point from left to right through the second and first stitches on the left hand needle and knit them together as one. The decreasing thus made slopes toward the right.

2. Knit two stitches together through the back of the loops. That is, pass the point of the right hand needle

through the back of the first and second stitches on the left hand needle and knit them together as one. The decreasing thus made slopes toward the left.

3. Slip the first stitch, knit the second stitch, then pass the slip stitch over the knit stitch and off the needle, the same as when binding off. This is sometimes written, slip, knit, pass. The decreasing thus made slopes toward the left.

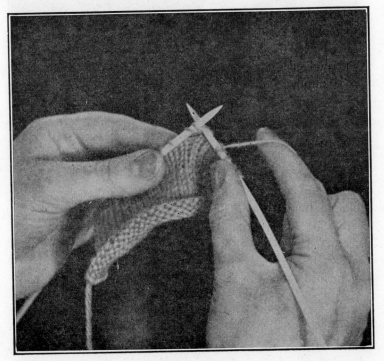

PLATE XXVI.

To Slip a Stitch

A slip stitch is also used for some lace patterns. If not otherwise stated, slip a stitch from the left hand needle to the right hand needle as if to purl and without working it.

Binding Off

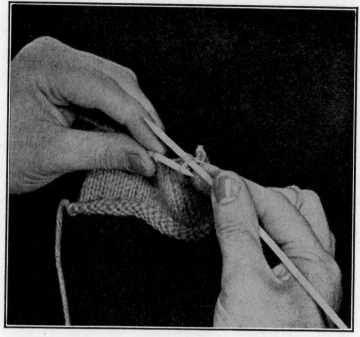

PLATE XXVII.

By binding off, the loops of the fabric are eliminated and a firm edge is formed. Binding off is necessary when the piece of fabric is completed or a straight piece of fabric is necessary as when binding off for an armhole or shoulder.

METHOD. Knit two stitches. * Pass the point of the left hand needle from left to right through the first of these stitches, lift it over the second stitch and off the needle point. Knit another stitch, again having two stitches on the right hand needle. Repeat from * until all the stitches are worked, then break off the yarn and draw it through the last loop.

NOTE. Bind off loosely. The edge should be as elastic as the rest of the knitting.

Stitch Gauge

The stitch gauge is the term given to the number of stitches to the inch that are obtained on the piece of fabric that is knitted. The number of stitches knitted to the inch depends upon the material used, the size of the needles and the tension of the work. As no two people knit exactly alike even when using the same material and the same needles, it is most important that a sample piece of fabric be knitted before starting either a garment or accessory; and as, throughout the book, everything is knitted from the stitch gauge and measurements, it is essential that the taking of a correct stitch gauge be thoroughly understood.

METHOD. With the yarn and the needles to be used for the actual work, cast on between 20 and 30 stitches, depending upon the weight of the yarn, and knit a piece of stockinette stitch about 2 inches wide.

NOTE. If a pattern stitch or lace stitch is to be used, make a sample of the actual stitch.

Taking the Stitch Gauge

Until accustomed to taking stitch gauges, it is advisable to steam the piece of fabric as one would a finished garment. This does not mean one should pin it down, in which case the piece of fabric would be pinned to a certain size. Simply steam over the piece, using a damp cloth and a hot iron, but keep the weight of the iron in the hand. Now the piece of fabric will be the same as the piece of fabric in the completed garment when blocked, and therefore correct for a stitch gauge.

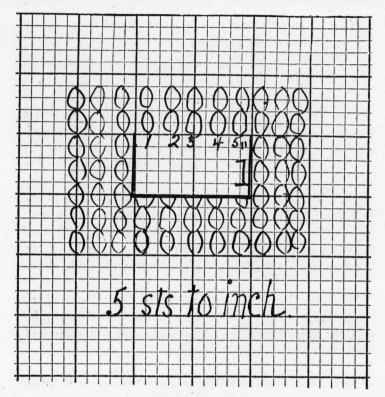

DIAGRAM 1.

METHOD. Place the piece of fabric on a flat surface and by means of either a steel ruler or linen tape, count the number of stitches to the inch as in diagram 1.

Do not measure near the loops on the needle or near the edges, but in the center of the fabric. Do this several times, over one inch then over two. Under no condition compute approximately 5 stitches to the inch. ½ a stitch to an inch makes a big difference when knitting a garment or accessory. The number of stitches to the inch is called the gauge, and this is measured horizontally for the number of stitches to the inch, and vertically for the number of rows to the inch. To know the number of rows to the inch is necessary when planning to increase or decrease to shape a garment.

> NOTE. Check the gauge as the work continues and, if necessary, make adjustments in calculation.

Abbreviations

K.—knit.

P.—purl.

P.S.S.O.—pass the slip stitch over.

Y.O.—yarn over.

st.—stitch.

= — equals.

— — minus.

x—multiply.

*—the directions have to be repeated.

Even—the rows have to be knitted without increasing or decreasing.

(   )—enclosing an explanation of something that has gone before.

CHAPTER IV

KNITTING OF GARMENTS

ONE might say that **KNITTING** is the twin sister of **DRESSMAKING**. The only difference between the two is that in dressmaking we have the fabric and cut the pattern to fit certain measurements, whereas in knitting, we knit our fabric and shape the garment to suit the measurements at the same time we are knitting. It is, therefore, very essential that in knitting, the stitch gauge, measurements and calculations are exact, as there can be no adding nor cutting away after the piece of garment has been shaped.

The principles of dressmaking apply equally to the principles of knitting and both are equally important when considering clothing; therefore, when one is selecting a knitted garment, if one thinks of it in the same terms as one does sewing, considering the line, texture, color and details on exactly the same principles, one will have no difficulty in choosing the yarn, needles and type, and finally charting the garment.

For the actual charting of a garment or accessory it is not at all necessary to have blocked paper. This is apt to confuse rather than help, because the figuring seems much more complicated than it really is.

SWEATERS WITH SET-IN SLEEVES

For the making of sweaters certain formulas have been computed and when these are understood one should be able to make any type or size of sweater, simply from the stitch gauge and measurements.

Stitch Gauge

As previously stated, the most important thing of all before starting any garment or accessory is to take a correct stitch gauge, i.e., the number of stitches to the inch we knit when we make our fabric. Imagine we wish to have a piece of material 14 inches wide, and we have measured our stitch gauge as 7 stitches to the inch instead of 6 stitches to the inch. That means one extra stitch for each inch. There will be, therefore, 14 stitches too many, and calculating 6 stitches to the inch our piece of material would be 2 1/3 inches too wide. This could easily be cut off if one were sewing, but not so in knitting, where we must know definitely and accurately the number of stitches. Therefore turn to instructions on STITCH GAUGE, read directions carefully and follow accordingly.

Measurements

Illustration 3 shows where to measure for sweaters. Naturally these measurements vary with style and individual necessity. They are for set-in sleeve sweaters and cardigans (coat sweaters). The other types will come later.

The following measurements are necessary for sweaters:

1. Waist
2. Chest or bust
3. Shoulder to shoulder
4. Waist to underarm
5. Wrist
6. Upperarm
7. Sleeve underarm length
8. Armhole

NOTE. In the case of man or boy, if he prefers a long sweater, take the measurement at the hip or the desired length instead of the waist measure.

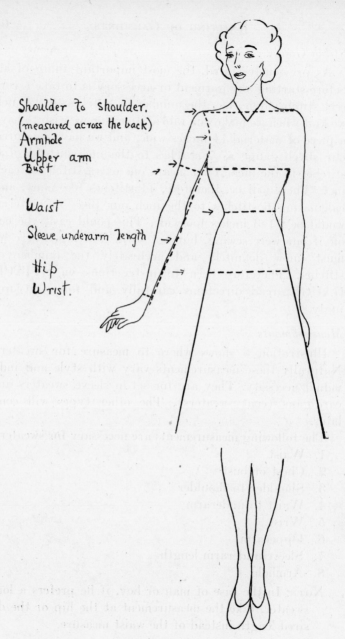

Shoulder to shoulder.
(measured across the back)
Armhole
Upper arm
Bust

Waist

Sleeve underarm length

Hip
Wrist.

ILLUSTRATION 3.   Necessary measurements for sweaters

It is impossible to take one's own measurements correctly, therefore, if making a sweater for oneself, have another person take measurements, using the following instructions:

1. The measurements taken are the measurements of the finished sweater and should not be taken tightly as if some one were measuring for a tight undergarment.

2. Sweaters should be made simple in construction and never fit tightly, as they are used for warmth and sportswear. They should, therefore, afford absolute freedom of action.

3. When measuring around any part of the body be sure the tape measure is on a straight line around that part of the body.

SPECIAL INSTRUCTIONS FOR DIFFERENT MEASUREMENTS

1. *Waist*

Take the waist measurement first because it is one of the natural divisions of the body. This measurement should be taken with a finger between the body and the tape measure, as ribbing for sweater is worn below the waist. This does not mean it has to be taken loosely, but so the measure may be moved around the waist without difficulty.

2. *Bust*

This measurement should be taken eased. Be sure the tape measure does not drop down at the back and that you are measuring the fullest part, which is approximately 2 inches below the underarm. Remember the measurement is the finished bust measurement, and if the sweater is to be a loose fitting one, add the necessary amount.

NOTE. The chest measurement is taken similarly.

3. *Shoulder to Shoulder*

This should be taken fairly snugly. Measure across the shoulders as in diagram, from the small bone that marks the tip of one shoulder, to the other. Too long a shoulder that droops off gives the wearer a sloppy appearance.

4. *Waist to Underarm*

This measurement should never be taken too short. Sufficient length should be allowed for when the arm is raised. If the sweater is desired long, add one or two inches extra as desired.

5. *Wrist*

This measurement is taken exactly. Special allowance is made as will be explained when we come to sleeves.

6. *Upperarm*

This is the measurement at the largest part of the upperarm and is taken exactly. Special allowance is made as in the case of the wrist, which will also be explained when we come to sleeves.

7. *Sleeve Underarm Length*

Take this from the armpit to the wrist and deduct one inch from the length.

8. *Armhole*

This measurement greatly depends upon the individual requirements of the wearer. There must be no constriction at the armhole and it should be sufficiently loose to conceal the actual outlines of the arm. Place the tape measure as in illustration around the armpit to the highest point of the small bone that marks the tip of the shoulder.

NOTE. In a man's sweater, if the measurement at the hip is greater than the chest measurement, compromise by allowing a little more width for the chest and a little less for hips. A hip measurement should never be larger than the chest in the actual sweater.

CHARTING OF A SAMPLE WOMAN'S SLIP-OVER SWEATER

The following measurements are the ones we shall use. They are not a standard size, but are an actual woman's measurements taken according to the way measurements should be for knitting a sweater.

1. Waist—29 inches
2. Bust—34 inches
3. Shoulder to shoulder—13½ inches
4. Waist to underarm—9 inches
5. Wrist—6 inches
6. Upperarm—10 inches
7. Sleeve underarm length—18 inches
8. Armhole—17 inches

    Gauge—6 stitches to the inch.

    8 rows to the inch.

BACK OF THE SWEATER

It is advisable for a beginner to chart one piece of the sweater at a time. For several reasons we begin our back piece first. It is simpler than the front in its shaping, there being no special neck line to consider; and once the back is completed, it is an easy matter to chart the front neck line. Often beginners knit too tight, making hard work of it instead of relaxing, hence the tension is too tight at the beginning. This change in stitch gauge can be rectified when knitting the front. Lastly, after working the back, the knitter is more skilled and hence the work will gradually be more even in tension.

The first thing is to draw a diagram.

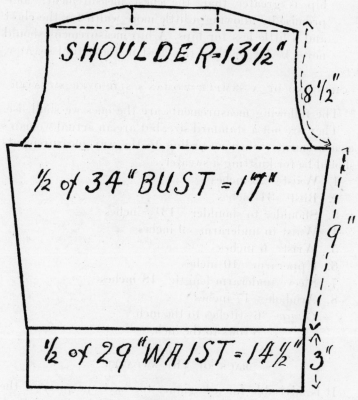

DIAGRAM 2.

NOTE. The back and front of all sweaters with set-in sleeves (not blouses) are made the same width unless the person has a particularly large bust, or there has been a change in tension, or for a cardigan which fastens up the front, in which case allowance is made for overlapping for buttons and buttonholes.

The way in which we chart this sweater is applicable to any slip-over sweater for any person, man, woman or child.

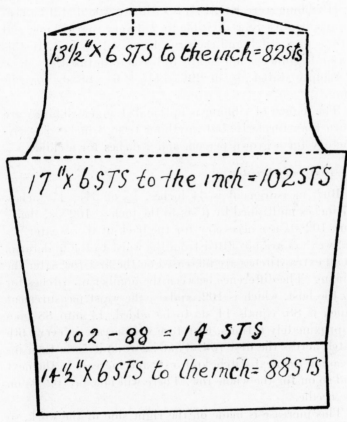

13½"× 6 STS to the inch = 82 STS

17"× 6 STS to the inch = 102 STS

102 - 88 = 14 STS

14½"× 6 STS to the inch = 88 STS

DIAGRAM 3.

1. *Waist Band or Ribbing*

We begin at the waist band with ribbing, which is worn below the waist. K.2, P.2, or K.1, P.1, are the best to use for ribbing. Any wider ribbing does not have such an elastic effect. In our case the waist measurement is 29 inches. ½ of this, or 14½ inches, multiplied by 6 stitches to the inch (the gauge) equals 87 stitches. If we make a ribbing of K.2, P.2, our number of stitches must be divisible by 4, therefore we require 88 stitches.

If ribbing were K.1, P.1, 88 stitches would still be necessary, because 88 is divisible by 2. Every row will now end with a purl stitch and each row begin with a knit. In this way a beginner is not so apt to become confused.

Simply stated: $\frac{1}{2}$ of $29 = 14\frac{1}{2} \times 6 = 88$ sts for ribbing.

The length of ribbing is optional. Longer ribbings are worn than formerly, but anything from 3 inches is satisfactory for a grown person, and 2 inches for a child.

2. *Body of Sweater*

Bust measurement is 34 inches. $\frac{1}{2}$ of $34 = 17$ inches. 17 inches multiplied by 6 sts to the inch $= 102$ sts, therefore 102 sts are necessary for the back of the sweater.

Sweaters are not fitted from the waist to the underarm, so all extra stitches are increased on the first row after the ribbing. The difference between the number of stitches for $\frac{1}{2}$ the bust, which is 102, and $\frac{1}{2}$ the waist measurement which is 88, equals 14 sts to be added. 14 into 88 goes approximately 6 times, therefore we increase in every 6th stitch across the first row. That is, we knit 5 sts then increase in the next stitch, knit 5 sts and increase in the next and so on for the whole row. There will now be 102 sts on the needle.

This increase is made on the right side of the work, so purl the next row, otherwise a ridge will show across the ribbing.

Stockinette stitch or texture stitches are shown in the chapter on stitches. These are most often used for sweaters. Garter stitch, all knitting, makes a sweater heavy and cumbersome and uses more yarn. Lace patterns are too dressy and should be used for blouses and dresses.

In this case we shall use stockinette stitch, therefore we knit one row and purl one row for desired underarm length, which is 9 inches.

3. Armhole Formation

The shoulder to shoulder measurement is 13½ inches.

13½ × 6 sts to the inch = 81 sts.

An even number of stitches is always better in calculating any change of shape in knitting, therefore we shall use 82 sts for the required number across the shoulders.

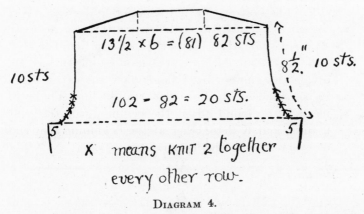

DIAGRAM 4.

The difference between the number of stitches required for the shoulder and the number of stitches across the back underarm gives us the number of stitches to take off for both armholes.

102 sts — 82 sts = 20 sts to be taken off for both armholes. That is 10 sts for each armhole.

As in sewing, we shape the armhole first in a straight line and then in a gradual curve. The rule for decreasing around the armhole is: ½ the total number of stitches are bound off for the straight line, and then knit 2 together every other row until the total number of stitches has been decreased. Therefore, we bind off 5 sts at the beginning of the next two rows—we can only bind off at the beginning of rows—then K 2 together at the beginning and end of the next 5 knitted rows.

Now work even in stockinette stitch until ½ the required armhole measurement is knitted, which is 8½ inches (measuring around, not straight, as this must give ½ the total armhole measurement).

NOTE.

1. Always begin any change of shaping on the right side of the work.

2. The knitter will find it better to decrease (K 2 together) the last two end stitches, then the decrease does not show when the parts are sewn together.

3. If the number to be taken off is uneven, say 13, divide the number by 2, and allow the extra stitch to be bound off, to form the straight line. That will mean 7 sts bound off at the beginning of the next 2 rows, and K 2 together at the beginning and end of every second row, 6 times.

4. *Shoulder*

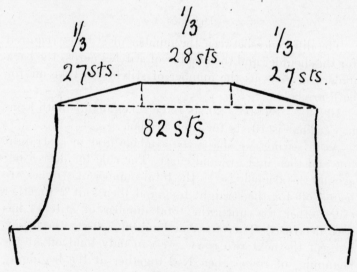

DIAGRAM 5.

As in sewing, the shoulders have a slight slope to conform to the shape of the body. Formerly this was overlooked in knitting, and there was an ill-fitting appearance at the underarm. The general rule is to allow 1/3 of the stitches for each shoulder and the remaining 1/3 for the back of the neck. The back of the neck stitches are never fewer than those allowed for the shoulders, and if a person has a larger neck than average, allow extra stitches for the back of the neck. For a high round neck or "V" neck sweater without an opening, allow 1 inch of stitches from each shoulder.

The shoulders are sloped in from 4 to 8 steps depending upon the weight of the yarn and the needles, or, in other words, the stitch gauge. In this way every succeeding row will be shorter than the previous row and the required slope will thus be made.

For 5 stitches to the inch allow 3 steps at each side.

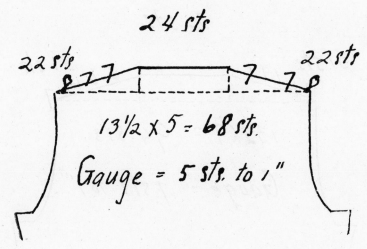

DIAGRAM 6.

For 6 stitches to the inch allow 4 steps at each side.

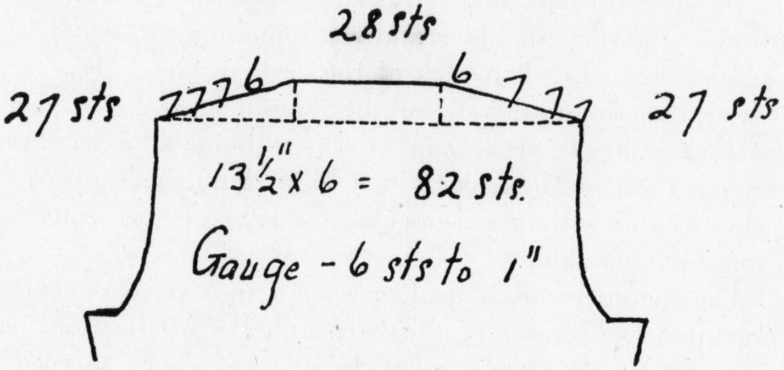

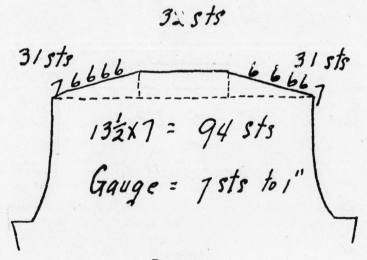

28 sts

27 sts   7 7 7 6   6 7 7 7   27 sts

$13\frac{1}{2}" \times 6 = 82$ sts.

Gauge - 6 sts to 1"

DIAGRAM 7.

For 7 stitches to the inch allow 5 steps at each side.

32 sts

31 sts   7 6 6 6 6   6 6 6 6   31 sts

$13\frac{1}{2} \times 7 = 94$ sts

Gauge = 7 sts to 1"

DIAGRAM 8.

For 8 stitches to the inch allow 6 steps, and so on.

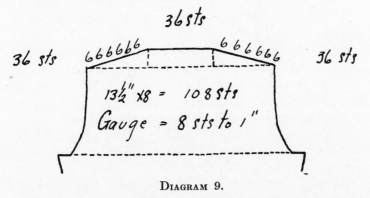

DIAGRAM 9.

The number of stitches across the shoulder is 82. Divided by $3 = 27$ plus 1 extra stitch, which is given to the back of the neck. Our sweater gauge is 6 sts to the inch, therefore 4 steps are necessary for each shoulder, making 3 steps of 7 sts to be bound off, and 1 step of 6 sts (See diagram 7). Remember we can only bind off at the beginning of rows, so it will take 8 rows to bind off the necessary number of stitches, leaving 28 sts for the back of the neck, which must either be bound off very loosely to be as elastic as the rest of the knitting, or placed on a stitch holder or safety pin if ribbing is going to be added.

NOTE. Sometimes smaller needles, usually 2 sizes smaller than those on which the body part of the sweater is knitted, are used to give the ribbing a tighter appearance. This is not necessary if one does not knit ribbing too loosely. (When knitting with 4 ply worsted or Angora some people knit ribbing more loosely.) If smaller needles are used, the stitch gauge is taken from the larger needles, and ½ the bust measurement instead of ½ the waist measurement is used for the waist, using the smaller needles, and no extra stitches are added when changing to larger needles.

FORMULA FOR BACK OF SWEATERS

1. ½ the waist measurement × the stitch gauge = number of stitches for ribbing.

2. ½ the bust or chest measurement × the stitch gauge = number of stitches for the body of sweater..

3. Difference between number of stitches for ½ the bust and ½ the waist measurement = the number of stitches to add on the first row after the ribbing.

4. Divide the number of stitches to be added into the stitches for the ribbing to learn at which intervals extra stitches have to be added.

5. Shoulder to shoulder measurement × the stitch gauge = the number of stitches necessary for shoulder.

6. The difference between the stitches for the shoulder and ½ the bust measurement = number of stitches to take off for both armholes.

7. Bind off ½ the total number of stitches for each armhole at one time, the remaining half decreased by knitting 2 together every other row.

8. Measure around the armhole, using ½ the armhole measurement.

9. Allow approximately 1/3 of the stitches for each shoulder and the remaining 1/3 for the back of the neck.

10. Slope shoulders in, from 4 to 8 steps depending upon the weight of the yarn and the needles—the smaller the stitch gauge the fewer steps necessary.

The following diagrams for the back of sweaters show the same measurements as the sample sweater but with different stitch gauges.

Measurements

Waist—29 inches   Waist to underarm—9 inches
Bust—34 inches   Shoulder to shoulder—13½ inches
Armhole—17 inches

1. Stitch gauge—5 sts to the inch

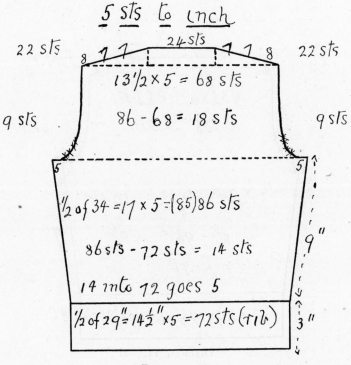

5 sts to inch

22 sts   8   1   1   24 sts   1   1   8   22 sts

$13\frac{1}{2} \times 5 = 68$ sts

9 sts $86 - 68 = 18$ sts   9 sts

5   5

$\frac{1}{2}$ of $34 = 17 \times 5 = (85)\,86$ sts

86 sts $- 72$ sts $= 14$ sts

14 into 72 goes 5

$\frac{1}{2}$ of $29'' = 14\frac{1}{2}'' \times 5 = 72$ sts (rib)   3''

9''

DIAGRAM 10.

2. Stitch gauge—6½ sts to the inch

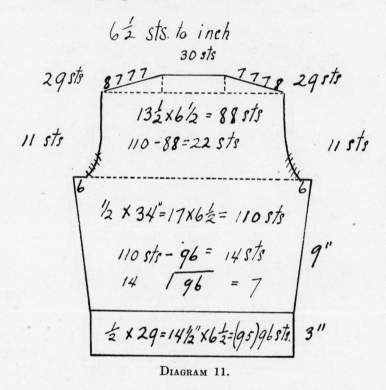

DIAGRAM 11.

3. Stitch gauge—7 sts to the inch

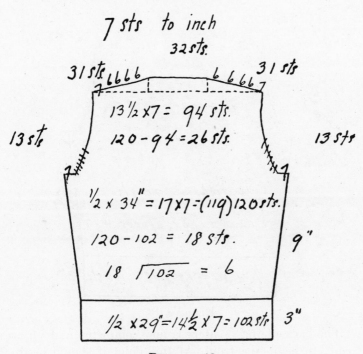

7 sts to inch

32 sts.

31 sts *6 6 6 6* *6 6 6 6 7* *31 sts*

7

13½ x 7 = 94 sts.

120 - 94 = 26 sts.

13 sts *13 sts*

7 *7*

½ x 34" = 17 x 7 = (119) 120 sts.

120 - 102 = 18 sts.

18 √102 = 6

9"

½ x 29" = 14½ x 7 = 102 sts. *3"*

DIAGRAM 12.

4. Stitch gauge—8 sts to the inch

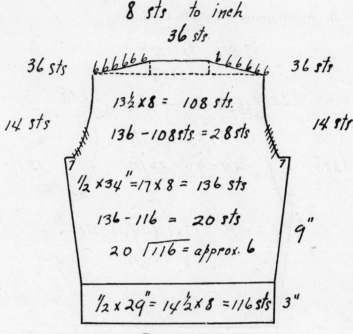

DIAGRAM 13.

The back of the sweaters is now completed and we are ready to begin the front. At this point it should be discernible that in calculating for knitted garments and accessories, our mathematics becomes very real and tangible.

FRONT OF SWEATER

The front of a slip-over sweater is charted the same as the back until the neck line is reached, with the exception of a woman's sweater, where 1 inch is added to the underarm to waist measurement to take care of the bust; and unless the stitch gauge has changed or allowances have to be made for a particularly large bust.

NECK LINES

A very important thing to remember is that the neck line must be large enough to allow the head to pass through, unless we intend to fasten the sweater across one or both shoulders, or to have an opening in the front. We generally have a ribbing around the neck of a slip-over sweater, so in gauging the depth for the neck line, this has to be taken into consideration. The ribbing is usually about 1 inch in depth.

ROUND NECK LINE FOR OUR SAMPLE SWEATER

A high round neck line should have a depth of at least 2 inches for adults and 1½ inches for the average child, measuring from the tip of the shoulder, to allow for the shape of the curve of the neck. If a high neck line is desired without an opening, allow approximately 1 inch of stitches fewer for each shoulder, the remaining stitches to be used for the neck. If lower neck line is required, determine with tape measure how many inches below tip of shoulder is the desired depth of neck, and start the neck line accordingly.

METHOD. For our sample sweater we shall start our round neck line 3 inches below the tip of the shoulder, or, in other words, work the armhole 3 inches shorter than the back armhole measurement, which is 8½ inches. We therefore work 5½ inches before starting the neck line. There are now 82 stitches on the needle, ending with a purl row. Knit over ½ the total number of stitches, that is ½ of 82, which is 41 stitches, placing the remaining 41 stitches on a stitch holder or large safety pin, as only ½ the neck line is worked at one time. As the front shoulder is shaped exactly like the back shoulder, we require 27 of the 41 stitches for the shoulder, that is 41 — 27 = 14 stitches for half the round neck line. The rule for a round neck is the

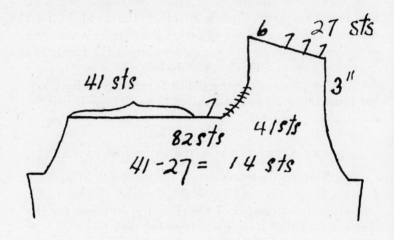

6 sts to 1"

27 sts

6 7 7 7

41 sts

3"

7

82 sts   41 sts

41 - 27 = 14 sts

× means knit 2 together

every other row

DIAGRAM 14.

same as for the armhole. Bind off ½ the total number of stitches at one time, the remainder to be decreased by knitting 2 together every other row. We shall, therefore, bind off 7 stitches in one straight line on the first row, (Bind off loosely so the neck will not bind), then knit 2 together at the neck edge every other row, 7 times. If the armhole is not deep enough after arriving at the necessary number of stitches for the shoulder, which is 27 stitches, knit even until the armhole measurement is reached.

Shoulder

Bind off the shoulder stitches in the same manner as the back shoulder; remember that the slope is up toward the neck, and therefore the binding off will always come at the armhole edge.

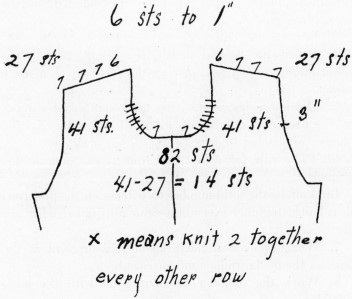

6 sts to 1"

27 sts   *7 7 6*   *6 7 7 7*   *27 sts*

41 sts.   *7   7*   *41 sts*   *3"*

82 sts

41-27 = 14 sts

X means knit 2 together

every other row

DIAGRAM 15.

When one side has been completed, the stitches on the stitch holder are placed on a needle and the other half of the neck line and shoulder are worked to correspond with the other side.

Opening

If an opening is desired in the front, measure with tape the point at which you are to begin, then knit half the stitches, placing the remaining half on a stitch holder. Work even until the neck line is reached, then decrease for the neck line and shoulder the same as previously.

Work the other half to correspond.

Formula for Round Neck Line

1. Work the front of the sweater the same as the back until the desired depth for neck line is reached.

2. A high round neck line is never higher than 2 inches for adult and 1½ inches for the average child, below the tip of the shoulder.

3. A round neck line is worked in two parts.

4. When the desired depth is reached knit ½ the total number of stitches, placing the other ½ on a stitch holder.

5. Difference between ½ the total number of stitches — the necessary number of stitches for shoulder = the number of stitches to decrease for ½ the neck line.

6. (The rule for round neck line is the same as for armhole.)

Bind off ½ the total number of stitches on the first row, then knit 2 together every other row until all stitches are decreased.

7. Work even until the armhole measurement is the same as the back armhole measurement.

8. Work the shoulder to correspond with the back shoulder.

NOTE. If extra stitches have been added because of large bust or change in tension, ½ the extra stitches are bound off at the armholes and the other ½ at the neck line.

Round Necks

The following diagrams show Round Neck Lines using the same measurements as the sample sweater but with different gauges.

1. Stitch gauge—5 sts to the inch.

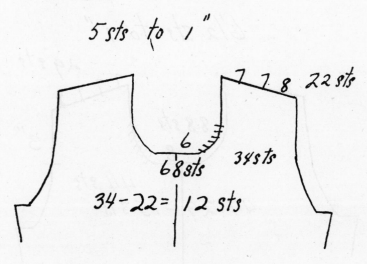

DIAGRAM 16.

2.   Stitch gauge—6½ sts to the inch.

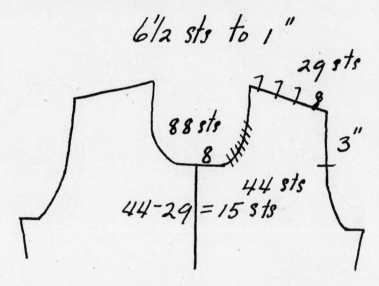

Diagram 17.

3. Stitch gauge—7 sts to the inch.

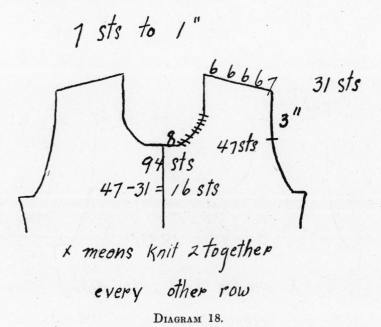

7 sts to 1"

6 6 6 7   31 sts

3"

8

94 sts

47 sts

47 − 31 = 16 sts

x means knit 2 together

every other row

DIAGRAM 18.

4. Stitch gauge—8 sts to the inch.

8 sts to 1"

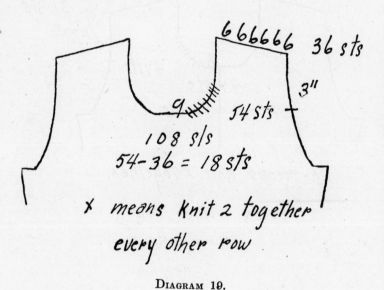

666666 36 sts

x 54 sts ⌐ 3"

108 s/s

54-36 = 18 sts

x means knit 2 together

every other row

DIAGRAM 19.

"V" NECK LINES

By this time one should see the value of diagrams and should almost be able to chart a "V" neck. No matter how rough or crude the drawing, always draw a diagram before changing the shape of the knitting. The principles are then easily understood.

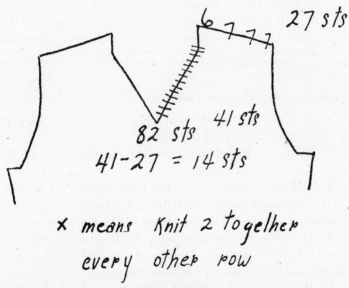

6 sts to 1"

27 sts

6 7 7 7

82 sts   *41 sts*

41-27 = 14 sts

X means Knit 2 together

every other row

DIAGRAM 20.

"V" Neck Line for Our Sample Sweater

A "V" neck is centered the same as a round neck. For our sample sweater we shall begin the "V" neck line after the decrease for the armhole has been completed. See diagram 20.

METHOD. Work to the center, that is 41 sts, which remain on the needle, then place the remaining 41 sts on a stitch holder. 41 sts — 27 sts for the shoulder = 14 sts. Therefore, 14 sts have to be decreased by knitting 2 together every other row at the neck edge 14 times. If the depth of the armhole is not the same as the back armhole, work even until it is, then bind off the shoulder the same as the back shoulder. Work the other side to correspond.

NOTE. If we wish the "V" neck to begin in a direct line with the underarm or a little higher, the decreases will have to be more gradual. A gradual slope has to be made to the shoulder to take care of the amount of stitches to be decreased. Suffice it to say at this point that if the neck line is started lower, decrease every 4th row for about ½ the distance, then every 2nd row.

Formula for "V" Neck Line

1. Begin "V" neck at point where decrease for armhole is completed, or lower if desired.

2. Work to the center, placing the other ½ of the stitches on a stitch holder.

3. Difference between ½ the total number of stitches — the necessary number of stitches for the shoulder = the number of stitches to decrease for ½ the neck line.

4. Decrease at the neck edge by knitting 2 together every other row or every 4th row at the beginning, if necessary, until the shoulder stitches remain.

5. Bind off the shoulder the same as the back shoulder.

SQUARE NECK LINE

The depth of a square neck line is for individual consideration. But no matter what depth is desired the general directions are the same. Measure with tape across the bust to determine the distance from the underarm to the tip of the shoulder, always remembering that if no fasteners are utilized, the neck must be deep enough for the head to pass through. Using a diagram as previously, it is a simple matter to chart a square neck.

Square Neck for Sample Sweater

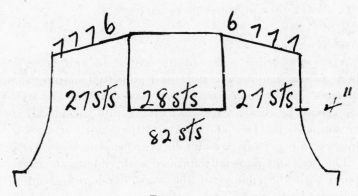

6 sts to 1"

7 7 7 6   6 7 7 7

27 sts   28 sts   27 sts   4"

82 sts

DIAGRAM 21.

We shall begin the neck line 4 inches below the tip of the shoulder. (See diagram 21.) That is, we shall knit 4½ inches of the armhole before we begin the neck line. As we require 27 of the 82 stitches for one shoulder, we knit these 27 stitches, which are placed on a stitch holder after binding off for the neck line. Now bind off, loosely, the next 28 stitches for the square neck, then work the other 27 stitches even until the tip of the shoulder is reached, that is, when the armhole measures 8½ inches. Next bind off the shoulder the same as the back shoulder, then transfer the 27 stitches from the stitch holder to a needle and work the other side to correspond.

FORMULA FOR SQUARE NECK

1. Decide at which point from shoulder tip to underarm the neck line is to be placed.

2. Work across the necessary number of stitches for the right shoulder and place these on a stitch holder.

3. Bind off loosely all the center stitches until the necessary number of stitches for the left shoulder remain.

4. Knit on the remaining stitches, working even until the tip of the shoulder is reached.

5. Bind off the shoulder the same as the back shoulder.

6. Work the opposite side to correspond.

CREW-NECK SWEATER

A crew-neck line is one of the easiest to knit because there are no shoulders to slope and no actual shaping for the neck line. One must remember, however, that the neck line should be chosen carefully, taking into consideration the shape of the face and chin and the length of throat. Only certain persons are able to wear crew-neck sweaters.

The neck line is usually finished with ribbing to correspond with the ribbing of the waist band and about 2 inches in depth.

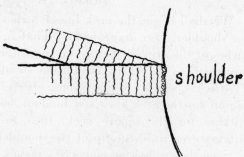

½ armhole measurement = 8½" + 1" = 9½"

Diagram 22.

1. The ribbings may cross at the shoulder, the center of each ribbing coming at the center of the top of the cap of the sleeve, in which case the armhole has to be knitted 2 inches bigger. In other words, the front and back armholes have each to be made 1 inch longer, the last 2 inches being ribbing.

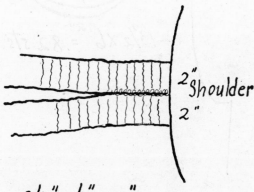

½ armhole = 8½" + ½" = 9"

DIAGRAM 23.

2. Instead of crossing at the shoulder the ribbing is joined at the shoulder seam for ¼ of the shoulder to shoulder measurement; and, as there is no shaping for the shoulders, the armhole has to be made approximately ½ inch larger at the front and back to prevent any binding at the shoulder seams. The last 2 inches are ribbed the same as previously.

BOAT-NECK SWEATER
(As in man's sweat shirt)

The front and back neck lines of a boat-neck sweater are knitted the same. The shoulders are short, approximately ¼ of the shoulder to shoulder measurement in width thus allowing for a wide neck line, which is bound off straight across. After the sweater has been sewn together the back neck line is turned down 1 inch toward the center and the front neck line 2 inches as in diagram 24 and hemmed.

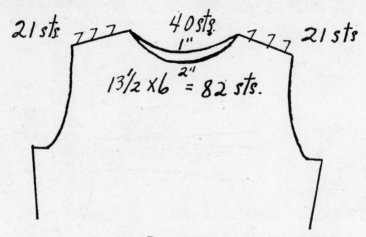

DIAGRAM 24.

In our sample sweater we allow 40 stitches for the neck and 21 stitches for each shoulder, which are bound off in 3 steps of 7 stitches.

TURTLE NECK SWEATER

Turtle neck sweaters are very smart, warm and popular for winter sportswear. They are knitted the same as a round neck sweater, allowing a little over 1/3 of the measurement from shoulder to shoulder for the back of the neck; also making sure that the front neck line is low enough so the head will pass through without difficulty—approximately 3 inches from the tip of the shoulder.

Diagram 25 for a turtle neck sample sweater should be self-explanatory.

The stitches are picked up on the right side of the neck and all at one time, necessitating the use of a small circular needle or a set of double pointed needles. The ribbing is then worked to match the waist band for 5 or 6 inches.

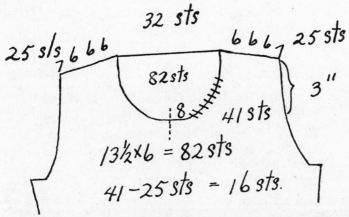

DIAGRAM 25.

NOTE. For completing different neck lines see the Chapter on Details.

EXCEPTIONS FROM MAKING THE FRONT AND BACK OF SWEATERS THE SAME WIDTH

For any of the following reasons, the front of the sweater must sometimes be made larger than the back:

1. To take care of a full bust measurement.

The measurement for the body of the back of the sweater is the measurement across the back from underarm to underarm. The measurement of the body for the front of the sweater is the fullest part of the bust.

For the back and front also, the extra stitches are added across the first row of ribbing, the same as for previous sweaters. When reaching the underarm at the front, the number of extra stitches necessary for the front is divided by two, allowing ½ the extra stitches to be taken off at the armholes and the other ½ to be used at the neck line.

2. If there has been a change in tension.

NOTE. If a beginner is knitting a sweater and the body part is a little large, never rip the work and start over. This is discouraging. Use this part for the front and knit to the front underarm, then place the stitches on another needle or stitch holder, and start the back, completing the back first.

a. If knitted too tightly (stitch gauge is too small), calculate how many inches short for both the waist band and the bust, then add the necessary extra inches to the front, using the correct stitch gauge.

b. If knitted too loosely (stitch gauge is too big), calculate how many inches too many, then allow the widest part for the front and deduct the necessary number of inches from the back.

3. For cardigan (coat sweater).

The previous sweater directions are applicable to a cardigan except in the following cases:

1. If the sweater begins at the hips. In that case no stitches are added after the band which should be narrow, from 1 to 1½ inches in width.

2. If the cardigan fastens with buttons and button-holes. The bands for the buttons and buttonholes are worked at the same time as the fronts and not knitted and sewn on afterwards. Generally, twice the number of stitches required for the buttonhole is used for the band, and ½ the width of the band is added to the width of each side. (Refer to Chapter on Details for the necessary directions on buttonholes and the size of bands.)

When working a "V" neck, the band is continued around the shaping of the neck line, the decreasing coming inside the width of the band, allowing the necessary number of stitches for shoulder stitches plus the number of stitches for the band. The shoulder stitches are then bound off as usual, the stitches for the band continuing for the back of the neck.

The Bands. As stockinette stitch curls, it is better for the bands to be knitted of a different stitch: garter, moss, cardigan or narrow ribbing are all suitable.

Note. If a sweater is knitted in one of the "texture" stitches, it is a piece of fabric of the actual stitch used, which must be measured for the stitch gauge.

SAMPLE CARDIGAN OR COAT SWEATER
(Round Neck)

The diagrams should be almost self-explanatory. The length of the sweater from the underarm is 13 inches, 1½ inches is made of garter stitch and the remaining 11½

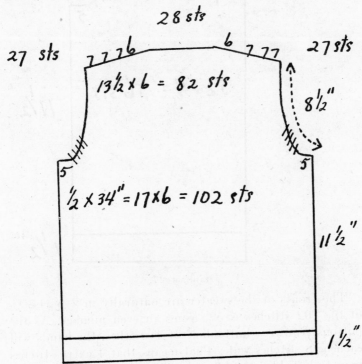

DIAGRAM 26.

inches in stockinette. From the underarm the back is worked the same as for the slip-over sweater.

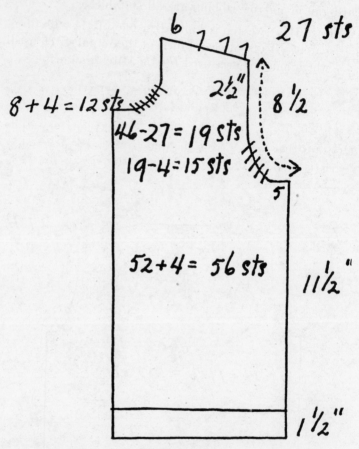

DIAGRAM 27.

The fronts of the sweater are naturally in 2 parts. ½ of the 102 stitches is 52, using an even number. As the buttons require a buttonhole of 4 stitches, the bands will each be 8 stitches wide. That means that 4 extra stitches have to be added to each side, which is 52 plus 4 stitches

= 56 stitches, 8 of these knitted of garter stitch for the band. The armhole is shaped the same as the back, and the neck line begins 2½ inches below the tip of the shoulder. The round neck line is figured the same as previously, except that allowances have to be made for the 4 extra stitches added for ½ the band. 56 stitches — 10 stitches for the armhole = 46 stitches. 27 of these are required for the shoulder, leaving 19 stitches. The 4 stitches extra for the band leave 15 stitches, and, following the rule, 8 plus 4 stitches = 12 stitches to be bound off in a straight line, the remaining stitches decreased by knitting 2 together every other row, 7 times.

FORMULA FOR CARDIGAN

1. The back is charted the same as a slip-over sweater unless it starts below the waist.

2. If longer sweater is desired use ½ the chest or bust measurement instead of ½ the waist measurement, and then no increasing is necessary until the underarm is reached.

3. For each front use ½ the total number of stitches required for the front plus ½ the number of stitches required for the width of each band.

4. Neck lines and shoulders are charted the same as for a slip-over sweater, binding off ½ the stitches of the band with the first bind off for a round neck, and decreasing inside the bands for a "V" neck.

SLEEVES

The sleeves should correspond in type and texture with the general style of the sweater. They should also fit comfortably, being adapted to the use of free and active exercise. That means they should have sufficient room at the elbow when the arm is bent, and should have sufficient length to enable the arm to be raised and bent without drawing away from the wrist or armhole.

LONG SLEEVES

The sleeve is started at the wrist band because it is the most logical place to begin. For the sample sweater the exact wrist measurement is 6 inches, but if the wrist band is knitted only 6 inches wide, it will be impossible for the hand to pass through the cuff. We have, therefore, to make allowances for the width of the hand. The measurement around the knuckles of the hand is generally about 1 inch greater than the wrist measurement for an adult and about ¾ inch for the average child. If, therefore, we allow 1 extra inch of stitches for the wrist measurement, or use the measurement around the knuckles of the hand for the wrist band measurement, the hand will be able to pass through. There are, however, other things to be considered.

1. Do we want a tight fitting cuff?

2. In the case of a child, do we want the cuff to be wide enough to turn back when the child is washing his hands?

3. How long do we wish the cuff?

Individual necessities have to be considered and the wrist band made accordingly.

SAMPLE SWEATER SLEEVE

Measurements

Wrist—6 inches

Upperarm—10 inches

Underarm sleeve length—18 inches

For the sample sweater we shall make a fitting cuff. The wrist measurement is 6 inches. Add 1 inch = 7 inches. The stitch gauge is 6 stitches to the inch, therefore $7 \times 6 =$

42 stitches. The number of stitches for the ribbing must be divisible by 4 for K.2, P.2, so that it matches the waist band. Therefore 44 stitches are used. We now work a ribbing of K.2, P.2 for 3 inches. (3 inches is an average length for an adult, 2 inches for a child.)

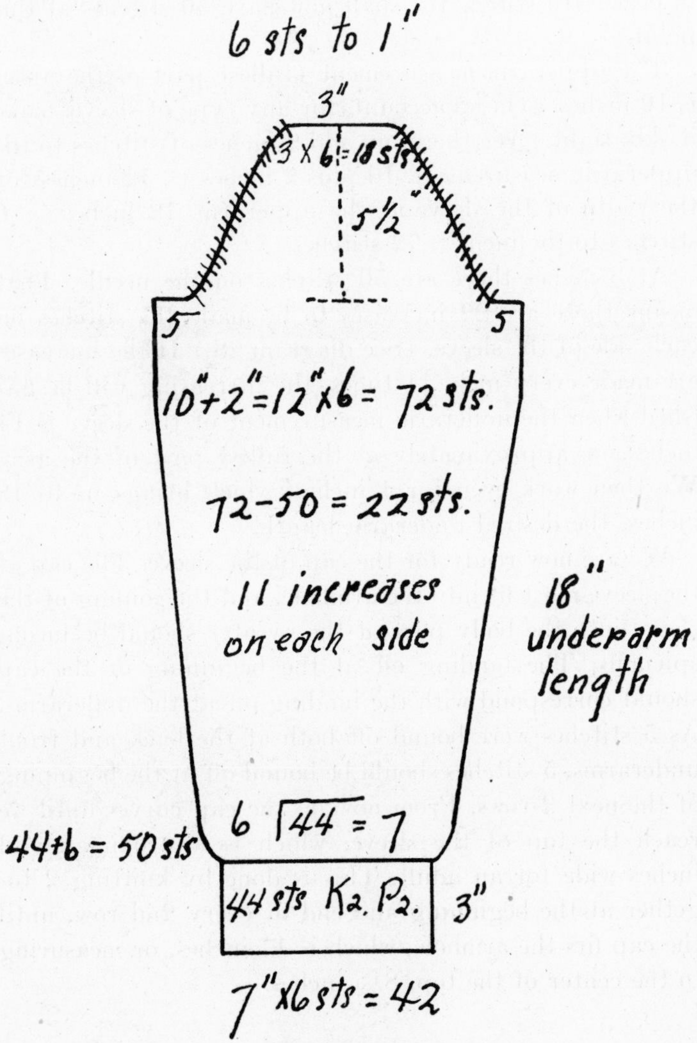

6 sts to 1"

3"

3 × 6 = 18 sts

5½"

5   5

$10'' + 2'' = 12'' \times 6 = 72$ sts.

$72 - 50 = 22$ sts.

11 increases on each side

18" underarm length

$6\overline{\smash{)}44} = 7$

$44 + 6 = 50$ sts

44 sts K2. P2.   3"

$7'' \times 6$ sts $= 42$

Diagram 28.

After knitting the cuff, we prevent the sleeve from being too tight fitting at this point by adding an inch of stitches across the first row after the ribbing, just as we added extra stitches across the first row after the waist band. 6 into 44 goes 7 times, therefore we increase a stitch in every 7th stitch. We shall now have 50 stitches at this point.

The upperarm measurement (fullest part of the arm) is 10 inches. (On no account, for any type of sleeve, make it skin tight.) We therefore add 2 inches of stitches to the upperarm measurement. 10 plus 2 inches = 12 inches for the width of the sleeve at the upperarm. 12 inches $\times$ 6 stitches to the inch = 72 stitches.

At 3 inches there are 50 stitches on the needle. That means there are 22 increases to be made, 11 stitches on each side of the sleeve. (See diagram 28.) If the increases are made every inch, 11 times, the increasing will be finished when the underarm measurement of the sleeve is 14 inches, or approximately at the fullest part of the arm. We then work even for 4 inches, which brings us to 18 inches, the desired underarm length.

We are now ready for the cap of the sleeve. The cap of the sleeve must fit into the armhole, and the joining of the sleeve into the body part of the sweater should be inconspicuous. The binding off at the beginning of the cap should correspond with the binding off at the underarms. As 5 stitches were bound off both at the back and front underarms, 5 stitches should be bound off at the beginning of the next 2 rows. From now on the cap curves until we reach the top of the sleeve, which is approximately 3 inches wide for an adult. This is done by knitting 2 together at the beginning and end of every 2nd row, until the cap fits the armhole, which is 17 inches, or measuring to the center of the top, 8½ inches.

NOTE.

1. If the sleeve has had to be made wider than usual, it may be necessary when decreasing near the top of the cap to knit 2 together at the beginning and the end of every row, so that the cap fits into the armhole.

2. The length of the cap for an average adult is 5½ inches. In knitted garments this is often made too short, so as to pull the shoulder and spoil the neck line.

FORMULA FOR LONG SLEEVES

1. The wrist measurement plus 1 inch, or the measurement around the knuckles of the hand × the stitch gauge = the necessary number of stitches for the cuff, more to be added if desired.

2. Add 1 inch of stitches on the first row after the cuff is completed.

3. Upperarm measurement plus 2 inches × the stitch gauge = the necessary number of stitches for the width of the sleeve. (1½ inches added to the width for an average child.)

4. Difference between the wrist stitches (after adding the extra inch of stitches) and the number of stitches necessary for the width of the sleeve = the number of times to increase on sides of sleeve.

5. Divide the number of times to increase, into the distance over which increases have to be made, to learn where to increase. (Should be completed between 3 and 4 inches from the armpit.)

6. After increasing the necessary number of stitches, knit even to the desired underarm length.

7. Number of stitches first bound off for the cap of the sleeve = the number of stitches bound off at the back and front underarms.

8. Knit 2 together at the beginning and end of every other row until the distance around the cap measures the same as the armhole.

9. The average length of cap for an adult is 5½ inches from the first bind off.

10. Approximate number of stitches along the top of the cap = 3 inches of stitches for an adult, 2 inches for an average child.

EXPLANATION OF THE FOLLOWING DIAGRAMS

For the diagrams, the same measurements are taken as those used for the sample sweater, but different stitch gauges are used.

EXPLANATION. a. Wrist measurement, 6 inches plus 1 inch = 7 inches × 5 stitches to the inch = 35 stitches for the cuff. To be divisible by 4 we shall use 36 stitches for the cuff, which is 3 inches long.

b. To add the extra inch of stitches increase in every 9th stitch across the cuff, which will make 40 stitches.

c. 10 inches is the width of the upperarm plus 2 inches = the width of the sleeve. 12 × 5 stitches to the inch = 60 stitches. 60 stitches — 40 stitches (the number of stitches already on the needle) = 20 stitches (the number to increase on both sides, 10 stitches on each side).

d. The sleeve underarm measurement is 18 inches. The cuff measures 3 inches, therefore in approximately 11 inches there are 10 increases on each side, so we increase each side 10 times, allowing a little over an inch for each increase. Now the sleeve is knitted without any increases until the underarm measurement is 18 inches.

e. For the cap bind off 5 stitches at the beginning of the next 2 rows, then knit 2 together at the beginning and end of every other row until approximately 3 inches of stitches remain, which is 16 stitches.

Stitch gauge—5 stitches to the inch.

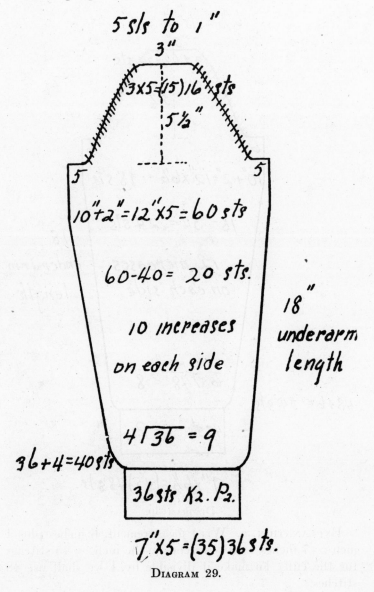

5 s/s to 1"

3"

3×5=(15)16 sts

5½"

5   5

10"+2"=12"×5=60 sts

60−40= 20 sts.

10 increases

on each side

18"
underarm
length

4⟌36 = 9

36+4=40 sts

36 sts K2. P2.

7"×5 =(35)36 sts.

DIAGRAM 29.

Stitch gauge—6½ stitches to the inch.

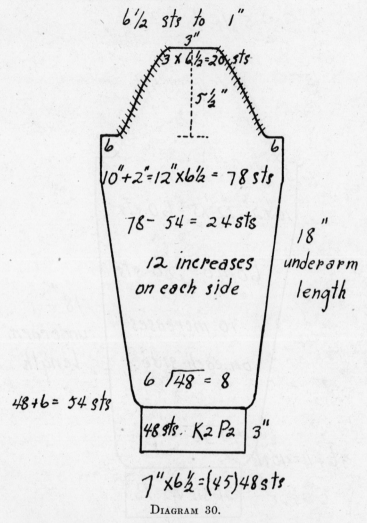

$6½$ sts to $1''$

$3''$

$3 \times 6½ = 20$ sts

$5½''$

6   6

$10'' + 2'' = 12'' \times 6½ = 78$ sts

$78 - 54 = 24$ sts

12 increases
on each side

18''
underarm
length

$6 \overline{)48} = 8$

$48 + 6 = 54$ sts

48 sts. K2 P2 $3''$

$7'' \times 6½ = (45) \, 48$ sts

DIAGRAM 30.

EXPLANATION. a. Wrist measurement, 6 inches plus 1 inch = 7 inches × 6½ stitches to the inch = 45 stitches for the cuff. To make it divisible by 4 we shall use 48 stitches.

b. To add the extra inch of stitches, increase in every 8th stitch across the cuff, which will make 54 stitches.

c. 10 inches is the width of the upperarm plus 2 inches = the width of the sleeve. 12 × 6½ stitches to the inch = 78 stitches. 78 stitches — 54 stitches = 24 stitches, the number to be increased on both sides, 12 on each side.

d. The sleeve underarm measurement is 18 inches, therefore if we increase at each side 12 times every inch, the increasing will be completed at 15 inches. Work even until the underarm measurement is 18 inches.

e. For the cap bind off 6 stitches at the beginning of the next 2 rows, then knit 2 together at the beginning and end of every other row until approximately 3 inches of stitches remain, which is approximately 20 stitches.

EXPLANATION. a. Wrist measurement, 6 inches plus 1 inch = 7 inches × 7 stitches to the inch = 49 stitches for the cuff. To be divisible by 4 we shall use 48 stitches.

b. To add the extra inch of stitches, increase in every 6th stitch across the cuff, which will make 56 stitches.

c. 10 inches is the width of the upperarm plus 2 inches = the width of the sleeve. 12 × 7 stitches to the inch = 84 stitches. 84 stitches—56 stitches = 28 stitches, the number to be increased on both sides, 14 stitches on each side.

d. The sleeve underarm measurement is 18 inches, therefore in 11 inches we have to increase 14 times, which means the increases come in a little less than an inch, approximately every 8th row, until there are 84 stitches. Work even until the underarm measurement is 18 inches.

e. For the cap bind off 7 stitches at the beginning of the next 2 rows, then knit 2 together at the beginning and end of every other row until approximately 3 inches of stitches remain, which is 22 stitches.

Stitch gauge—7 stitches to the inch.

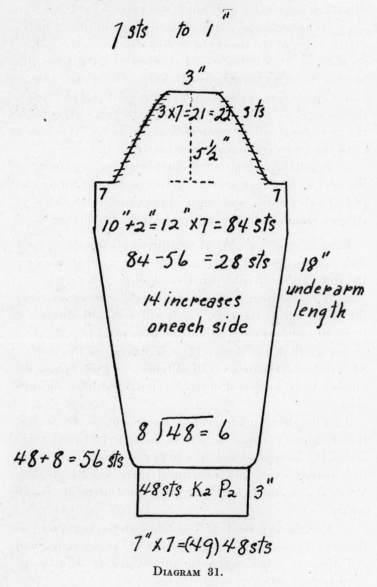

7 sts to 1"

3"

3 × 7 = 21 = 22 5 ts

5½"

7   7

10" + 2" = 12" × 7 = 84 sts

84 − 56 = 28 sts   18" underarm length

14 increases on each side

8)̄48 = 6

48 + 8 = 56 sts

48 sts K2 P2   3"

7" × 7 = (49) 48 sts

DIAGRAM 31.

Stitch gauge—8 stitches to the inch.

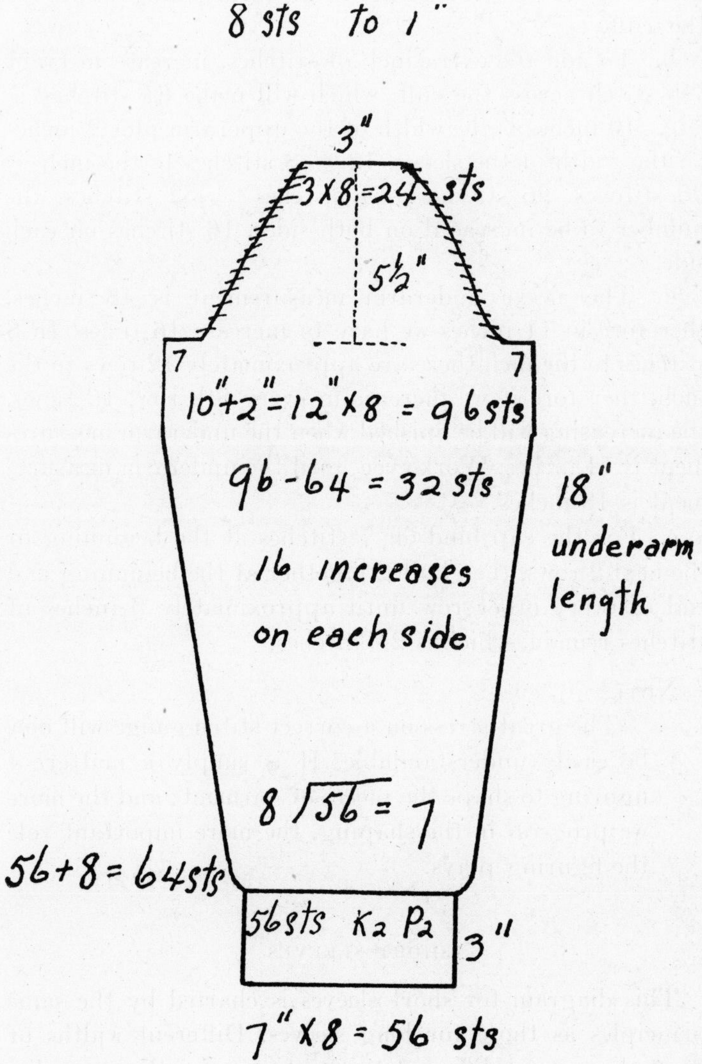

8 sts   to 1"

3"

3 x 8 = 24 sts

5½"

7   7

10" + 2" = 12" x 8 = 9 6 sts

9 6 - 6 4 = 3 2 sts

16 increases

on each side

18"
underarm
length

8)56 = 7

56 + 8 = 64 sts

56 sts K2 P2   3"

7" x 8 = 56 sts

DIAGRAM 32.

EXPLANATION. a. Wrist measurement, 6 inches plus 1 inch = 7 inches × 8 stitches to the inch = 56 stitches for the cuff.

b. To add the extra inch of stitches, increase in every 7th stitch across the cuff, which will make 64 stitches.

c. 10 inches is the width of the upperarm plus 2 inches = the width of the sleeve. 12 × 8 stitches to the inch = 96 stitches. 96 stitches—64 stitches = 32 stitches, the number to be increased on both sides, 16 stitches on each side.

d. The sleeve underarm measurement is 18 inches, therefore in 11 inches we have to increase 16 times. In 8 stitches to the inch there are approximately 12 rows to the inch, therefore if we increase in every 8th row, 16 times, the increasing will be finished when the underarm measurement is 14 inches. Work even until the underarm measurement is 18 inches.

e. For the cap bind off 7 stitches at the beginning of the next 2 rows, then knit 2 together at the beginning and end of every other row until approximately 3 inches of stitches remain, which is 24 stitches.

NOTE.

The great stress on a correct stitch gauge will now be easily understandable. It is simply a matter of figuring to shape the pieces of garment; and the more we progress in the shaping, the more important role the figuring plays.

SHORT SLEEVES

This diagram for short sleeves is charted by the same principles as those for long sleeves. Different widths of short sleeves and different types of caps for them are discussed later.

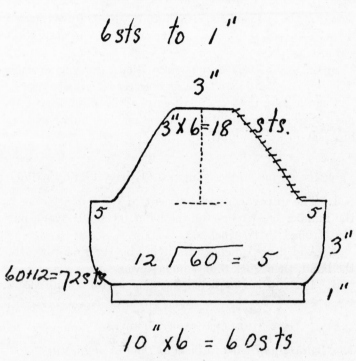

6 sts to 1"

3"

3" X 6 = 18 sts.

5   5

3"

60+12=72 sts.   12 / 60 = 5

1"

10" x 6 = 60 sts

DIAGRAM 33.

SHORT STRAIGHT SLEEVE FOR SAMPLE SWEATER

EXPLANATION. The ribbing or band for a short sleeve is the same as the upperarm measurement, which is 10 inches in the sample sweater. 10 inches × 6 stitches to the inch = 60 stitches. The ribbing on short sleeves is narrow, varying from 1 to 1½ inches in width.

The 2 inches extra for the width of the sleeve is added on the first row after the band. That is 12 more stitches. 12 into 60 goes 5, therefore we increase in every 5th stitch, making 72 stitches. (This will be a fairly tight-fitting short sleeve.)

If one desires to add 3 inches extra after the cuff, that

would be 18 stitches more. 18 into 60 goes approximately 3 times, therefore increase in every 3rd stitch, making 78 stitches.

Short sleeves are seldom more than 4½ inches long. This, of course, depends upon the needs of the wearer.

For the cap, bind off 5 stitches at the beginning of the next 2 rows, then knit 2 together at the beginning and end of every other row until 18 stitches remain.

FORMULA FOR SHORT SLEEVES (Fairly Tight-Fitting)

1. The upperarm measurement × the stitch gauge = the number of stitches for the band. (Usually made narrow, from 1 to 1½ inches.)

2. Add 2 or 3 inches of stitches on the first row after the band, then work 3 or 4 inches even.

3. The cap is completed the same as for a long sleeve.

FULLER SHORT SLEEVES

1. *Medium puff with fullness at the top of the cap*

Medium puff sleeves may be made by increasing in every 2nd stitch after the band, and decreasing for the cap the same as for tight short sleeves, until the cap is the necessary length, as in diagram.

The fullness at the top of the sleeve may be knitted in one of the following ways:

a. Knitting 2 together across the top of the sleeve, which in sewing takes the place of gathering.

b. Completing the top as one would turn the heel of a sock. (See Chapter on Socks.) This gives a wide, tailored effect.

c. Binding off all the stitches across the top; in this case, when sewing the sleeve into the armhole, form a box pleat at the top.

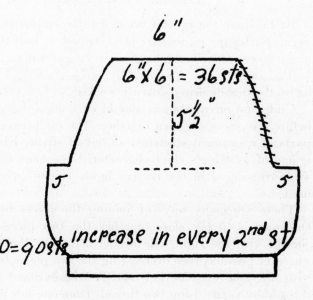

DIAGRAM 34.

2. Medium Puff with Fitted Cap

Medium puff sleeves with a fitted cap may be made to fit into the armhole by binding off 2 stitches at the beginning of every row, instead of knitting 2 together at the beginning and end of every other row.

3. Full Puff

Full puff sleeves may be made by increasing in every stitch after the band, and the decreasing for the cap worked more rapidly according to the type of fullness required.

FINISHING OF SWEATER

By finishing the sweater, we mean the completing of the sweater after the pieces have been shaped. It is of the most importance and should be done very carefully. A well-knitted sweater can be spoiled by careless sewing together or by the details being slovenly worked.

Under no circumstances should each piece be steamed before the pieces are sewn together. Too often have I seen parts of a garment stretched all out of shape. Elasticity is one of knitting's chief characteristics—most desirable when considered in the correct light, ruinous when misused.

There are many ways of joining the pieces together. One way is to lay close together the two pieces to be joined, with the right side inside, matching the stitches wherever possible, then overcasting the two pieces together with the same yarn as that used for the garment (unless it is nubby yarn) using two threads from one side and two threads from the other. This is as smooth and unnoticeable as any way. One thing to be especially remembered is that the seams must have the same stretch as the rest of the garment, so be careful not to overcrowd the stitches nor tighten them too much.

In a woman's sweater, when sewing the front and back together, we have to take care of the extra inch in length of the front from the waist to the underarm. Generally this is eased into the 4 inches below the underarm.

The shoulder seams are often a little tiresome. The stitches, where they are bound off, have two parts, so be sure both of these are sewn when joining. When coming to the different steps that slope the shoulder, overcast a little deeper. To insure that the shoulders retain their fit and to prevent them from sagging, it is advisable to tape the shoulders with ribbon binding.

Sleeves

Sew the sleeve seams, then baste the sleeves to the armholes with seam at the center underarm and the center of the top of the cap at the shoulder seam. If there is a little fullness, ease this around the top of the armhole. Do not let it protrude at the shoulder seam. Be very careful not to bind the armhole with the overcasting. Often this is done, and the armhole is considered too small.

The stitches for the ribbing of the neck should be picked up on the right side, not an extra piece sewn on. It is not necessary to use a small circular needle or a set of needles, but pick up the stitches from shoulder to shoulder, working the front first, then the back, and join at the shoulder seams on the wrong side. (Refer to Chapter on Details for miter of "V" neck.)

The ends of the yarn on the wrong side should be woven into the fabric.

Steaming Sweaters

It should not be necessary to block a sweater, that is, pin it out to shape, if it is knitted correctly and made to fit. The sweater should be steamed (*not pressed*) ; that is, hold the weight of the iron in the hand, just as the piece of fabric was steamed when we were measuring the stitch gauge. Use a damp cloth with the sweater turned on the wrong side, allowing the steam to pass through the cloth to the sweater. Under no consideration allow the weight of the iron to rest on the garment.

Leave the sweater on the table or board until thoroughly dry, then steam the seams, having the cloth not too damp.

SLEEVELESS SWEATER

Sample Sleeveless Sweater

Measurements

1. Waist—29 inches
2. Bust—34 inches
3. Shoulder to shoulder—13½ inches
4. Waist to underarm—9 inches
5. Armhole—17 inches

Stitch gauge—6 stitches to the inch

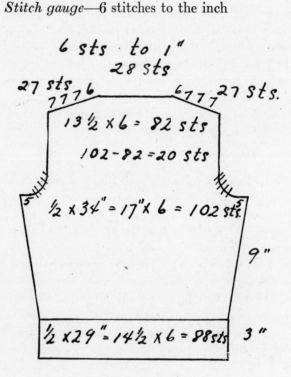

6 sts to 1"
28 sts
27 sts 7 7 6   6 7 7 7 27 sts.
13½ x 6 = 82 sts
102 - 82 = 20 sts
½ x 34" = 17" x 6 = 102 sts.
9"
½ x 29" = 14½ x 6 = 88 sts   3"

DIAGRAM 35.

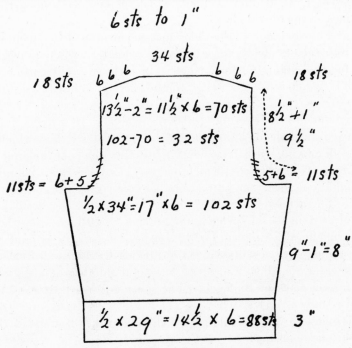

6 sts to 1"

34 sts

18 sts   6 6 6   6 6 6   18 sts

$13\frac{1}{2}" - 2" = 11\frac{1}{2}" \times 6 = 70$ sts $8\frac{1}{2}" + 1"$

$102 - 70 = 32$ sts $9\frac{1}{2}"$

11 sts = 6 + 5   5 + 6 = 11 sts

$\frac{1}{2} \times 34" = 17" \times 6 = 102$ sts

$9" - 1" = 8"$

$\frac{1}{2} \times 29" = 14\frac{1}{2} \times 6 = 88$ sts   3"

DIAGRAM 36.

Following the diagrams and comparing them, it should be a simple matter to chart any sleeveless sweater.

Back

The waist measurement is 29 inches. ½ of 29 = 14½ inches × 6 stitches to the inch = 88 stitches for the ribbing.

The bust measurement is 34 inches. ½ of 34 = 17 inches × 6 stitches to the inch = 102 stitches.

102 stitches — 88 stitches = 14 stitches to be added after the ribbing.

14 into 88 goes 6 therefore increase in every 6th stitch.

The underarm measurement is 9 inches. For a sleeveless

sweater we deduct 1 inch, which makes the underarm measurement 8 inches.

The shoulder to shoulder measurement is 13½ inches. Subtract 2 inches for a sleeveless sweater, which is used for the ribbing. 13½ inches — 2 inches = 11½ inches. 11½ inches × 6 stitches to the inch = 69 stitches, 70 stitches for an even number. 102 — 70 stitches = 32 stitches to be taken off for both armholes. 16 stitches for each armhole. We now subtract 1 inch of stitches, which is 6, making 10 stitches left, then follow the rule for binding off the armholes, which makes 11 stitches to be bound off at one time, then knit 2 together every other row, 5 times.

The armhole is made 2 inches larger than the armhole measurement. 17 inches plus 2 inches = 19 inches, ½ the armhole measurement = 9½ inches, measuring around.

There are now 70 stitches on the needle. For a sleeveless sweater we allow almost ½ the total number of stitches for the back of the neck. (The same as for a boat neck.) In this case 34 stitches for the back of the neck and 18 stitches for each shoulder, which is sloped in 3 steps of 6 stitches each.

Front

The front is worked exactly the same as the back with the exception of the neck line, which is charted the same as previous round neck lines.

DIFFERENCES BETWEEN SLEEVELESS SWEATER AND SWEATER WITH SET-IN SLEEVES

The differences between a sleeveless sweater and a sweater with set-in sleeves are these, that the neck line is wider and the armholes made larger. These are readily understandable when one realizes that the ribbing around a sleeveless sweater should not protrude over the shoulder, giving the wearer a sloppy appearance, but should be included in the actual shoulder to shoulder measurement, and the ribbing around the armhole should not fit too tightly around the armpit. We therefore make the underarm to waist measurement 1 inch shorter, which necessitates the armhole being 2 inches longer (1 inch for the back and 1 inch for the front).

FORMULA FOR SLEEVELESS SWEATER

Back

1. ½ the waist measurement × the stitch gauge = number of stitches for the waist band.

2. ½ the bust or chest measurement × the stitch gauge = the number of stitches for the body of the sweater.

3. The difference between the number of stitches for ½ the bust and ½ the waist measurement = the number of stitches to add on the first row after the ribbing.

4. Subtract 1 inch from the waist to underarm measurement, this inch to be added to the length of the armhole.

5. Subtract 2 inches from the shoulder to shoulder measurement, using these 2 inches later for the bands around the armholes.

6. The difference between the stitches for the shoulder and ½ the bust measurement = the number of stitches to take off for both armholes, ½ for one armhole.

7. Subtract 1 inch of stitches from the number and follow the rule for binding off at the armholes, that is, ½ the stitches at the first bind off, then knit 2 together for the remaining ½ of the stitches, adding the 1 inch of stitches to the first bind off.

8. Knit the armhole 1 inch longer than ½ the armhole measurement.

9. Almost ½ the shoulder to shoulder stitches used for the back of the neck (Requires one or two fewer steps to take care of the shoulders).

Front

1. Work the front the same as the back with the exception of the neck line.

2. The front neck line is charted the same as other neck lines for sweater with set-in sleeves.

When the back and front are knitted, sew together and work a 1 inch band around the armholes and neck. (See Chapter on Details.)

MAN'S SLEEVELESS SWEATER WITH "V" NECK

PLATE XXVIII.

Measurements

    Waist—32 inches

    Chest—38 inches

    Shoulder to shoulder—16 inches

    Underarm to waist—10 inches

    Armhole—19 inches

Materials

    Yarn—Worsted 12 ounces or 10 ounces of sport yarn

    Needles—#4 steel or aluminum needles

Stitch gauge—6 stitches to the inch

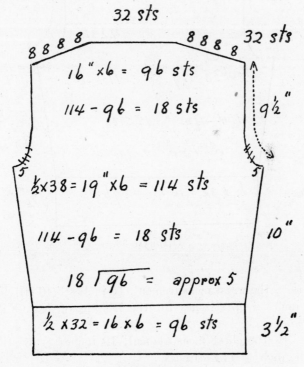

DIAGRAM 37.

The diagrams, comparing the backs of the same sized sweater with set-in sleeves, and sleeveless, should be helpful and practically self-explanatory.

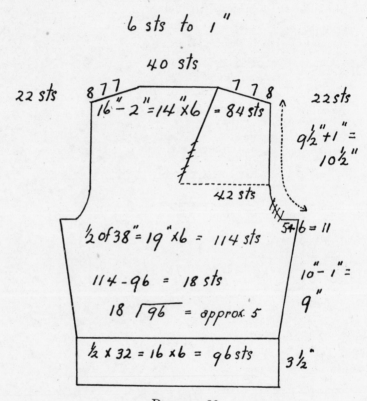

DIAGRAM 38.

Back

1. ½ the waist measurement, 16 inches × 6 stitches to the inch = 96 stitches for the ribbing of K.2, P.2 for 3½ inches.

2. ½ the chest measurement, 19 inches × 6 stitches to the inch = 114 stitches.

3. 114 stitches — 96 stitches = 18 stitches to be added after the ribbing, therefore increase in every 5th stitch across the ribbing.

4. Work the stockinette stitch for 9 inches, which is 1 inch less than the underarm to waist measurement.

5. Shoulder to shoulder measurement 16 inches — 2 inches = 14 inches for a sleeveless sweater. 14 × 6 stitches to the inch = 84 stitches for the shoulders.

6. 114 stitches — 84 stitches = 30 stitches to be taken off for both armholes, 15 stitches for each armhole. (Follow the rule in the formula.)

7. ½ the armhole measurement, 9½ inches plus 1 inch = 10½ inches.

8. 40 stitches used for the back of the neck — a little under ½ the total number.

Front

The front is knitted the same as the back with the exception of the "V" neck line, which begins after the stitches for the armholes are decreased.

Work to the center, 42 stitches, then place the other 42 stitches on a stitch holder, and knit 2 together every other row until the 22 stitches for the shoulder remain and the armhole measures 10½ inches.

Work the other side to correspond.

Pick up the stitches and work ribbing of K.2, P.2 around the neck and the armholes. (See Chapter on Details for miter.)

BOY'S SWEATER (AGE 14)

As can be seen from the illustration, this boy's sweater has an opening in the front, round neck line and set-in sleeves.

PLATE XXIX. Boy's sweater, opening in front, round neck, long sleeves.

Measurements

Waist—28 inches
Chest—34 inches
Underarm to waist—9 inches
Shoulder to shoulder—14 inches
Armhole—20 inches
Wrist—6 inches

Upperarm—10 inches
Sleeve underarm length—17 inches

Materials

Yarn—15 oz. of 4 ply Worsted
Needles—#4 steel or aluminum

Stitch gauge—5 stitches to the inch

BACK OF SWEATER

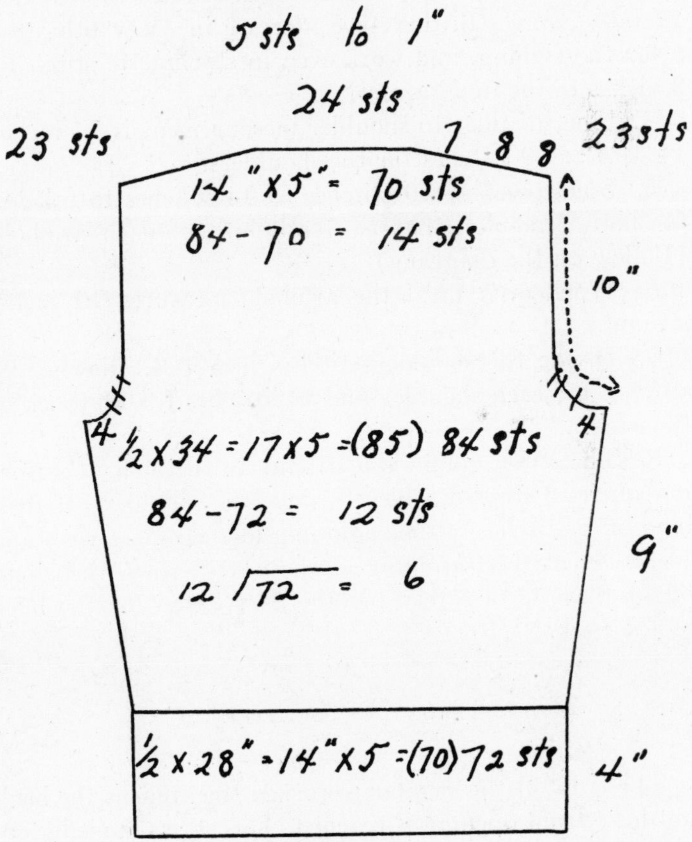

5 sts to 1"

24 sts

23 sts   7 8 8   23 sts

14"x5" = 70 sts
84 - 70 = 14 sts

10"

$\frac{1}{2}$ x 34 = 17x5 = (85) 84 sts

84 - 72 = 12 sts

12 $\overline{)72}$ = 6

9"

$\frac{1}{2}$ x 28" = 14" x 5 = (70) 72 sts   4"

DIAGRAM 39.

Back

1. Waist measurement 28 inches. ½ of 28 = 14 × 5 stitches to the inch = 70 stitches; to make it divisible by 4 we require 72 stitches for ribbing of K.2, P.2 for 4 inches.

2. The chest measurement is 34 inches. ½ of 34 = 17 × 5 stitches = 85 stitches for the chest, 84 stitches, an even number.

3. 84 stitches — 72 stitches = 12 stitches to be added. 12 into 72 goes 6, therefore increase in every 6th stitch after the ribbing, and work even in stockinette stitch for 9 inches to the underarm.

4. The shoulder to shoulder measurement is 14 inches. 14 × 5 = 70 stitches for the shoulders.

5. 84 stitches — 70 stitches = 14 stitches to take off for both armholes, that is, 7 stitches for each armhole. (Follow on the diagram.)

6. Work even until the armhole measures 10 inches around.

7. Divide the shoulder stitches into 1/3, allowing 23 stitches for each shoulder and 24 stitches for the back of the neck.

8. The stitch gauge is 5 stitches to the inch, therefore it requires 3 steps in which to slope the shoulders, that is, bind off 8 stitches at the beginning of the next 4 rows and 7 stitches at the beginning of the next 2 rows, then bind off or place on a safety pin the 24 stitches for the back of the neck.

FRONT OF SWEATER

Front

The front of the sweater is worked the same as the back until the front opening is reached. This starts immediately after the decreasing for the armholes. (When putting zipper fastening be sure the opening measures equal inches.) Knit across ½ the total stitches, which is 35 stitches, placing the remaining 35 stitches on a stitch holder. Knit until the armhole measurement is 8 inches, or 2 inches from the tip of the shoulder.

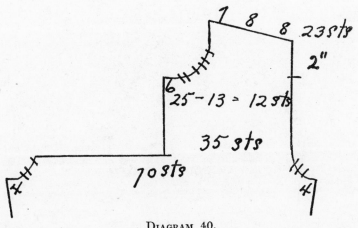

DIAGRAM 40.

Neck Line and Shoulder

The difference between the number of stitches on the needle, which is 35 stitches, and the shoulder stitches, 23, = 12 stitches to be decreased at the neck edge. Therefore bind off ½ the stitches in a straight line which is 6 stitches, then knit 2 together every other row, 6 times, leaving 23 stitches for the shoulder. (Front and back armhole to measure the same.) Shoulder is bound off to correspond with the back shoulder.

The wrist measurement is 6 inches. In this case 2 inches extra are added. 8 ×5 stitches to the inch = 40 stitches of K.2, P.2 for 3 inches. As 2 inches of stitches were added to the cuff measurement, it is not necessary to add 1 inch of stitches immediately after the ribbing for the cuff. The

Sleeve

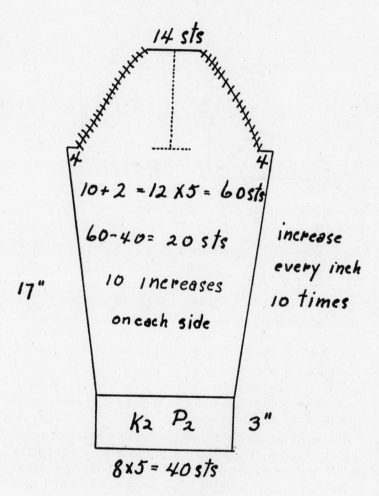

5 sts to 1"

14 sts

4   4

$10 + 2 = 12 \times 5 = 60$ sts

$60 - 40 = 20$ sts

10 increases

on each side

17"

increase
every inch
10 times

K2 P2   3"

$8 \times 5 = 40$ sts

DIAGRAM 41.

upperarm measurement is 10 inches plus 2 inches for the width of the sleeve. 12 $\times$ 5 stitches to the inch = 60 stitches for the sleeve width. 60 — 40 = 20 stitches to be increased, 10 stitches at each side of the sleeve; therefore increase every inch at both sides of the sleeve 10 times. The last 4 inches knitted even.

Cap of sleeve

Bind off 4 stitches at the beginning of the next 2 rows, then knit 2 together at the beginning and end of every other row until the cap fits the armhole, which, when approximately 3 inches of stitches remain, will be 16 stitches.

Work the other sleeve to correspond.

Completing the sweater

Work one row of single crochet around the opening in the front, baste and sew the zipper in the opening. Sew parts together as in previous directions for sweaters. Pick up the stitches around the neck line; the number should be divisible by 2 so both sides of the ribbing are the same. Knit ½ inch of K.2, P.2. Bind off 4 stitches at the beginning of the next 4 rows, then bind off all the stitches, knitting the knit stitches and purling the purls.

WOMAN'S SLIP-ON SWEATER WITH ROUND NECK

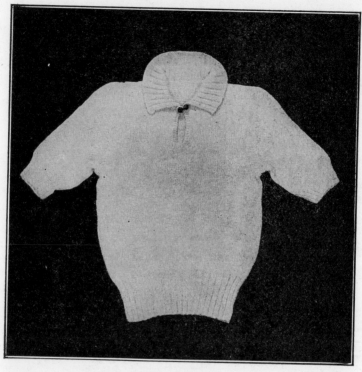

Plate XXX.

Measurements

    Waist—26½ inches
    Bust—34 inches
    Shoulder to shoulder—14 inches
    Waist to underarm—10 inches
    Upperarm—10 inches
    Armhole—18½ inches

Materials

    6 oz. of Shetland floss
    A pair of #3 steel or aluminum needles

Stitch gauge—6 stitches to the inch

Back

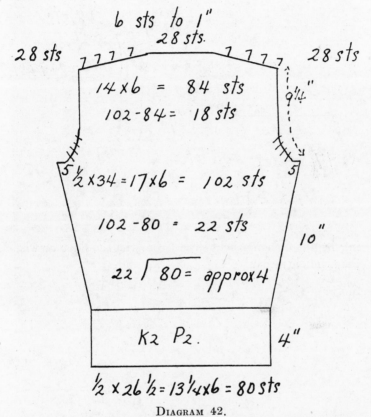

6 sts to 1"

28 sts.

28 sts   28 sts

14 x 6 = 84 sts

102 - 84 = 18 sts

9¼"

5¼

5

½ x 34 = 17 x 6 = 102 sts

102 - 80 = 22 sts

22 ⟌ 80 = approx 4

10"

K2 P2.

4"

½ x 26½ = 13¼ x 6 = 80 sts

Diagram 42.

This is a simple sweater, therefore few directions are necessary. The diagrams should be easily understandable.

Front

The opening in the front is 3 inches long with 3 stitches of garter stitch on each side. The round neck line begins 2 inches below the tip of the shoulder, therefore the open-

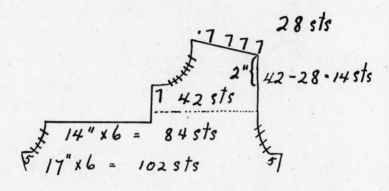

6 sts to 1"

28 sts

.7 7 7 7

2" 42 - 28 - 14 sts

7 42 sts

14" × 6 = 84 sts

17" × 6 = 102 sts

102 - 84 sts = 18 sts

DIAGRAM 43.

ing begins 5 inches below the tip of the shoulder or when the armhole measures 4¼ inches around.

Sleeve

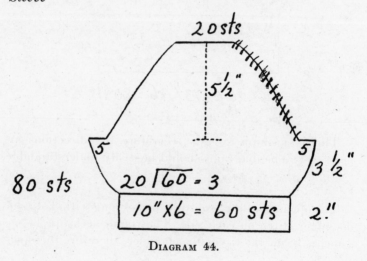

20 sts

5½"

80 sts

20 ⟌60 = 3

10" × 6 = 60 sts

3½"

2"

DIAGRAM 44.

Collar

The stitches for the collar are picked up on the wrong side. It is impossible to shape a collar made of ribbing, therefore 1½ inches are worked on #3 needles, and 1½ inches with #4 needles.

WOMAN'S CREW-NECK ANGORA SWEATER

Measurements

Waist—26 inches
Bust—34 inches
Underarm to waist—8 inches
Shoulders—13½ inches
Armhole—18 inches
Upperarm measurement—9 inches

Materials

6 oz. of sport angora
Pair of #2 steel needles

Stitch gauge—8 sts to the inch. 12 rows to the inch.

The armhole measurement is 18 inches. ½ of 18 inches is 9 inches, but according to the charts the armhole measurements are 7½ inches worked in stockinette stitch and 2 inches of ribbing, making 9½ inches altogether. This is explained in the discussion on crew-neck sweaters earlier in the book.

ILLUSTRATION 4.   Woman's crew-neck sweater.

8 sts to 1"

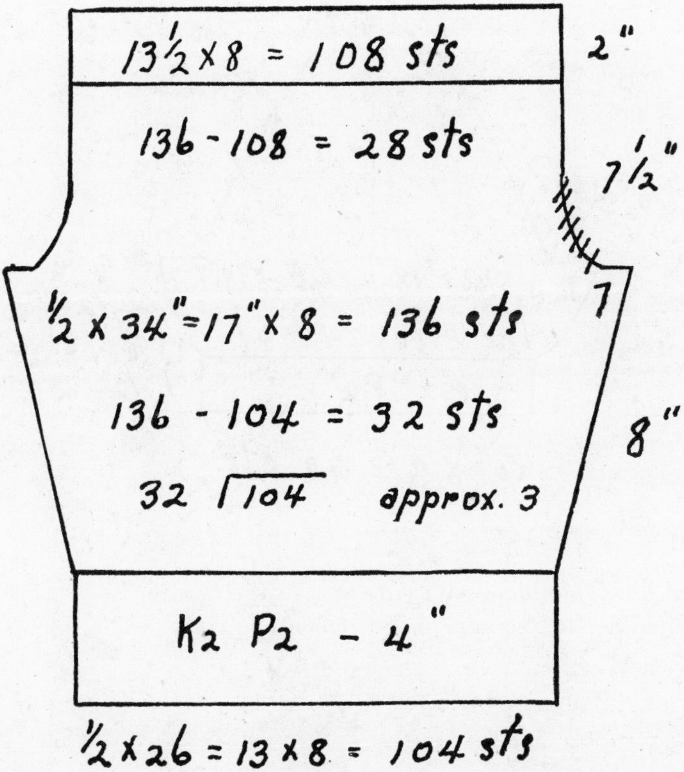

$13\frac{1}{2} \times 8 = 108$ sts   2"

$136 - 108 = 28$ sts $7\frac{1}{2}$"

$\frac{1}{2} \times 34" = 17" \times 8 = 136$ sts   7

$136 - 104 = 32$ sts   8"

$32 \overline{)104}$ approx. 3

K2 P2 – 4"

$\frac{1}{2} \times 26 = 13 \times 8 = 104$ sts

DIAGRAM 45.

Sleeves

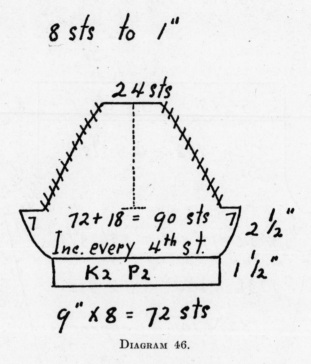

8 sts to 1"

24 sts

$72 + 18 = 90$ sts
Inc. every 4th st.

7   7 $2\frac{1}{2}$"

K2 P2 $1\frac{1}{2}$"

$9" \times 8 = 72$ sts

DIAGRAM 46.

The shoulder seams are sewn together for a ¼ of the shoulder to shoulder measurement.

MAN'S CARDIGAN (COAT SWEATER)

ILLUSTRATION 5.

Measurements

    Chest—44 inches
    Hip—44 inches
    Underarm to desired length (hip)—19 inches
    Shoulder to shoulder measurement—17 inches
    Wrist—8 inches
    Upperarm—14 inches
    Sleeve underarm—20 inches
    Armhole—23 inches

Materials

    24 oz. of knitting worsted
        or
    20 oz. of sport yarn or fingering
    A pair of #4 steel or aluminum needles

Stitch gauge—6 stitches to the inch. 8 rows to the inch

Back

The hip measurement is 44 inches. ½ of 44 is 22 inches × 6 stitches to the inch = 132 stitches. Knit 1½ inches in garter stitch (all knitting) and the remaining 17½ inches in stockinette stitch, making the total length of the underarm.

The shoulder to shoulder measurement is 17 inches. 17 × 6 stitches to the inch = 102 stitches. The difference between 132 stitches and 102 stitches = 30 stitches, which is the number to be taken off for both armholes, therefore 15 stitches to be taken off for each armhole. Following the rule, bind off 8 stitches at the beginning of the next 2 rows, then knit 2 together at the beginning and end of every other row, 7 times. The total armhole measurement is 23 inches, therefore knit even until the armhole measurement is 11½ inches (measuring around).

The general rule for binding off shoulders is to allow approximately 1/3 of the stitches for each shoulder and

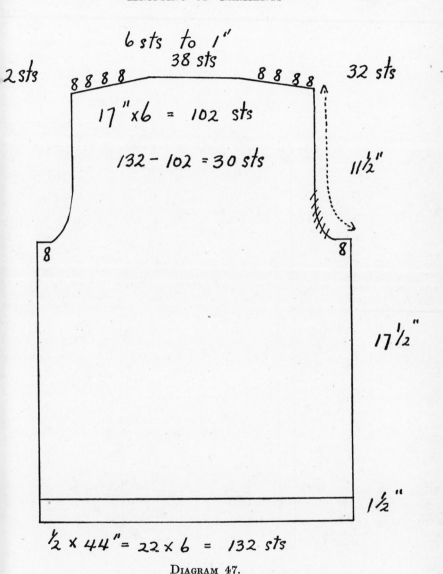

6 sts to 1"

38 sts

2 sts

8 8 8 8

17" × 6 = 102 sts

132 − 102 = 30 sts

32 sts

8 8 8 8

11½"

8

8

17½"

1½"

½ × 44" = 22 × 6 = 132 sts

DIAGRAM 47.

the remaining 1/3 for the back of the neck. In this case a few extra stitches are allowed for the back of the neck (see diagram)—38 stitches, and 32 stitches for each shoulder. The gauge is 6 stitches to the inch, therefore

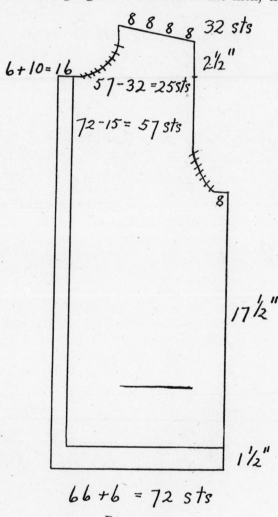

8 8 8 8   32 sts

6 + 10 = 16

2½"

57 − 32 = 25 sts

72 − 15 = 57 sts

8

17½"

1½"

66 + 6 = 72 sts

Diagram 48.

4 steps are required to slope the shoulder. Bind off 8 stitches at the beginning of the next 8 rows, then lastly the 38 stitches for the back of the neck.

Front

For each front the stitches for the band have to be added. (See Chapter on Details for Buttonholes.) The buttonholes require 6 stitches, therefore each band is 12 stitches wide. Remembering that the bands overlap, 6 stitches or ½ the width of the band is added to each front. This insures no gaping at the opening.

½ of 132 stitches = 66 stitches, the necessary number of stitches for each front. 66 stitches plus 6 stitches = 72 stitches with the band.

Work garter stitch on 72 stitches for 1½ inches to match the back, then continue in stockinette stitch, keeping 12 stitches at the front edge in garter stitch for buttons. (Buttonholes for man's sweater are on the left side, so work the right side first to learn the position of the buttonholes.) The opening for the pocket is made 6 inches from the bottom (See diagram and also refer to Chapter on Details for Pockets) and is 4 inches wide, therefore knit 14, bind off 24 stitches, knit 34 stitches. On the wrong side add the 24 stitches that were bound off for the pocket. Work even until the front underarm measures the same as the back underarm, then shape the armhole the same as the back armhole.

Neck line

The neck line is started 2½ inches below the tip of the shoulder. 32 of the 57 stitches are required for the shoulder, therefore 25 stitches remain for the neck line. 6 of these 25 stitches overlap at the band, leaving 19 stitches, therefore 10 plus 6 stitches are bound off in a straight line and the remaining 9 stitches decreased by knitting 2 together every other row.

Shoulder

The front shoulder is bound off the same as the back shoulder.

Left Front

The left front is knitted to correspond with the right front, the buttonholes starting 3½ inches from the bottom and every 3 inches thereafter, making 7 buttonholes altogether, allowing 6 stitches for each buttonhole in the center of the band.

Pockets

The stitches for the 2 parts of the pocket are picked up on the right side and knitted in stockinette stitch for 4 inches, then the sides and bottom sewn together.

Sleeves

10 inches of stitches for the wrist. 10 ×6 stitches to the inch = 60 stitches for the cuff, which is 4 inches wide. Increase 1 inch of stitches on the first row after the cuff is knitted. 6 into 60 goes 10, therefore increase in every 10 stitches, making 66 stitches. Width of the upperarm is 14 inches. Add 2 inches to the width, making 16 inches for the width of the sleeve. 16 × 6 stitches to the inch = 96 stitches. That is, 30 stitches are to be increased on both sides, 15 stitches on each side. The sleeve underarm length is 20 inches, 4 inches of which have been knitted, leaving 16 inches, therefore increase every 6th row until 96 stitches are formed, then knit even until the underarm measurement of the sleeve is 20 inches.

Cap of Sleeve

Bind off 8 stitches at the beginning of the next 2 rows, then knit 2 together at the beginning and the end of every

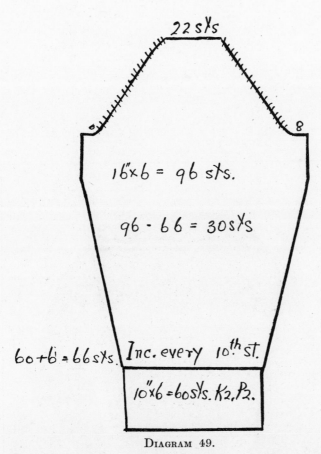

6 sts to 1"

22 sts

16"×6 = 96 sts.

96 - 66 = 30 sts

60+6 = 66 sts. Inc. every 10th st.

10"×6 = 60 sts. K2, P2.

DIAGRAM 49.

other row until 3½ inches of stitches remain, which is 22 stitches.

Collar

Pick up all the stitches around the neck on the wrong side, starting and ending in the center of each band. There should be approximately 108 stitches. Work in ribbing of K.2, P.2 for 2½ inches. Bind off 4 stitches at the begining of each row, 16 times, then bind off the remaining stitches.

Finishing

Sew together the same as in directions for sample sweater and steam.

YOUTH'S CABLE STITCH SWEATER (AGE 16-18 YEARS)

PLATE XXXI.

Measurements

Waist—30 inches
Chest—32 inches
Underarm to waist—12 inches
Shoulder to shoulder—15 inches
Wrist—7 inches
Upperarm—12 inches
Sleeve underarm length—20 inches
Armhole—20 inches

Materials

14 oz. of sport yarn
1 pair of #2 steel needles for ribbing
1 pair of #3 steel needles for the body
a double pointed needle
18 inch zipper
#4 or #5 steel crochet hook

Stitch gauge with #2 needles—7 stitches to the inch
     "   "   " #3 needles—6 "   " " "

PLATE XXXII. Cable stitch.

PATTERN FOR CABLE STITCH
Multiple of 14 plus 4.

Row 1. K.4 * P.2, K.6, P.2, K.4. *
Row 2. P.4 * K.2, P.6, K.2, P.4. *

Repeat these 2 rows.

The cable is twisted every 6th row. (See Chapter on Stitches.)

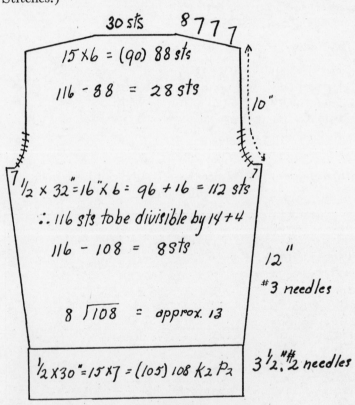

30 sts   8 7 7 7

15 × 6 = (90) 88 sts

116 - 88 = 28 sts

10"

7   7

$\frac{1}{2}$ × 32" = 16" × 6 = 96 + 16 = 112 sts

∴ 116 sts to be divisible by 14 + 4

116 - 108 = 8 sts

12"

#3 needles

8 $\overline{)108}$ = approx. 13

$\frac{1}{2}$ × 30" = 15 × 7 = (105) 108 K2 P2

3$\frac{1}{2}$" #2 needles

DIAGRAM 50.

Back

Cast on 108 stitches and work in ribbing of K.2, P.2 for 3½ inches with #2 needles. ½ of 32 = 16 inches × 6 stitches to the inch = 96 stitches plus 16 stitches (2 stitches for each cable) = 112 stitches for the body of the sweater. 116 is divisible by 14 plus 4 stitches for the cable pattern.

With #3 needles work 12 inches to the underarm, twisting the cables on every 6th row.

To form the armholes bind off 7 stitches at the beginning of the next 2 rows, then knit 2 together at the beginning and end of every other row, 7 times. Work even on the remaining 88 stitches until around the armhole measures 10 inches.

To shape the shoulders, bind off 7 stitches at the beginning of the next row, knit in pattern the next 22 stitches, purl 30 center stitches (for back of the bands), then knit in pattern the last 22 stitches. Continue in this manner, purling (on the right side) the center 30 stitches until 7, 7, 7, 8 stitches have been bound off on each shoulder, then bind off the remaining 30 purled stitches.

Front

Cast on 60 stitches and work in ribbing with #2 needles for 3½ inches. Increase in every 4th stitch, making 74 stitches. With #3 needles knit in pattern, purling the 6 stitches on the center front. Knit in pattern until the work measures 12 inches from the ribbing. Decrease the armholes the same as the back armholes, and when the center front measures 18 inches from the bottom of the ribbing, knit 2 together every other row on the center front to form the "V" neck, keeping 6 purled stitches on the front and decreasing inside the purls, dropping the cables as decreasing, until 29 stitches remain. Bind off the shoulder the same as the back shoulder.

Work the other front to correspond.

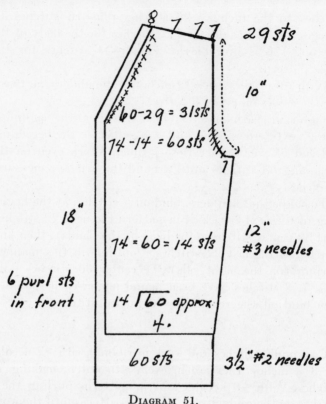

8 7 7 7 7   29 sts

10"

60-29 = 31 sts

74-14 = 60 sts

7

18"

12"
#3 needles

74 = 60 = 14 sts

6 purl sts
in front

14 √60 approx
4.

60 sts   3½" #2 needles

DIAGRAM 51.

Sleeve

Cast on 60 stitches and work in ribbing with #2 needles for 3½ inches. Increase in every 4th stitch, making 74 stitches. With #3 needles, work in pattern increasing a stitch each side every inch 13 times until 100 stitches on the needle. Do not add more cables on the extra stitches but make them stockinette stitch. When the sleeve measures 20 inches, bind off 7 stitches at the beginning of the next 2 rows, then knit 2 together at the beginning and end of every other row until 26 stitches remain. Bind these off.

The two sleeves are knitted the same.

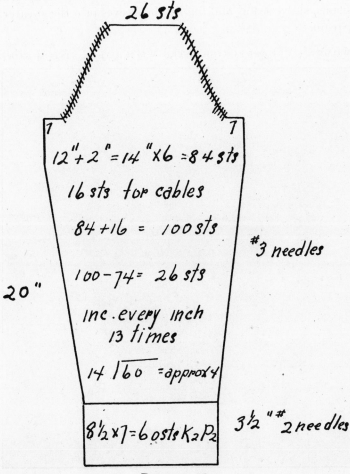

26 sts

$12'' + 2'' = 14'' \times 6 = 84$ sts

16 sts for cables

$84 + 16 = 100$ sts

$100 - 74 = 26$ sts

Inc. every inch
13 times

$14 \overline{)60} =$ approx 4

$8\frac{1}{2} \times 7 = 60$ sts $K_2 P_2$

20"

#3 needles

$3\frac{1}{2}$" #2 needles

DIAGRAM 52.

Finishing

Sew the shoulder seams. Single crochet tightly, beginning on the right front at the bottom of the ribbing (on the right side) and working around the neck and down the other side to the bottom of the ribbing. Pin the zipper in place. Baste. Sew on the machine, then sew the underarm seams, sleeve seams and finally the sleeves into the sweater. Steam.

WOMAN'S CREW-NECK SWEATER WITH CABLE STITCH YOKE

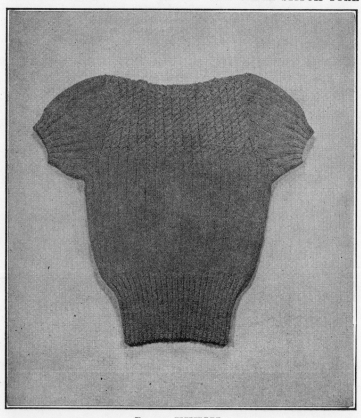

PLATE XXXIII.

Measurements

    Waist—27 inches
    Bust—34 inches
    Underarm to waist—8 inches

Armhole—17 inches
Shoulder to shoulder—13½ inches
Upperarm—9 inches

Materials

8 oz. of 3 ply fingering or sport yarn
1 pair of #2 steel needles for ribbing
1 pair of #4 steel needles for body
A double-pointed needle #12

Stitches

1. Multiple of 6 plus 5.
   Row 1. * K.5, P.1. * K.5.
   Row 2. * P.5, K.1. * P.5.

   Repeat these 2 rows for the body of sweater.

2. Multiple of 5 plus 5.
   Row 1. K.2, P.1. * K.4, P.1. * K.2.
   Row 2. P.2, K.1. * P.4, K.1. * P.2.

   Repeat these 2 rows for the yoke twisting the cable every 4th row.

Back and Front of Sweater

Follow the diagrams. The #2 needles are used for the ribbing and the #4 for the remainder.

½ of 27 inches = 13½ inches × 8 stitches to the inch = 108 stitches for ribbing of K.2, P.2 for 5 inches with #2 needles.

½ of 34 inches = 17 inches × 6 stitches to the inch = 102 stitches. (Has to be divisible by 6 plus 5.) Work #1 pattern on 107 stitches for 8 inches.

13½ inches for shoulder × 6 stitches to the inch = 80 stitches plus 10 stitches for the cables = 90 stitches.

Work until the armhole measures 8¼ inches (measuring around) then rib in K.2, P.2 ¾ inch, making 9 inches altogether.

The back and front are made the same with the exception of the pocket. The yoke in each case starts immediately after the armhole stitches have been taken off.

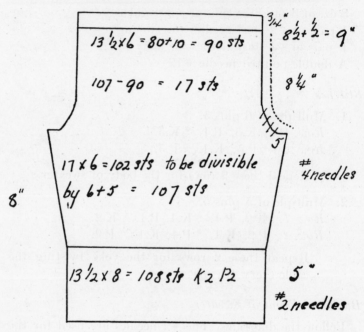

DIAGRAM 53.

Pocket

The pocket begins after 2 twists of the cables and requires 4 cables. On the row the pocket is bound off, K.2, P.1, K.4, then bind off * P.1, K.4. * 4 times and P.1, making 21 stitches. Continue working the pattern across the row.

Have a piece for the pocket already knitted, 21 stitches wide and 2½ inches in stockinette stitch and 1 inch in cable to match the stitches which were bound off, ending on the right side. On the way knitting back, this piece of fabric is used to take the place of the stitches which were bound off.

Sleeve

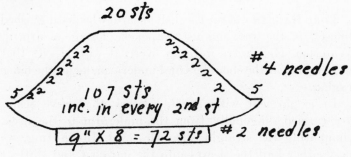

DIAGRAM 54.

The sleeve is a wide short sleeve and fits into the armhole, therefore we bind off 5 stitches at the beginning of the first two rows then bind off 2 stitches at the beginning of every row until the cap fits into the armhole and approximately 20 stitches remain.

Finishing

The seams are sewn together the same as in the sample sweater and 14 stitches are joined across the shoulders.

CHAPTER V

RAGLANS

LORD RAGLAN was an English general who distinguished himself in the wars against Napoleon, losing an arm at Waterloo. He always wore an overcoat with sleeves that were roomy at the shoulders and underarm, hence the name raglan.

In a garment with raglan sleeves the sleeve seams are carried diagonally from the underarm to the neck, eliminating the straight shoulder seam. In knitting, we may either knit the sleeves into the garment and start at the neck, or make a set-in raglan in which case each piece is knitted separately and then sewn together.

Before deciding on a raglan sleeve garment, it is advisable to consider the following:

1. Raglan sleeves bring down the shoulders and make them appear less square.

2. Raglan sleeves exaggerate stooped, rounded, narrow and sloping shoulders, making them appear worse than they really are.

KNIT-IN RAGLAN USED FOR SWEATER, BLOUSE OR COAT

We begin a knit-in raglan at the neck, and work the fronts, sleeves and back all in one piece until we reach the underarm. Starting at the neck with the necessary number of stitches allotted for front, sleeves and back, we have to widen the material as we knit. This widening or increasing may be done in many ways. The simplest way, I believe, is where the necessary stitches for the front, sleeves and back are marked by markers (small rings or pieces of thread which stay right on the needles, passing along as one knits) and the increases made by knitting first in the front of the stitch and then in the back of the same stitch. In other words, 2 stitches are made from one, every other row before and after these markers. This eliminates counting and is easily followed. As the fabric is increasing 8 stitches every other row, 2 stitches for the front, 2 stitches for each sleeve and 2 stitches for the back, the material widens considerably, hence a circular needle is required to take care of all the stitches.

At the underarm the fabric is separated into sleeves, back and front. If no underseam is desired, the sleeves are knitted first, then the front and back worked together. It is possible to knit a raglan sweater, blouse or coat without a single seam. In that case we require 2 circular needles, one short one, 16 inches long, and one 27 inches long.

NOTE. The sleeves must be knitted first if no small circular needle is to be used.

As we continue, the mathematics are becoming a little more complex, but if we understand what has previously been stated, and are able to apply the formulas which have already been explained, the charting of raglans will not be difficult.

For a raglan sleeve sweater or blouse, 2 additional measurements from those already taken are necessary; the neck measurement and the length from the top of the shoulder at the neck line to the underarm, i.e., the diagonal line of the raglan.

By the neck measurement, we mean the exact neck measusement, not the neck line of the garment after it is finished. The measurement should be exact and taken around the smallest part of the neck. This is most important because if measured too large the whole top of the garment will be too large and there is no way to rectify it. If a man's sweater is being made, the neck measurement of his shirt will be satisfactory.

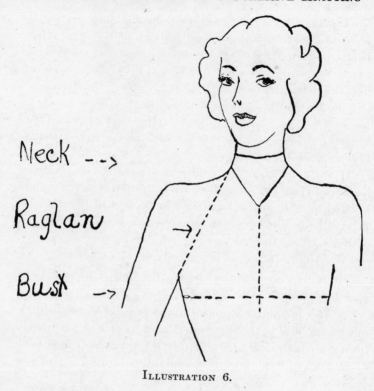

Neck --->

Raglan

Bust -->

ILLUSTRATION 6.

SAMPLE RAGLAN

Measurements
  Neck—14 inches
  Raglan—10 inches

Stitch gauge
  6 stitches to the inch
  8 rows to the inch

We shall take for the sample raglan, a neck measurement of 14 inches, because it is one from which all other raglans may be charted. A smaller neck measurement as well as a larger one will later be charted for a raglan.

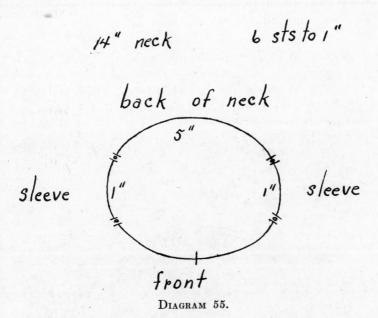

14" neck   6 sts to 1"

back of neck

5"

sleeve   1"   1"   sleeve

front

DIAGRAM 55.

14 inches × 6 stitches to the inch = 84 stitches for the neck line. At this point we shall not consider the type of neck we desire but the number of stitches to be allotted for the back, the sleeves and the front of the neck.

We require approximately 5 inches of stitches for the back of the neck. 5 inches × 6 stitches to the inch = 30 stitches for the back of the neck. For each sleeve allow 1 inch of stitches, which is 6 stitches, therefore the 2 sleeves will require 12 stitches.

The 8 slanting lines represent the stitches on which the increases are made. (The small circles are not stitches but markers which separate the front from the sleeves, the sleeves from the back, etc.)

We have used, therefore,

> 30 stitches for the back of the neck
> 12 stitches for the sleeves
> 8 stitches for the increases

—

50 stitches of the 84 stitches, which leaves 34 stitches for the front, 17 stitches for each side, if we are having an opening.

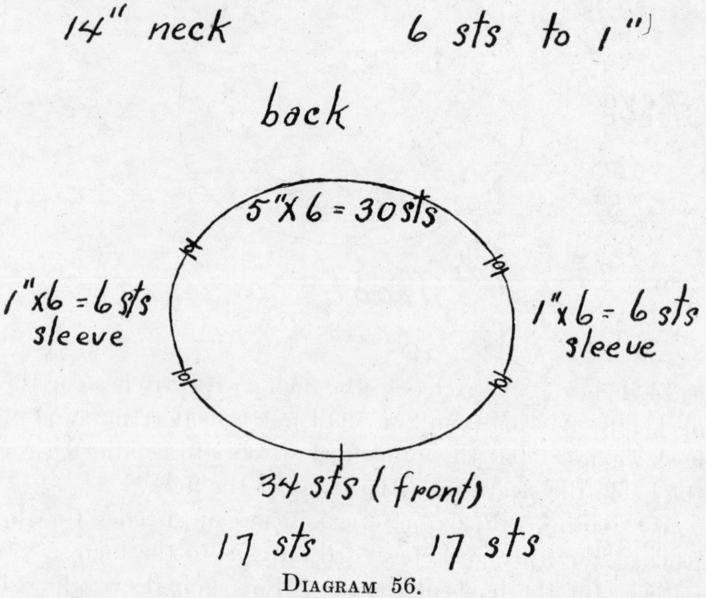

DIAGRAM 56.

We have, therefore, 4 stitches more for the front of the neck than the back. This is permissible and correct. Generally from ¾ of an inch to 1 inch of stitches more than the back stitches is allowed for an adult, and sometimes more, depending upon the size of the bust, in which case some of the back of the neck stitches are added to the front.

We now know the number of stitches for each part of the neck. We may cast on all the 84 stitches at one time if we are going to have an opening in the front and a turned back lapel for either sweater, blouse or coat; but when a shaped neck line is desired, even if it be a high round neck, if the stitches are cast on all at one time, there will be a bulge in the garment below the throat. We shall, therefore, have to chart the neck line to learn how to shape it gradually, the same as we did for the sweater with set-in sleeves.

As it is the easiest to understand, when all the stitches are cast on at one time, this is explained first.

METHOD. (Follow the diagram as we proceed.)

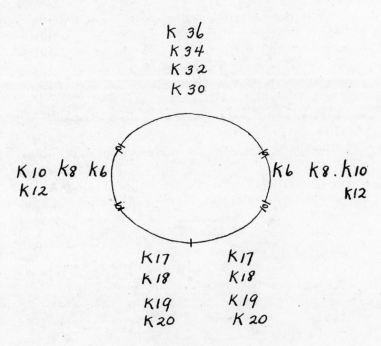

DIAGRAM 57.

Cast on 84 stitches on a circular needle but do not join. Knit 17 for a front, increase in the next stitch, place a marker on the needle, increase in the next stitch, knit 6 stitches for sleeve, increase in the next stitch, place a marker on the needle, increase in the next stitch, knit 30 stitches for the back of the neck, increase in the next stitch, place a marker on the needle, increase in the next stitch, knit 6 stitches for sleeve, increase in the next stitch, place a marker on the needle, increase in the next stitch, knit 17 stitches for the front.

Each of the increases made a new stitch. We have, therefore, 8 more stitches on the needle, making 18 stitches for each front, 8 stitches for each sleeve and 32 stitches for the back. 84 stitches plus 8 stitches = 92 stitches altogether.

As there is an opening in the front, every 2nd row is purled (no increases on the purl row) passing the markers from one side to the other.

The second knit row will now read:

Knit 18 stitches (front), increase before and after the marker, knit 8 stitches (sleeve), increase before and after the marker, knit 32 stitches (back) increase before and after the marker, knit 8 stitches (sleeve), increase before and after the marker, knit 18 stitches (front). Then purl back.

The seam stitch will readily be seen as we proceed.

We continue in this manner, increasing before and after the markers on every knit row and purling every other row, until the raglan (seam stitch) measures 10 inches. At this point the underarm is reached.

The markers now separate the fronts, sleeves and back, and, as before stated, the sleeves are finished first.

Leave all the stitches, but the stitches for one of the sleeves, on the circular needle and work the sleeve stitches back and forth with straight needles, the same size as the circular needle. Usually ½ inch of stitches, 3 stitches in this case, is added to each side of the sleeve, as well as the fronts and back, to give shape at the underarm. This is the same as the first bind·off when set-in sleeves are knitted.

PLATE XXXIV.   Shows raglan increase.

From now on the sleeve is charted the opposite from set-in sleeves, i.e., the decreases are made when knitting down the sleeve, instead of the increases being knitted when working up. (See formulas for long and short sleeves.)

Work the other sleeve to correspond.

Body

Add to each underarm, ½ inch of stitches, 3 stitches in this case, the same as for the sleeves, and work the fronts and back together, joining the fronts. This means that every row will be knitted. If a sweater or loosely-fitting blouse is being made, work even to the waist and decrease instead of increase as for sweater with set-in sleeves.

RAGLANS WITH DIFFERENT STITCH GAUGES

1.

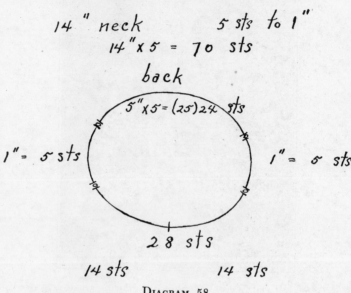

DIAGRAM 58.

The diagrams are for the same size neck line as the sample raglan but use a different stitch gauge.

A little explanation should be all that is necessary.

Neck measurement—14 inches
Stitch gauge—5 stitches to the inch

14 inches × 5 stitches to the inch = 70 stitches for the neck. 5 inches for the back of the neck—5 × 5 stitches to the inch = 25 stitches, 24 stitches (even number).

1 inch for sleeve = 5 stitches, 10 stitches for both sleeves.

8 stitches for increases, therefore:

    24 stitches for the back of the neck
    10 stitches for the sleeves
     8 stitches for the increases
    ——
    42 stitches

70 stitches — 42 stitches = 28 stitches, 14 stitches for each front.

2.

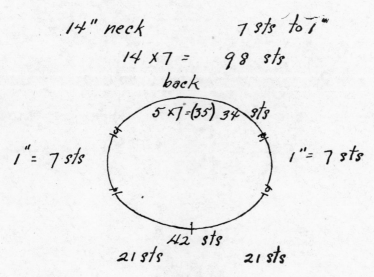

DIAGRAM 59.

Neck measurement—14 inches
Stitch gauge—7 stitches to the inch

14 inches × 7 stitches to the inch = 98 stitches for the neck. 5 inches for the back of the neck—5 ×7 stitches to the inch = 35 stitches, 34 stitches (even number).

1 inch for sleeve—7 stitches, 14 stitches for 2 sleeves.

8 stitches for increases, therefore:

> 34 stitches for the back of the neck
> 14 stitches for sleeves
> 8 stitches for increases
> —
> 56 stitches

98 stitches — 56 stitches = 42 stitches for both fronts, 21 stitches for each front.

3.

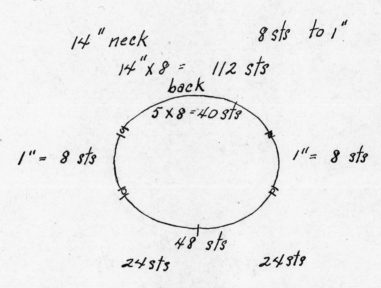

DIAGRAM 60.

Neck measurement—14 inches
Stitch gauge—8 stitches to the inch

14 inches × 8 stitches to the inch = 112 stitches. 5 inches for the back of the neck = 5 × 8 stitches to the inch = 40 stitches.

1 inch for sleeve = 8 stitches, 16 stitches for 2 sleeves.

8 stitches for increasing, therefore:

    40 stitches for the back of the neck

    16 stitches for 2 sleeves

     8 stitches for increases

    ——

    64 stitches

112 stitches — 64 stitches = 48 stitches for front, 24 stitches for each front.

EXPLANATION OF THE NUMBER OF STITCHES FOR SLEEVES, BACK AND FRONT

The stitch gauge for the sample raglan is 6 stitches to the inch and 8 rows to the inch. From these, one is able to calculate how many stitches there are at the underarm, in other words, the chest or bust measurement and the width of the sleeves. The measurements are the same as for sweater with set-in sleeves.

Sleeve

There are 10 inches to the underarm. There are 8 rows to the inch, therefore 80 rows have been knitted. Increasing every other row, there are 40 increases on one side of the sleeve and 40 increases on the other side, making 80 increases altogether.

80 stitches plus 6 stitches = 86 stitches.

86 stitches divided by 6 stitches to the inch = 14 inches, the width of the sleeve, before adding any stitches at the underarm.

Back

Similarly there are 80 stitches increased at the back, plus 30 stitches allotted for the back = 110 stitches for the back underarm.

Front

Similarly there are 80 stitches increased at the front, plus 34 stitches allotted for the front = 114 stitches.

110 stitches plus 114 stitches = 224 stitches, the total number of stitches for the chest or bust.

224 stitches divided by 6 stitches to the inch = 37 inches before adding any stitches at the underarm.

> NOTE. It will be seen that the different measurements may be changed, if the proportions for certain figures are not the same. For example, by increasing every 4th row the width is lessened, or by increasing every row the width is increased, but the length of the raglan is maintained. Also the stitches for the bust may be increased every 2nd row while the sleeves are only increased every 4th row and vice versa.

HOW TO PROPORTION STITCHES FOR KNIT-IN RAGLANS FOR DIFFERENT SIZE NECK LINES USING DIFFERENT STITCH GAUGES

1.

Neck measurement—16 inches
Stitch gauge—6 stitches to the inch

The diagram is almost self-explanatory.

16 inches × 6 stitches to the inch = 96 stitches for the total neck line.

Proportioning the stitches from a 14 inch neck line, there is required for the back of the neck:

$^{16}/_{14}$ of 5 inches × 6 stitches to the inch = 34 stitches.

Similarly:

$^{16}/_{14}$ of 1 inch × 6 stitches to the inch = 7 stitches for each sleeve.

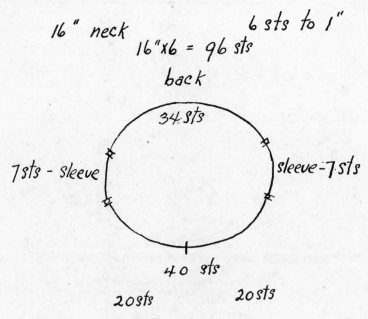

16" neck   6 sts to 1"

16" x6 = 96 sts

back

34 sts

7 sts - sleeve   sleeve - 7 sts

40 sts

20 sts   20 sts

DIAGRAM 61.

Therefore,   34 stitches for the back of the neck
             14 stitches for both sleeves
              8 stitches for the increases
             ──
             56 stitches

96 stitches — 56 stitches = 40 stitches for the front of
the neck as shown on the diagram.

2.

Neck measurement—13 inches
Stitch gauge—8 stitches to the inch

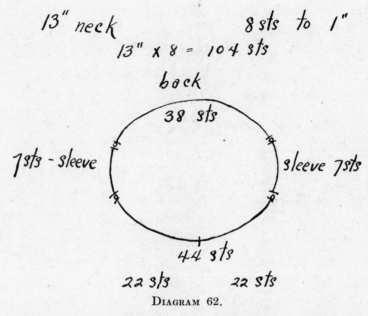

13" neck   8 sts to 1"

13" × 8 = 104 sts

back

38 sts

7 sts - sleeve   sleeve 7 sts

44 sts

22 sts   22 sts

DIAGRAM 62.

13 inches × 8 stitches to the inch = 104 stitches for the total neck line.

Proportioning the stitches from a 14 inch neck line, for the back of the neck is required:

$1\frac{3}{14}$ of 5 inches × 8 stitches to the inch = 37 stitches, 38 stitches (even number).

Similarly:

$1\frac{3}{14}$ of 1 inch × 8 stitches to the inch = 7 stitches for each sleeve.

Therefore, 38 stitches for the back of the neck
            14 stitches for both sleeves
             8 stitches for the increases
            ——
            60 stitches

104 stitches — 60 stitches = 44 stitches for the front of the neck as shown on the diagram.

3.

Neck measurement—12 inches
Stitch gauge—5 stitches to the inch

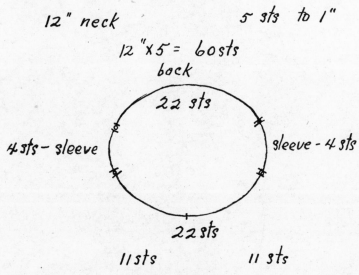

12" neck   5 sts to 1"

12"x5 = 60sts
back

22 sts

4 sts - sleeve   sleeve - 4 sts

22 sts

11 sts   11 sts

DIAGRAM 63.

12 inches × 5 stitches to the inch = 60 stitches for the total neck line.

Proportioning the stitches from a 14 inch neck line, for the back of the neck is required:

$\frac{12}{14}$ of 5 inches × 5 stitches to the inch = 22 stitches.

Similarly:

$\frac{12}{14}$ of 1 inch × 5 stitches to the inch = 4 stitches for each sleeve.

Therefore,   22 stitches for the back of the neck
           8 stitches for both sleeves
           8 stitches for the increases

          ——

        38 stitches

60 stitches — 38 stitches = 22 stitches for the front of the neck as shown in the diagram.

4. For baby—

Neck line—9 inches
Stitch gauge—6 stitches to the inch

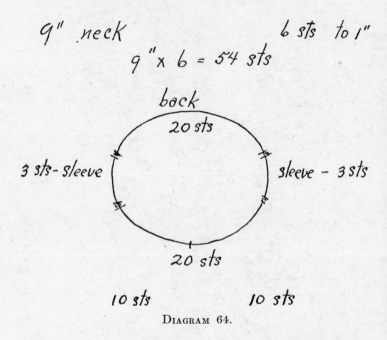

9" neck   6 sts to 1"

9" x 6 = 54 sts

back

20 sts

3 sts- sleeve   sleeve - 3 sts

20 sts

10 sts   10 sts

DIAGRAM 64.

9 inches × 6 stitches to the inch = 54 stitches for the neck line.

Proportioning the stitches from a 14 inch neck measurement, there is required for the back of the neck:

$9/14$ of 5 inches × 6 stitches to the inch = 20 stitches.

Similarly:

$9/14$ of 1 inch × 6 stitches to the inch = 3 stitches for each sleeve.

Therefore, 20 stitches for the back of the neck
6 stitches for both sleeves
8 stitches for the increases

—

34 stitches

54 stitches — 34 stitches = 20 stitches for the front of the neck as shown on the diagram.

Formula for Raglans with Knit-In Sleeves

1. Taking an average neck measurement of 14 inches, allot 5 inches of stitches for the back of the neck, 1 inch of stitches for each sleeve, 8 stitches for the increases and the remaining stitches for the front of the neck.

2. For charting larger or smaller neck lines, proportion the stitches as for a 14 inch neck line.

3. Increase every other row to widen for fronts, sleeves and back.

4. Chart neck lines the same as the neck lines in sweater or blouse with set-in sleeves.

5. When depth of raglan is reached, add ½ inch of stitches to the underarms of fronts, sleeves and back for adults.

6. Complete the garment the same as for sweater or blouse with set-in sleeves, working downwards.

RAGLANS WITH DIFFERENT NECK LINES

HIGH ROUND NECK LINE

As has been previously stated, if a high round neck line is desired, the stitches for the front will have to be put on gradually to correspond with the curve at the throat.

The neck line has to be charted the same as the round neck for the sweater with set-in sleeves. (Turn to formula for round neck line given previously.)

NOTE. If no opening is desired, care must be taken to insure that the head will pass through the neck line. It is advisable to knit 1 inch even, in front, for an adult before any extra stitches are added.

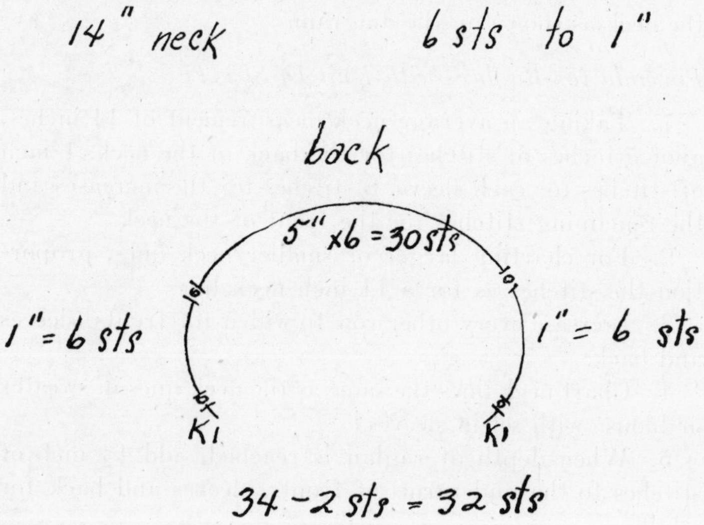

14" neck   6 sts to 1"

back

5" x 6 = 30 sts

1" = 6 sts   1" = 6 sts

K1   K1

34 – 2 sts = 32 sts

DIAGRAM 65.

The measurements are the same as for the sample raglan.

Neck measurement—14 inches
Stitch gauge—6 stitches to the inch

(Follow the diagram.)

There are 34 stitches allotted for the front of the neck. 2 of these stitches are cast on with the stitches for the sleeves and the back of the neck, leaving 32 stitches to be added when the neck line is shaped.

Therefore, on the needle are now required:

  2 stitches for the fronts
30 stitches for the back of the neck
12 stitches for the sleeves
  8 stitches for the increases

—

52 stitches

Therefore, 52 stitches are cast on the needle and the first row reads as follows:

Knit 1, (front) increase in the next stitch, put a marker, increase in the next stitch, knit 6, (sleeve) increase in the next stitch, put a marker, increase in the next stitch, knit 30, (back) increase in the next stitch, put a marker, increase in the next stitch, knit 6, (sleeve) increase in the next stitch, put a marker, increase in the next stitch, knit 1 (front).

Round neck line for Raglan.

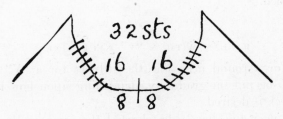

DIAGRAM 66.

The first row is now complete and the markers separating the fronts, sleeves and back are in position. As for previous raglan every second row is increased, before and after the markers, to widen the fabric, and, until the fronts are joined, every 2nd row is purled.

We are chiefly concerned with the shaping of the neck line. First calculate the stitches as though the neck line were for a sweater with set-in sleeves, then reverse the order, increasing the stitches instead of decreasing. As the diagram indicates, each front is increased a stitch every other row, 8 times, then 8 stitches are added all at one time, making 16 stitches on each side, 32 stitches on both sides, which is the necessary number.

LOWER ROUND NECK LINES

If a lower round neck line is desired, widen the material by increasing at the sleeves, back and fronts without adding any stitches at the neck line for the desired depth, then increase for the round neck the same as for former round neck.

If no opening is desired, after adding the stitches for the neck, finish on a knit row, then join across the front and continue knitting every row, with the increases on every second row, until the depth of the raglan is reached.

RAGLAN WITH A "V" NECK LINE

As for a round neck line the stitches for a "V" neck have to be put on gradually, depending upon how low a "V" neck is desired.

The neck line has to be charted the same as the "V" neck for the sweater with set-in sleeves. (Turn to formula for "V" necks given previously) increasing as we knit from the neck line down, instead of decreasing as we knit up.

Follow Diagram 65.

Neck measurement—14 inches
Stitch gauge—6 stitches to the inch
There are 34 stitches allotted for the front of the neck. Two of these stitches are cast on with the stitches for the sleeves and the back of the neck, leaving 32 stitches to be added when the neck line is shaped.

We require now on the needle:

    2 stitches for the fronts
  30 stitches for the back
  12 stitches for the sleeves
    8 stitches for the increases
    —
  52 stitches

Therefore, 52 stitches are cast on the needle and the first row reads as follows:

"V" neck line for Raglan.

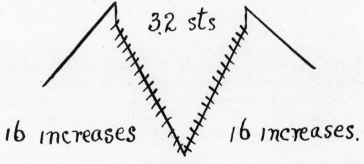

DIAGRAM 67.

Knit 1, (front) increase in the next stitch, put a marker, increase in the next stitch, knit 6 (sleeve) increase in the next stitch, put a marker, increase in the next stitch, knit 30 (back) increase in the next stitch, put a marker, increase in the next stitch, knit 6, (sleeve) increase in the next stitch, put a marker, increase in the next stitch, knit 1 (front).

The first row is now complete and the markers separating the fronts, sleeves and back are in position. As for previous raglan every 2nd row is purled and every other row increased to widen the fabric for fronts, sleeves and back.

We now continue to increase before and after the markers every second row, at the same time adding a stitch every other row, 16 times, to each front, making 32 stitches altogether.

When the necessary stitches for the neck line have been added, join the fronts and knit every row to the underarm.

NOTE. If a lower "V" neck is desired, calculate how often to increase to reach the desired depth.

RAGLAN WITH A SQUARE NECK LINE

As for a round and "V" neck line, cast on one stitch on each side of the front with the sleeves and back stitches, that is 52 of the 84 stitches, leaving 32 stitches for the square neck line.

Increase the fabric for the fronts, sleeves and back without adding the front neck line stitches, until the depth for the completion of the square neck is reached—anything from 3 inches without a back opening—then add the 32 stitches all at one time, and continue as for previous raglans to the underarm.

CHILD'S RAGLAN SWEATER, ROUND NECK, OPENING UP
THE FRONT AND LONG SLEEVES

(AGE 8 TO 10 YEARS)

PLATE XXXV.

Measurements

Neck—10 inches
Raglan—7½ inches
Chest—26 inches
Underarm to waist—7½ inches
Sleeve underarm—14 inches
Wrist—5½ inches

Materials

9 ounces of sport yarn (Medium weight yarn)
#3 circular needle
1 pair #3 straight needles

Stitch gauge

6 stitches to the inch
8 rows to the inch

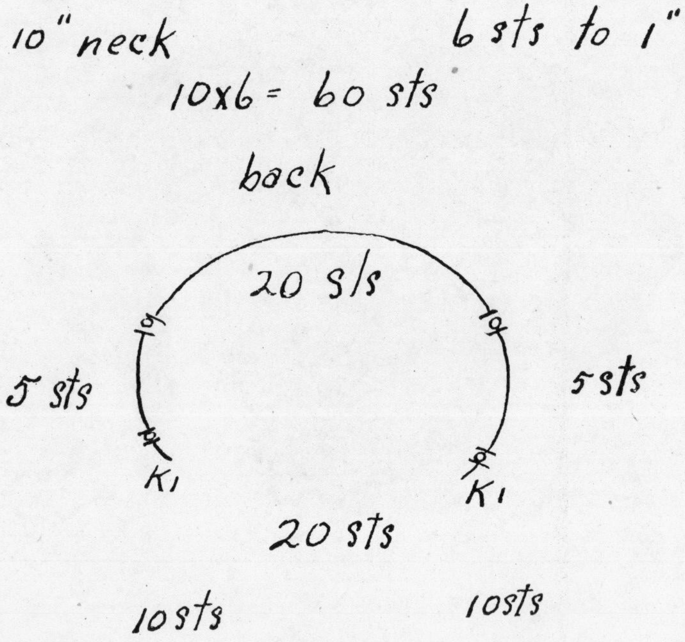
10" neck
6 sts to 1"
10x6 = 60 sts
back
20 sts
5 sts
5 sts
K1
K1
20 sts
10 sts
10 sts

DIAGRAM 68.

Follow charts

10 inches × 6 stitches to the inch = 60 stitches
20 stitches for the back of the neck
10 stitches for both sleeves
8 stitches for the increases

2 stitches for the fronts

———

40 stitches to be cast on at the beginning

60 stitches — 40 stitches = 20 stitches to be added gradually at the neck.

METHOD. Cast on 40 stitches on the circular needle.

Row 1. Knit 1, (front) increase in a stitch, put a marker, increase in a stitch, knit 5, (sleeve) increase in a stitch, put a marker, increase in a stitch, knit 20, (back) increase in a stitch, put a marker, increase in a stitch, knit 5, (sleeve) increase in a stitch, put a marker, increase in a stitch, knit 1, (front) making 40 plus 8 stitches = 48 stitches.

Row 2. Purl (Every 2nd row purled).

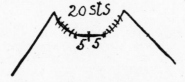

Round neck for child's raglan.

20 sts

5 5

DIAGRAM 69.

Continue in this way, increasing before and after each marker, every other row, at the same time adding for the round neck, 1 stitch each side every other row 5 times, then 5 stitches all at one time. This makes 10 stitches added to each side, 20 stitches at both sides. (See diagram.)

After these stitches are added the neck line is completed,

but continue to increase before and after the markers every other row, working 3 stitches at each front edge in garter stitch until the raglan measures 7½ inches. Now there will be approximately 64 stitches for each sleeve, 80 stitches for the back and 41 stitches for each front. If fewer or more stitches are desired at this point, or if there has been a change in tension, make the raglan shorter or longer as necessary.

sleeve

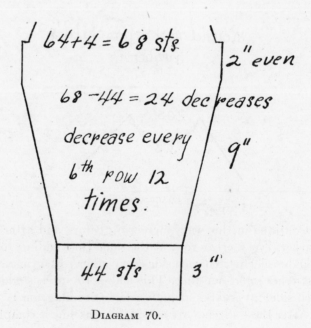

$64 + 4 = 68$ sts

2" even

$68 - 44 = 24$ decreases

decrease every 6th row 12 times.

9"

44 sts

3"

DIAGRAM 70.

Sleeves

Leave all the stitches but the stitches for one sleeve on the circular needle and use the straight needles for the sleeve. (The markers separate the fronts, sleeves and the back.) Add 2 stitches at each side of the sleeve, making 68 stitches. Work 2 inches even on the 68 stitches, then decrease by knitting 2 stitches together every 6th row on both sides, 12 times. The sleeve underarm measurement will now be 11 inches and there will be 44 stitches on the needle for the cuff. Knit 2 and purl 2 for 3 inches, then bind off loosely, knitting the knit stitches and purling the purl stitches.

Work second sleeve to correspond.

Body of the Sweater

The body of the sweater is worked in one piece. Add 2 stitches at each side of both back and front underarms, then there will be 43 stitches for each front and 84 stitches for the back, making 170 stitches altogether. Work back and forth on the circular needle, keeping 3 stitches at each front edge in garter stitch. Continue in this way for 7½ inches to the waistline (or the desired length).

Waist Band

Knit every 5th and 6th stitch together across the row, reducing the stitches to 140 stitches for the ribbing, which is 3 inches wide.

Collar

On the wrong side of the sweater pick up the stitches at the neck from one center of the stitches for a sleeve to the other—28 stitches. Work in stockinette stitch, picking up 2 stitches at the beginning of every row until all the neck stitches have been picked up. Continue working in stockinette stitch for 2½ inches keeping 3 stitches at each front

edge in garter stitch and increasing at each front edge
every other row (inside garter stitch) also working the
last 6 rows in garter stitch. Bind off loosely.

Finishing

Pin, baste and sew in the zipper on a machine. Sew
underarm seams and steam the sweater as in the directions
for steaming.

MAN'S RAGLAN SWEATER

PLATE XXXVI.

Measurements

Neck—16 inches

Raglan—11½ inches

Chest—44 inches
Waist—37 inches
Sleeve underarm length—20 inches
Underarm to waist—12 inches

Materials

24 ounces of knitting worsted
#4 circular needle
1 pair #4 straight steel needles

Stitch gauge

6 stitches to the inch
8 rows to the inch

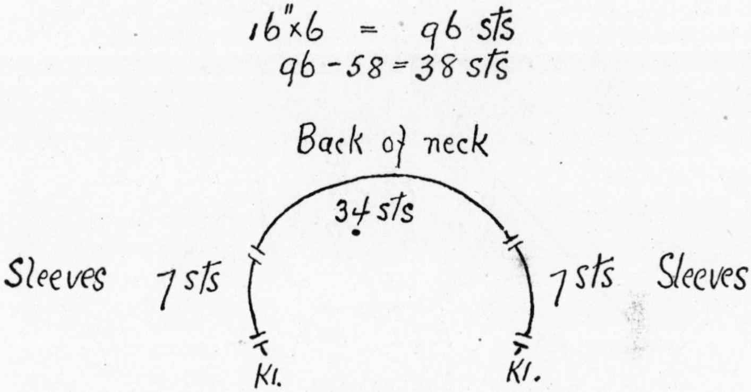

$$16'' \times 6 = 96 \text{ sts}$$
$$96 - 58 = 38 \text{ sts}$$

Back of neck

34 sts

Sleeves 7 sts 7 sts Sleeves

K1. K1.

DIAGRAM 71.

Follow diagram

16 inches × 6 stitches to the inch = 96 stitches
34 stitches for the back of the neck
14 stitches for both the sleeves
8 stitches for the increases
2 stitches for the fronts
___
58 stitches to be cast on at the beginning

96 stitches — 58 stitches = 38 stitches to be added gradually at the neck line.

Cast on 58 stitches.

Row 1. Knit 1, (front) increase in a stitch, put a marker, increase in a stitch, knit 7, (sleeve) increase in a stitch, put a marker, increase in a stitch, knit 34, (back) increase in a stitch, put a marker, increase in a stitch, knit 7, (sleeve) increase in a stitch, put a marker, increase in a stitch, knit 1, (front) making 58 stitches plus 8 stitches = 66 stitches now on the needle.

Row 2. Purl. (Every second row is purled.)

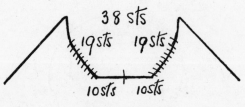

Round neck for man's raglan.

38 sts
19 sts   19 sts
10 sts   10 sts

DIAGRAM 72.

Continue in this way, increasing before and after the markers, every other row, at the same time increasing a stitch at each front edge, every other row 9 times, then cast on 10 stitches at the end of each of the next 2 rows, completing the round neck line.

Work back and forth, increasing before and after the markers every second row and purling every other row, keeping 4 stitches at each front edge in garter stitch (knitting) until the raglan measures 11½ inches. There will now be 96 stitches for the sleeves, 124 stitches for the back and 64 stitches for each front, each separated by the markers.

Sleeve – working downwards

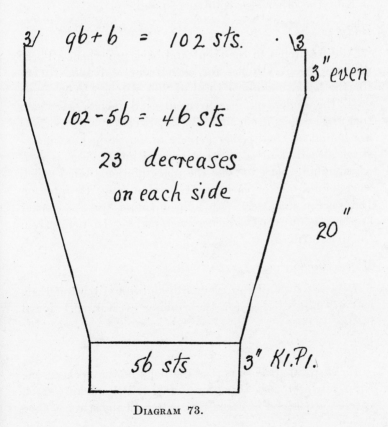

3/ 96 + 6 = 102 sts. · 3

3" even

102 − 56 = 46 sts

23 decreases on each side

20"

56 sts   3" K1.P1.

DIAGRAM 73.

Sleeves

Keep all the stitches but the stitches for one sleeve on the circular needle and work the sleeves on the straight needles. Add 3 stitches at each end of the sleeve to shape the underarm, making a total of 96 stitches, plus 6 stitches = 102 stitches. Work 3 inches even, then knit 2 together at the beginning and end of every 5th row until 56 stitches remain. The underarm sleeve measurement will now be 17 inches. Work ribbing of K.1, P.1 for 3 inches, then bind off loosely.

Knit the other sleeve to correspond.

Body

Add 3 stitches to the front and back underarms. There will now be 67 stitches for each front and 130 stitches for the back, making a total of 264 stitches. Work even until the underarm measurement is 8 inches, at which time the pockets are made. The 24 stitches for the pockets are bound off, and either a piece of fabric or stockinette stitch already knitted of 24 stitches, 4 inches deep, is used when coming back to take the place of the stitches which were bound off; or cast on 24 stitches. (See Chapter on Details for Pockets.) After the opening for the pocket has been made, work 4 inches even, making 12 inches from the underarm.

Waist Band

Decrease by knitting every 5th and 6th stitch together, leaving 220 stitches for the ribbing of K.1, P.1 for 3 inches.

Collar

Pick up 36 stitches across the back of the neck on the right side and work in ribbing of K.1, P.1, picking up 2 stitches at the end of every row. After all the stitches have been picked up, work the ribbing until the front of the collar band measures ½ inch, then bind off all the stitches, knitting the knit stitches and purling the purl stitches.

Tabs for Pockets

The stitches for the tabs are picked up on the right side, after the pockets have been completed. Work ½ inch even in stockinette stitch then decrease every other row both sides, until 3 stitches remain. Work the buttonholes according to the directions in Chapter on Details.

Finishing

Pin, baste and sew in zipper by machine. Sew underarm seams of the sleeves and steam the sweater as in directions for steaming.

CHAPTER VI

RAGLANS WITH YARN OVERS FOR THE INCREASES

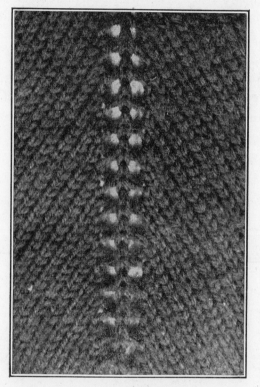

PLATE XXXVII.

THE photograph represents a piece of fabric increased, at one point, by means of yarn overs, every other row, instead of by increasing in the front and the back of the stitch. It will be noticed that the yarn overs widen the material more than an ordinary increase, therefore in charting raglans using yarn overs, the exact neck measurement minus 1 inch of stitches, is used.

The yarn overs give a raglan a hemstitched effect. This, of course, is not suitable for every occasion.

Raglans with yarn overs are charted by the same principle as raglans increased in the stitches themselves and the same measurements are necessary.

FORMULA FOR RAGLANS USING YARN OVERS

1. The exact neck measurement minus 1 inch of stitches is used.

2. Taking an average neck measurement of 14 inches, allow approximately 5 inches of stitches for the back of the neck, 1 inch of stitches minus 1 stitch for each sleeve, 4 stitches for the seam stitches, and the remaining stitches for the front of the neck.

3. For charting larger or smaller neck lines, proportion the stitches as in the 14 inch neck measurement.

4. Increase every other row by means of yarn overs to widen fabric for fronts, sleeves and back.

5. Chart the neck lines the same as the neck lines in sweater or blouse with set-in sleeves.

6. When depth of raglan is reached add ½ inch of stitches to the underarm of fronts, sleeves and back.

7. Complete the garment the same as for sweater or blouse with set-in sleeves, working downwards.

RAGLAN WITH YARN OVERS FOR SAMPLE SWEATER

We shall take for our sample raglan a neck measurement of 14 inches and a raglan measurement of 10 inches, the same as the previous sample raglan, using 6 stitches to the inch as our stitch gauge. We shall require 14 inches minus 1 inch or 13 inches × 6 stitches to the inch = 78 stitches for the total neck measurement.

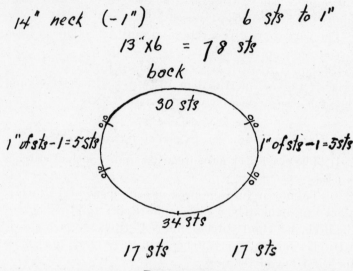

14" neck (-1") 6 sts to 1"

13"×6 = 78 sts

back

30 sts

1" of sts - 1 = 5 sts

1" of sts - 1 = 5 sts

34 sts

17 sts 17 sts

DIAGRAM 74.

Following the diagram, the 4 slanting lines represent the seam stitches and the circles before and after the slanting lines, the yarn overs.

Allowing 5 inches for the back of the neck, 5 inches × 6 stitches to the inch = 30 stitches for the back of the neck, 1 inch of stitches or 6 stitches minus 1 stitch, which leaves 5 stitches for each sleeve. We therefore require

    30 stitches for the back of the neck
    10 stitches for both sleeves
     4 stitches for seam stitches
    ──
    44 stitches

78 stitches — 44 stitches = 34 stitches for the front.

If all the stitches were cast on at one time, the directions would read:

Row 1. Knit 17, (front) yarn over, knit 1 (seam stitch) yarn over, knit 5, (sleeve) yarn over, knit 1 (seam stitch) yarn over, knit 30 (back) yarn over, knit 1, (seam stitch) yarn over, knit 5, (sleeve) yarn over, knit 1, (seam stitch) yarn over, knit 17, (front) making 8 more stitches, 2 for the fronts, 2 for each sleeve, and 2 for the back. 78 stitches plus 8 stitches = 86 stitches.

Row 2. Purl, using the overs as stitches.

Row 3. Knit 18, (front) yarn over, knit 1 (seam stitch) yarn over, knit 7, (sleeve) yarn over, knit 1 (seam stitch) yarn over, knit 32, (back) yarn over, knit 1, (seam stitch) yarn over, knit 7, (sleeve) yarn over, knit 1 (seam stitch) yarn over, knit 18, (front) making 8 more stitches, 2 for the fronts, 2 for each sleeve and 2 for the back. 94 stitches now on the needles.

Row 4. Purl, using the overs as stitches.

Continue in this manner, increasing by means of the yarn overs before and after the seam stitches until the raglan measurement is reached.

Complete the garment the same as the previous garment made with raglan sleeves.

NOTE. The various types of neck lines and sleeves are charted the same as in the sweater or blouse with set-in sleeves, the only difference being that we work downwards instead of upwards.

CHAPTER VII

RAGLANS WITH SET-IN SLEEVES

THE difference between a raglan with set-in sleeves and a raglan with knit-in sleeves, is that the diagonal line of the raglan is worked upwards from the underarm to the neck (and not knitted from the neck to the underarm) and the pieces, the back, fronts and sleeves knitted separately and then sewn together.

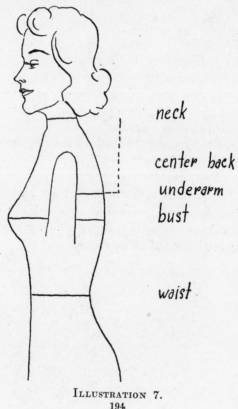

neck

center back
underarm
bust

waist

ILLUSTRATION 7.
194

Three additional measurements are required to those for the sweater or blouse with the set-in sleeves.

1. The neck measurement
2. The raglan measurement
3. The length from the center back from underarm to underarm to the back of the neck. (See illustration 7.)

The back, sleeves and front are knitted the same as the sweater or blouse with set-in sleeves until the underarm is reached and the raglan begun. As in the case of the knit-in raglan, 1 inch of stitches is generally bound off at the underarms of the sleeves, back and fronts, i.e., ½ inch of stitches on each side.

FORMULA FOR RAGLAN WITH SET-IN SLEEVES

Back

Bind off ½ inch of stitches on each side of the back underarm, then knit 2 together at the beginning and the end of every other row for the desired length of raglan

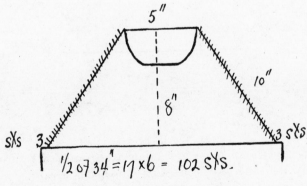

DIAGRAM 75.

and approximately 5 inches of stitches are left. Smaller sizes vary proportionately.

Front

The front raglan is decreased in the same way as the back raglan, and the neck line is charted the same as the neck line for the sweater with set-in sleeves.

> NOTE. From where the front neck line begins, the back raglan will give the necessary number of decreases for completing the front raglan. The number of stitches necessary for the decreases subtracted from the stitches for the front at this point, will give the stitches to be taken off for the neck.

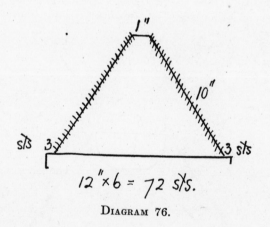

6 sts to 1"

1"

10"

sts 3

3 sts

12" x 6 = 72 sts.

DIAGRAM 76.

Sleeves

The sleeves in a set-in raglan are decreased approximately the same as the back raglan and the raglan must be the same length.

NOTE. If the raglan is being reduced too quickly, figure the number of rows from the center of the back to the back of the neck, hence the number of decreases, which will have to be made on each side.

CHARTING OF A SAMPLE SWEATER
SLIP-OVER, ROUND NECK, SET-IN RAGLAN SLEEVES

Measurements (Same as those used for sweater with set-in sleeves)

Waist—29 inches
Bust—34 inches
Waist to Underarm—9 inches
Neck—12½ inches
Raglan—10 inches
Upperarm—10 inches
Wrist—6 inches
Center back underarm to back of neck—8 inches
Sleeve underarm length—18 inches

Stitch gauge

6 stitches to the inch
8 rows to the inch

NOTE. A sweater with the above measurement and set-in sleeves has been charted previously, therefore, the same directions are applicable up to the underarm, from which point set-in raglan sleeves will be charted.

Back

At the underarm there are 102 stitches. Bind off ½ inch of stitches from each end. 102 minus 6 stitches = 96 stitches.

The distance from the center back underarm to the back of the neck is 8 inches. Having 8 rows to the inch, there

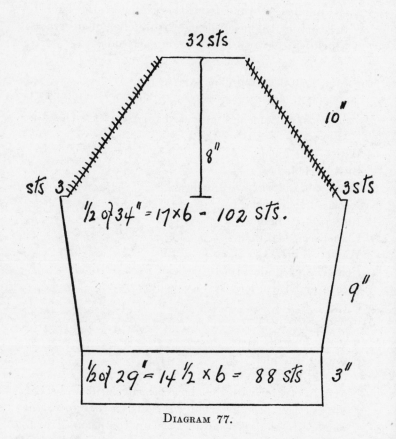

32 sts

10"

8"

sts 3

3 sts

½ of 34" = 17×6 - 102 sts.

9"

½ of 29" = 14½ × 6 = 88 sts

3"

DIAGRAM 77.

will be 8 inches × 8 rows = 64 rows. Decreasing every other row would give 32 decreases on each side, leaving 96 stitches minus 64 stitches or 32 stitches. At 6 stitches to the inch this is 2 stitches over 5 inches for the back of the neck, which follows the general formula for set-in raglans and proves how easy they are to chart.

Sleeves

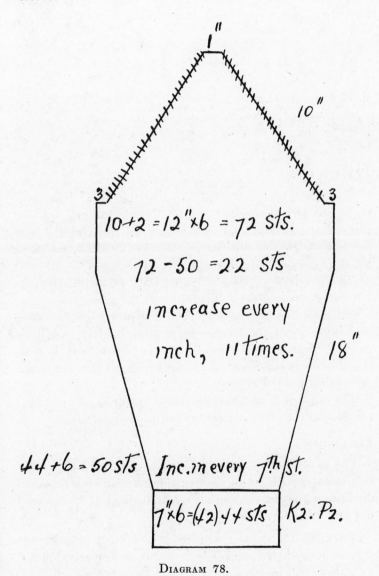

1″

10″

3   3

10 + 2 = 12″ × 6 = 72 sts.

72 - 50 = 22 sts

increase every

inch, 11 times.   18″

44 + 6 = 50 sts   Inc. in every 7th st.

7″ × 6 = (42) 44 sts   K2. P2.

Diagram 78.

At the underarm there are 72 stitches. Binding off ½ inch of stitches on each side, there will be 72 stitches minus 6 stitches or 66 stitches.

To make the raglan the same length as the back raglan, there will be 64 rows knitted, 32 decreases on each side of the sleeve, leaving 2 stitches at the top of the sleeve. There should be approximately 1 inch of stitches remaining, that is, 6 stitches, therefore 30 decreases are made every other row and the last 2 every fourth row instead of every 2nd row.

Front

The front is charted the same as the back, therefore there are 102 stitches at the underarm. Binding off ½ inch of stitches on each side, there will be 102 stitches minus 6 stitches or 96 stitches. Decreasing the front raglan the same as the back raglan, 32 stitches will be reduced on each side. 96 stitches minus 64 stitches = 32 stitches, left for the round neck. Therefore at the place where the round neck line begins, work to the center and place the remaining ½ of the stitches on a stitch holder. (See diagram.) Bind off 8 stitches on the next row, and knit 2 together every other row at the neck edge, at the same time decreasing for the raglan.

The stitches from the stitch holder are placed upon the needle and the other side is worked to correspond.

Finishing

The sweater with set-in raglans is completed the same as a sweater with set-in sleeves; therefore follow the same directions, sewing the raglan seams instead of the shoulder and armhole seams.

Note. As for sweater with set-in sleeves, if no opening is desired, the neck line is begun sufficiently low so there will be room for the head to pass through.

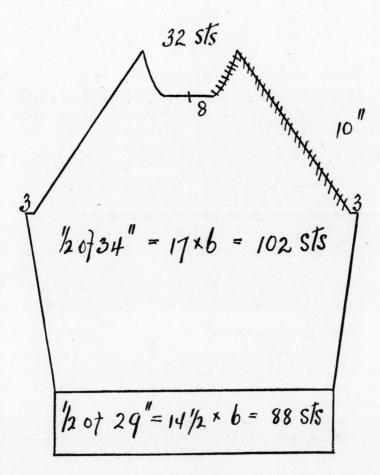

32 sts

8

10″

3

3

½ of 34″ = 17 × 6 = 102 sts

½ of 29″ = 14½ × 6 = 88 sts

DIAGRAM 79.

CHAPTER VIII

DETAILS

Joining Yarns

YARNS should never be knotted when knitting. If a knot is found in the yarn it should be broken and the ends joined. It has been found that the following method is the most satisfactory, especially for beginners.

Place the new end of yarn over the short end, pointing in the opposite direction, and knit about 5 stitches with both strands. The ends are woven into the fabric on the wrong side after the garment is completed.

If very thick yarn is being used, it may be necessary to "splice" the yarn, that is, untwist each end of yarn for several inches, then break off one or two strands as the case may be, depending upon the size of the yarn, then twist the remaining ends firmly together.

Dropped Stitches

It is essential that one know how to pick up dropped stitches. No matter how far a stitch has been dropped, unless a lace pattern is being knitted, it is easy to pick it up over the horizontal bars which are formed by the dropped stitches. When knitting stockinette stitch, turn to the right side of the work, that is the knit side, or when ribbing is being knitted, to the knit side of the rib. It is easier to pick up knit stitches.

METHOD. Place the loop of the dropped stitch on the left hand needle and the horizontal bar of the dropped stitch at the right hand side of the loop. Pass the loop over the thread to the back of the work. If many stitches have been dropped, use a crochet hook instead of placing the loop on the needle.

Grafting or Weaving

Grafting is the name given to weaving two pieces of fabric together. For example, toes of stockings, mitten tops and seams that should be soft.

When weaving the toe of a sock or the top of a mitten together, the stitches remain on two needles with the yarn attached to the first stitch on the back needle.

METHOD. Thread the yarn through a blunt pointed or worsted needle.

1. Pass the needle through the first stitch on the front needle as if to knit, draw the yarn through then slip the stitch from the needle.

2. Pass the needle through the second stitch on the front needle as if to purl, draw the yarn through, but leave the stitch on the needle.

3. Pass the needle through the first stitch on the back needle as if to purl, draw the yarn through, then slip the stitch from the needle.

4. Pass the needle through the second stitch on the back needle as if to knit, draw the yarn through, but leave the stitch on the needle.

Repeat these four steps until the stitches on both needles have been used.

NOTE. Do not draw the yarn too tight nor have it too loose. The joining should look like a continuation of the fabric.

Weaving Stockinette Stitch

PLATE XXXVIII.

Thread a worsted needle. Draw the yarn through the first stitch on the lower piece, inserting the needle from the wrong side. Draw the yarn through. Next, insert the needle from the right in the first stitch on the upper part and bring through the next stitch on the upper piece from the wrong side. Draw the yarn through. * Now insert the needle from the right side in the same stitch as previously on the lower piece and bring through the next stitch on the lower piece from the wrong side. Draw the yarn through. Insert the needle from the right side in the same stitch as previously on upper piece and bring up through the next stitch on upper piece. Draw the yarn through. Repeat from * until all the stitches are joined.

NOTE. Before starting to weave, read the directions, following them through using the illustration. This will help you to understand the directions.

Picking up Stitches

It is necessary to pick up stitches when making a ribbing around a neck line or armhole, or when a piece for a pocket is added after the hole for the pocket has been made, or for collars, etc.

METHOD. Hold the edge of the knitted garment, where the stitches are going to be picked up, in the left hand and the yarn and needle in the right hand. * Put the point of the needle into a stitch where a new stitch has to be formed, pass the yarn around the point of the needle as when knitting and draw it through the stitch to make a loop on the right hand needle. This is the "picked up" stitch. Repeat from * until all the stitches have been picked up.

NOTE.
1. The picked up stitches should resemble a continuation of the fabric.
2. For a round piece of work, e.g., neck line or armhole, a small circular needle or a set of needles may be used. In this case there would be no joinings in the work. If a pair of needles is used for a ribbing around a neck, the stitches are picked up from the shoulder to shoulder and the ribbing joined on the wrong side. For an armhole the ribbing is joined under the arm and at the shoulder.

3. There should be approximately as many stitches picked up as there are rows of the fabric—in other words, the distance multiplied by the stitch gauge.

Buttonholes

PLATE XXXIX.

Buttonholes are knitted as the fabric is being made, not slashed as in sewing. Therefore, it is advisable when knitting garments, to knit the side on which the buttons are to be fastened first. In this way the position of the buttons may easily be ascertained and marked, and hence be a guide for the buttonholes. This is important especially where the last buttonhole should be at the neck line.

Decide upon the size of the buttonhole. In knitting this may be same as the width of the button. If bands are used, the buttonhole is made in the center of the band. The width of the band usually depends upon the size of the button-hole, that is, if a buttonhole requires 4 stitches, the band should be at least 8 stitches wide, allowing ½ the width of the button on each side of the buttonhole.

METHOD. The position and size of each buttonhole having been ascertained, bind off the necessary number of stitches at this point. Continue to complete the row as previously, and back again to where the stitches have been bound off. The stitches are added the same way as the second method in the Chapter on Fundamentals.

NOTE. Turn the work to the wrong side to add the stitches and back again to the right side after they have been added.

After the garment is completed, the buttonholes should be finished with buttonhole stitches, using the same yarn if possible, or should be reinforced with binding on the wrong side.

Pockets

There are many different types of pockets in knitting, just as there are in sewing, but instead of "slashing" the hole for the pocket, the pieces for the pocket have to be either first worked, then knitted into the desired position, or the stitches for the pocket bound off as for a buttonhole, and the stitches picked up afterwards and the pieces knitted the last.

The position of the pocket is a matter of individual taste, but a safe rule for all pockets is to subtract the

PLATE XL.

number of stitches required for the pocket, this, of course, depends upon the stitch gauge and the size desired, from the total number of stitches from the underarm seam to the center front. Divide the remaining stitches into thirds, allowing two-thirds of the stitches at the front edge and one third toward the underarm seam.

The lower edge of a pocket in a cardigan or coat sweater should reach the top of the border, the depth varying from 3 inches in children's garments to 5 inches for men.

From experience, it has been found that if the stitches are bound off as for a buttonhole and the stitches picked up after that portion of the garment is completed, there is the advantage of a firm joining, which is an asset, especially for much-used pockets.

If a pouch pocket is desired, it may be made in either of the following ways:

1. Bind off the stitches the desired width of the pocket, then add the same number of stitches on the next row.

After the garment is completed, pick up the stitches and knit each piece to the desired length of the pocket. Sew together.

2. Knit the necessary number of stitches with a piece of fine string. Slip these stitches back on the left hand needle, then knit over them with the yarn. After the piece of garment has been completed, take out the string, place the loops on a needle and knit the desired length for both pieces. Sew together.

3. Knit to where the pocket is to be made, then continue knitting on the stitches for the pocket until the desired length; finish this piece on a knit row, or on the right side of the work. Continue knitting the row, and use these stitches for the return row for the actual piece of garment. Sew the sides together.

Welt Pocket

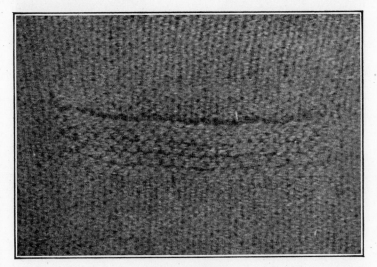

PLATE XLI.

If a one piece welt pocket is desired, a welt may be first knitted of either garter or single moss stitch, before the stitches are bound off, and then the stitches for the pocket are either picked up or the piece already knitted and the stitches used on the return row.

Miter for a "V" Neck

There are several ways to miter a "V" neck. Two ways are given here.

PLATE XLII.

1. The stitches are first picked up, then a row of K.2, P.2 is knitted, allowing 4 purled stitches at each side of the two knit stitches, which come exactly in the center of the "V" neck (that is, on the right side). The decreasings are made in the purled stitches by purling two stitches together at both sides of the two knit stitches, every other

row. In that way, two decreasings are made only on the right side of the work. Continue in this manner for desired width of the band, which varies from ¾ to 1 inch.

Plate XLIII.

2. The 8 center stitches are knitted, having 2 purled stitches on each side. One row of ribbing is first worked, then the decreasing, which is done on the 8 knitted stitches, is begun. The decreasings are made on the right side of the work on the knit stitches as follows: slip a stitch, knit a stitch, pass the slip stitch over the knit stitch and on the left side of the knit stitches, by knitting the last two knit stitches together. These two decreasings are made every second row until the knitted stitches are used, then the decreasings are made in the purled stitches at each side until the band is the desired length.

Openings

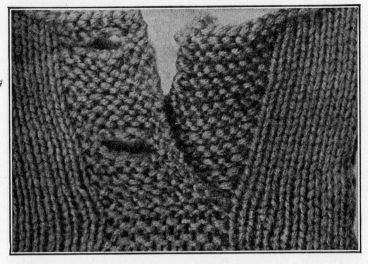

Plate XLIV.

First decide what size band is desired for the opening. The one shown has eight stitches worked in garter stitch. That means there are 4 stitches on each side of the center front. The left side, the button side, is knitted first. (This is the right side of the illustration.)

Method. Work to the center of the front, then pick up and knit in the horizontal bars at the back of the next 4 stitches. Place the stitches of the right front on a stitch holder, then work the left side, keeping the eight stitches in garter stitch. Knit the desired length.

Right Side. Place the stitches on a needle. Attach yarn and work to the center front, then pick up the purled way, the next four stitches belonging to the band on the left side. Work the band in garter stitch, working the buttonholes where necessary.

Round Knitting

Knitting on a Set of Needles or Circular Needle

The knitting is worked continuously in rounds from right to left without turning the work. This method is employed, using a set of needles, for mittens, gloves, hats or socks, and a circular needle for skirts, raglans, etc.

Knitting on a set of needles is no more difficult than using a pair of needles, if the needles are held correctly. The empty needle knits off the stitches of each needle in turn, therefore only two needles are in use at one time. These are the only two actually held during the process while one of the other needles crosses the palm of the hand and the other hangs loosely.

Sewing on Zippers

When a zipper is to be used for a fastening in knitting, it is advisable to knit several stitches either in garter stitch or moss stitch at each side of the opening to prevent the edges from rolling. If this is not desired, a row of single crochet may be worked around the opening before the zipper is attached.

METHOD. Lay the garment flat on a table, the right side up, and place the zipper in the opening. The fastener must face the outside. First pin and then baste the zipper in place, the edge of the fabric being less than $\frac{1}{16}$ of an inch away from the hooks. Then sew the zipper on by machine, $\frac{1}{8}$ of an inch from the hooks so the edges will not catch.

Beading for Elastic for Skirts, Etc.

With a crochet hook, a steel hook preferred, work a treble crochet, that is, the yarn twice around the hook, in a stitch on the waist line. * Chain 2, skip 2 stitches, a treble crochet in the next stitch. Repeat from * around the waist, then join with a slip stitch and fasten.

It is advisable to make a single crochet in each stitch afterwards. This gives a firmer edge.

Casing for Elastic

This is worked inside the top of the skirt after several rows of single crochet have been worked.

METHOD. With the work inside out, make a slip stitch on the top of the skirt. Chain 4, make a slip stitch in the second stitch to the left in the fourth row below.* Chain 4, make a slip stitch 4 stitches to the left of the last stitch at the top of the skirt. Chain 4, make a slip stitch 4 stitches to the left of the last stitch at the bottom of the casing. Repeat from * around the top of the skirt.

Round or Dutch Collar

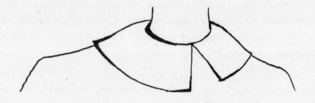

Round or Dutch Collar

ILLUSTRATION 8.

If there is an opening in the blouse on which a round collar is to be added, it is advisable not to make the collar separately but to pick up the stitches around the neck line on the wrong side. If, however, the collar is knitted separately, the amount of stitches to put on the needle should be equal to the number of stitches around the neck line.

For a grown person, it is advisable to make 5 increases every 4th row until the width of the collar is reached. That is, pick up the stitches on the wrong side, then purl a row, knit a row, purl a row, and on the 4th row, which is knit, increase about 1 inch before and after each shoulder seam and once in the center of the back.

For a child's collar, where the neck line is necessarily smaller, it is necessary to increase only every 4th row, 4 times in the row, that is, about 1 inch before and after each shoulder seam.

Blocking

It is generally but erroneously thought that all hand-knitted garments have to be blocked. This is not the case. A sweater, for example, if knitted to measurement and not knitted too loosely will keep its shape after washing and all that is necessary is to steam, not press, the fabric, and flatten the seams.

From experience, I consider that if a fitted garment has been knitted, for example a jacket or coat, it should be given for the first blocking to an experienced and reliable cleaning and blocking establishment. They understand their job. A well-knitted garment can be absolutely spoiled by bad blocking.

After the first blocking, if one desires to block it one-self, trace a chart of the garment on a piece of old sheeting, and after washing carefully and partially drying, pin, using bank (non-rustable) blocking pins, to the desired measurements on the wrong side of the garment, using a heavy pad as a base. Lay a damp Turkish towel over the garment and steam with hot iron (never ribbing) and leave on the pad until dry. Take out the pins, steam the seams and remove the pin marks.

CHAPTER IX

SKIRTS

Knitted skirts, the same as any other garment, must conform to all forms of visual art, line, texture and color; and the same principles which we apply when sewing apply equally to knitted skirts.

Skirts may either be joined to a bodice or blouse to make a full length one piece garment, or be unattached forming complete lower garments in themselves. A dress skirt should closely follow the lines, texture and color of the bodice or blouse, while an unattached skirt should conform harmoniously to the sweater, blouse or coat with which it is to be worn.

Knitted skirts may be worn on every occasion, in the morning, for sportswear, in the afternoon and also for evening wear. Naturally, the style of skirt depends upon the character of the clothes to be worn. For morning wear, skirts should be simple and the contour and length governed not so much by prevailing fashion as by the needs of the wearer.

Knitted skirts for sportswear are very comfortable, durable and practical. They require little care, and knitting's chief characteristic, elasticity, is never more welcome. Skirts for sportswear should be plain and simple, permitting freedom of movement. This may be achieved by means of inverted pleats of varying heights and widths to meet the necessary requirements, in the front or at the sides, for tennis or golf, or a skirt may be pleated all around for skating.

The bottom of the skirt may also be widened by means

of godets, their height, width and position varying with individual requirements and taste.

Fullness may also be added below the hip line in a paneled skirt. Again the number of panels is a matter of requirement and should be planned to enhance the proportions of the figure. Narrow panels, forming straight perpendicular lines, tend to make the figure more slender, but it must also be remembered that too evenly spaced panels may not carry the eye up and down, but across, emphasizing the width rather than the height. The decreasing of a gored skirt is most important. Decreasing before the hip line too quickly makes the skirt "cup" below the hip, and decreasing too quickly toward the waist makes the hips look large.

Afternoon skirts may be more elaborate, employing godets, gores or panels and using either simple or complex lace patterns for insertions or the entire skirt.

For evening wear, skirts may be as simple or as elaborate as the occasion demands. Here is an opportunity for indulgence of individual taste, but above all, skirts must be becoming and appropriate to the age of the wearer.

Incredible as it may seem, a skirt knitted on a circular needle is the simplest form of knitting. Remember, I refer to the actual knitting, not the charting. For a plain skirt the only manipulations are casting on, knitting around and around, the decreasing and the binding off. Where to decrease means the charting of the skirt from a correct stitch gauge, i.e., the number of stitches to the inch. Where so large a garment is concerned, this is a very important factor.

Three measurements are required for a skirt for a grown person:
1. Waist
2. Hip
3. Length

The waist measurement should be taken eased. That is, allow sufficient room to place a finger between the tape and the person when the measurement is taken.

The hip measurement for a knitted garment is taken around the fullest part. The distance from the waist down varies with the individual, from 7 to 9 inches approximately. Care must be taken when measuring, that the tape does not drop down either at the front or back, but is held at the same distance from the waist line. It must be understood that this measurement is the actual hip measurement of the skirt when completed and ready to be worn, not the measurement for an undergarment.

Note.

1. Care must be taken not to tighten the tape around the front of the body of a large person, as this emphasizes defects.

2. The hip is the most important measurement when knitting a skirt, for no matter what type of knitted skirt is desired, it should fit from the hips to the waist.

The length of a skirt should not be determined solely by prevailing fashion, although it should vary with it. At all times the length of a skirt should be becoming to the height and weight of the wearer.

This measurement is taken from the waistline over the hips to the desired distance from the floor. This may be either 10, 12, 14 or 16 inches for a short skirt. A long skirt may reach the instep or further, according to individual taste.

CHARTING OF A KNITTED STRAIGHT SKIRT

Once again mathematics plays a major role in the construction of a knitted skirt, which, if correctly charted and measured, need not be taken off the needle or needles until the last stitch is bound off.

There are on the market different types of needles and devices for measuring skirts when so much has been knitted. These are not necessary unless the skirt is made by guesswork, which is usually never satisfactory no matter what is being constructed. Above all else, accuracy in measuring and calculating is one of our aims.

The most satisfactory way to knit a skirt is on a circular needle, the length of the needle varying with the size of the waist. The needle cannot be longer than the actual waist measurement which is required. Naturally the size of the needle varies with the weight of the yarn to be used. It is not advisable to knit a skirt too loosely or use yarn that is too soft. In either case the skirt will not hold its shape so well.

Skirts may be knitted on straight needles, in two pieces or in a number of panels, as desired. In these cases, the seams have to be sewn together and the decreasing generally is made at the sides of the pieces or panels. When the same effect can be obtained using a circular needle, it is advisable to do so because the knitting is simplified and the skirts hang better.

As stated at the beginning of the chapter, knitting a plain skirt on a circular needle is one of the simplest forms of knitting; and by the time a person has knitted several inches of fabric she will have become accustomed to the feel of the needles, and as she progresses will be more proficient; therefore the tension will be more even, i.e., the number of stitches knitted to the inch will remain the same throughout the fabric. This is why it is advisable to begin knitting a skirt from the bottom and decrease toward the hip, especially if one is not a proficient knitter or if the material to be used is new to the individual. Any change in tension may be rectified when knitting up to the hips and then to the waist, which is where the skirt should fit.

No plackets are used in knitted skirts. In sewed garments, plackets provide sufficient room to don a garment, whereas the natural elasticity of knitted goods makes them unnecessary. If the tension, that is the stitch gauge, is too small, it cannot be rectified when knitting from the waist down, and nothing is worse than a knitted skirt too large from the waist to the hips.

DIRECTIONS FOR A SAMPLE SKIRT

The following average measurement will be used:
Waist—28 inches
Hip—38 inches — 9 inches below the waist
Length—30 inches

Stitch gauge

6 stitches to the inch
8 rows to the inch

A straight skirt will first be charted to learn the principle by which it is done.

It is from the hip measurement that the width of the bottom of the skirt is figured, for either a straight or a flared skirt. Ten inches added to the hip measurement is the average width for the bottom of a straight skirt, and fifteen inches or more for a flared skirt, depending upon the tastes and needs of the wearer.

The hip measurement is 38 inches; therefore 48 inches will be used for the width at the bottom of the skirt. At 6 stitches to the inch, 48 inches × 6 stitches = 288 stitches, the necessary number of stitches for the bottom of the skirt. As it simplifies the system of decreasing, it is advisable to use the next higher number divisible by 10, if the units figure is 5 or above, and the next lower number divisible by 10, if it is below 5; therefore 290 stitches are

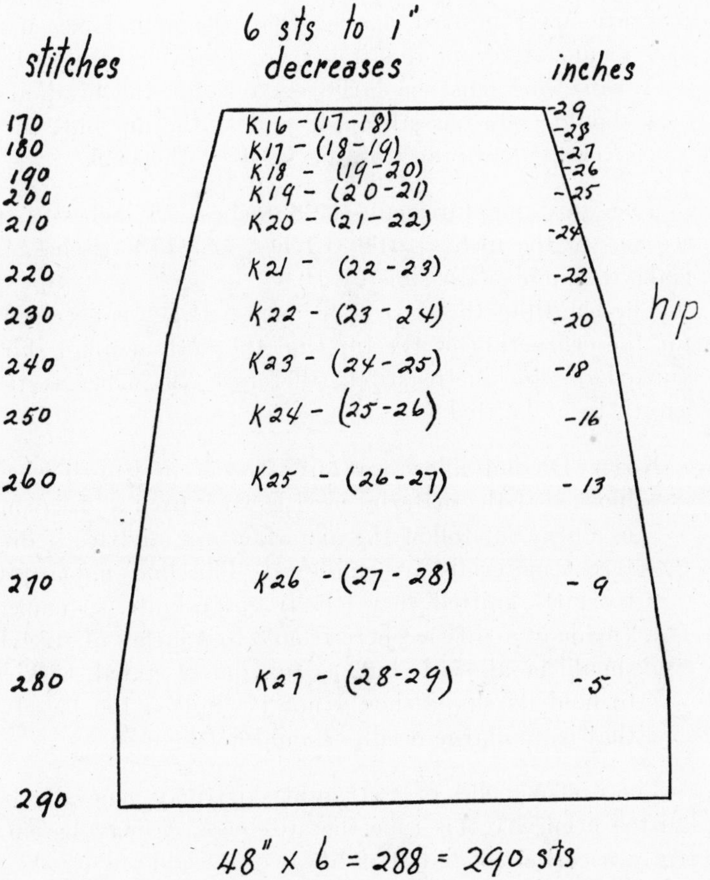

6 sts to 1"

stitches	decreases	inches
170	K16 - (17-18)	-29
180	K17 - (18-19)	-28
190	K18 - (19-20)	-27
200	K19 - (20-21)	-26
210	K20 - (21-22)	-25
220	K21 - (22-23)	-24
230	K22 - (23-24)	-22
240	K23 - (24-25)	-20
250	K24 - (25-26)	-18
260	K25 - (26-27)	-16
270	K26 - (27-28)	-13
280	K27 - (28-29)	-9
290		-5

hip

48" × 6 = 288 = 290 sts

DIAGRAM 80.

the number of stitches to be used for the bottom of the skirt.

The hip measurement is 38 inches. 38 inches × 6 stitches to the inch or 228 stitches, i.e., 230 stitches making the number divisible by 10.

NOTE. The number of stitches at the waist line and hip are never figured smaller than the actual measurements. A few more stitches are desirable because the waist line must be large enough for the head and shoulders to pass through, and at the hip line, they prevent "cupping" of the skirt at the back.

The waist measurement is 28 inches. 28 inches × 6 stitches to the inch = 168 stitches, i.e., 170 stitches, to make the number divisible by 10.

The length of the skirt is 30 inches. 1 inch is necessary for the crocheting at the top and the bottom for a skirt knitted of stockinette stitch, therefore 29 inches is the length to be knitted.

NOTE. Do not allow for any stretch in length when blocked if the material used is wool, wool and rayon, or linen, but follow the manufacturer's advice if different materials are employed. This does not apply to skirts knitted very loosely, jiffy knits, so named (made in a jiffy), where from 3 to 4 inches of stretch should be allowed; but, as previously stated, a skirt to hold its shape should not be knitted too loosely, that is, too large needles should not be used.

The first 5 inches of a straight skirt may generally be knitted even. By this time the stitch gauge may be correctly ascertained, but it is always advisable to check it again at the hip line, where any change may be rectified.

To have a well-shaped skirt the decreases or narrowings must be gradual, the narrowings coming closer toward the hip, and upwards to the waist line.

Following the chart, 230 stitches for the hip from 290 stitches at the bottom, gives a difference of 60 stitches or 6 decreases of 10 stitches each. In 290 stitches there are 29 tens, therefore to decrease a stitch in each 29 stitches,

27 stitches are knitted and a decrease is made by knitting the 28th and 29th stitches together. To distribute evenly the 10 decreases, 27 stitches are knitted and the 28th and 29th stitches knitted together around the whole width making 10 decreases.

So that the decreases may come at regular intervals throughout the skirt, it is advisable to mark the beginning of the first decreased row with a marker and keep this on the needle throughout the whole skirt.

The hip line is 9 inches from the waist, therefore there are 20 inches from the bottom of the skirt to the hip.

The next decrease comes at 9 inches, therefore knit even until the skirt measures 9 inches from the bottom or 4 inches from the first decrease. (Of course, the distance between the decreases varies with individual skirts.)

Following the chart, there are at present 280 stitches on the needle, i.e., 28 tens. To decrease a stitch in every 28 stitches, knit 26 stitches, the 27th and 28th stitch being knitted together for the decrease. Repeat this manner of decreasing for the complete round.

NOTE. When decreasing by knitting 2 stitches together, be sure the yarn is pulled tightly. The actual decreasing of stitches should not be visible to any marked degree.

The next decrease is made at 13 inches, therefore knit evenly until the skirt from the bottom measures 13 inches. (When measuring, place the skirt flat on a table and smooth out the fabric, as it will appear after the skirt is blocked.)

There are now 270 stitches on the needle, and 260 stitches are all that are necessary at this point, therefore to decrease 10 times in the round, knit 25 stitches, and the 26th and 27th stitches are knitted together for the whole round.

Continue to decrease in this manner, following the chart, until 230 stitches remain on the needle and the hip line is reached at 20 inches. It will be noticed that the decreasing rows come closer together as they near the hip line.

When the hip line is reached, the stitch gauge should be checked. The decreases from the hip line to the waist are figured in the same manner. The last decreasing row never comes at the waist line, but varies from ½ inch to an inch below the waist.

170 stitches are required at the waist line. There are 230 stitches at the hip. 230 stitches minus 170 stitches = 60 stitches, i.e., 6 decreases of 10 stitches each. As will be seen from the diagram, the decreases come closer together nearer the waist line, the last at 28 inches, then 1 inch is knitted even to complete the length of the skirt of 29 inches. The knitting of the skirt is now completed and the stitches bound off loosely so the binding off will have the same stretch as the rest of the skirt.

Finishing

Top. Work a row of single crochet around the top of the skirt, working in every stitch and keeping the same tension. Then make the beading for the elastic. (See Chapter on Details.)

Bottom. Work as many rows of single crochet around the bottom of the skirt, working in every stitch, as will prevent the skirt from rolling at the bottom.

NOTE. This is necessary only when the skirt is made of stockinette stitch throughout.

FORMULA FOR CHARTING KNITTED STRAIGHT SKIRTS

1. Three measurements are necessary:
    The waist, taken eased
    The hip, at the fullest part
    The length, depending upon the wearer

2. Add approximately 10 inches to the hip measurement for the bottom of a straight skirt.

3. Multiply the waist, hip and bottom of the skirt measurement by the stitch gauge to ascertain the necessary number of stitches at these points.

4. Deduct 1 inch from the length of the skirt to allow for crocheting at the top and bottom.

5. To simplify the charting of skirts, use the next highest number divisible by 10 for the waist and hips, and the nearest number divisible by 10 for the bottom.

6. Knit 5 inches even then decrease.

7. Decrease 10 stitches or 20 stitches evenly around the skirt, the decreasing rows coming closer toward the hip and then the waist.

8. First calculate how many decreases from the bottom to the hip, then from the hip to the waist, checking the stitch gauge at the hip.

9. Bind off loosely when the desired length is reached.

CHARTING SKIRTS WITH DIFFERENT STITCH GAUGES

In the diagram the same measurements are used as for sample skirt, but a different stitch gauge is taken.

Measurements

    Waist—28 inches
    Hip—38 inches
    Length—30 inches
    Width at the bottom of the skirt—48 inches

1. *Stitch gauge*—5 stitches to the inch

The width at the bottom is 48 inches, therefore 48 inches × 5 stitches to the inch = 240 stitches.

The hip measurement is 38 inches, therefore 38 inches × 5 stitches to the inch = 190 stitches.

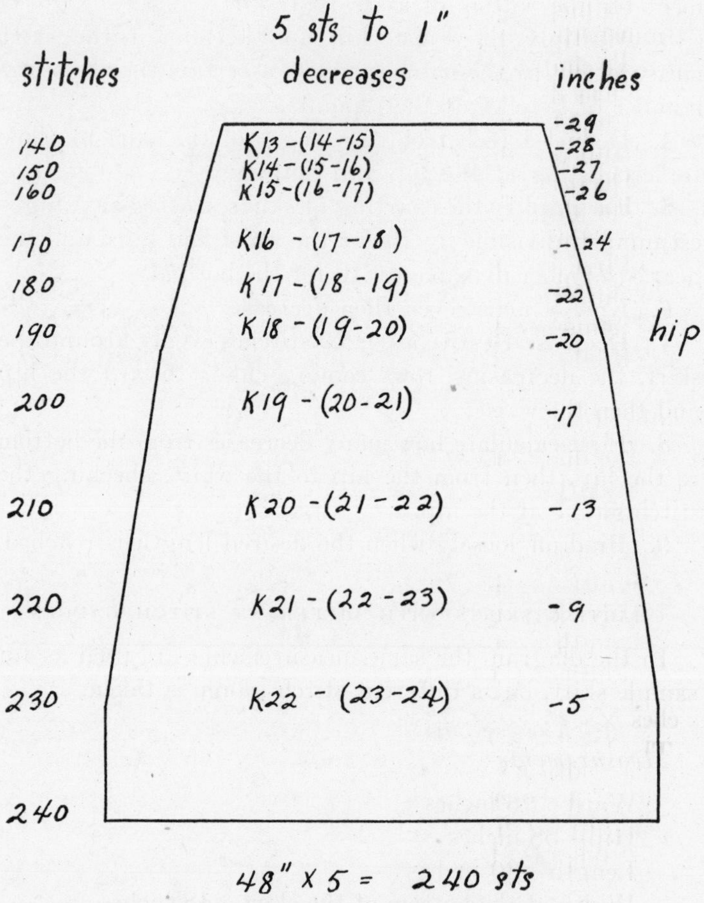

5 sts to 1"

stitches	decreases	inches
		-29
140	K13 –(14–15)	-28
150	K14 –(15–16)	-27
160	K15 –(16 –17)	-26
170	K16 – (17 –18)	– 24
180	K17 – (18 –19)	-22
190	K18 – (19-20)	-20 hip
200	K19 – (20-21)	-17
210	K20 –(21 – 22)	– 13
220	K21 – (22 – 23)	-9
230	K22 – (23 –24)	-5
240		

48" × 5 = 240 sts

DIAGRAM 81.

The waist measurement is 28 inches, therefore 28 inches
× 5 stitches to the inch = 140 stitches.

The diagram is self-explanatory.

2. *Stitch gauge*—7 stitches to the inch.

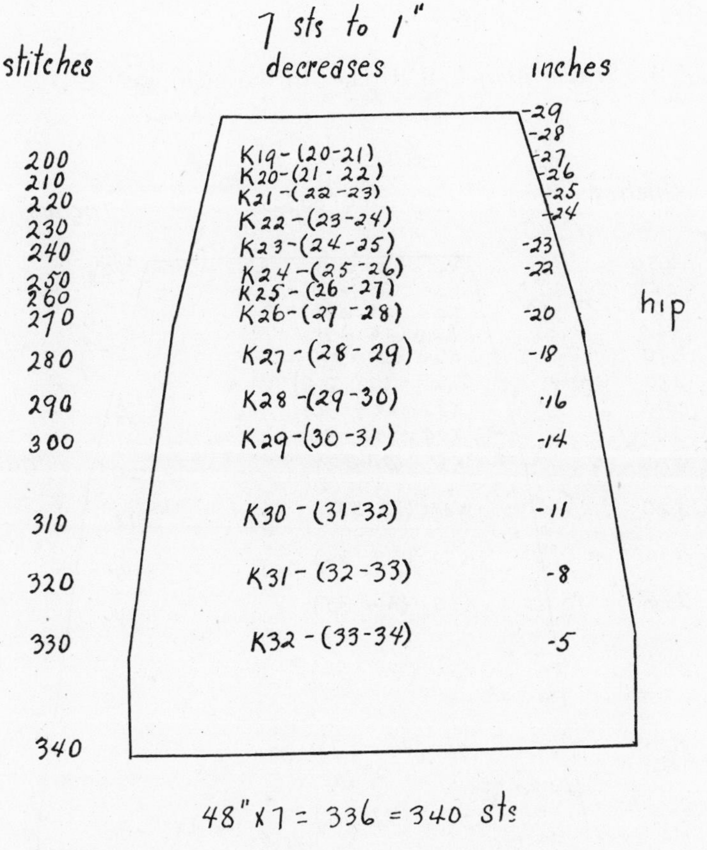

7 sts to 1″

stitches	decreases	inches
		-29
		-28
200	K19-(20-21)	-27
210	K20-(21-22)	-26
220	K21-(22-23)	-25
230	K22-(23-24)	-24
240	K23-(24-25)	
250	K24-(25-26)	-23
260	K25-(26-27)	-22
270	K26-(27-28)	-20
280	K27-(28-29)	-18
290	K28-(29-30)	·16
300	K29-(30-31)	-14
310	K30-(31-32)	-11
320	K31-(32-33)	-8
330	K32-(33-34)	-5
340		

hip

48″ × 7 = 336 = 340 sts

DIAGRAM 82.

The width at the bottom of the skirt is 48 inches, therefore 48 inches × 7 stitches to the inch = 336 stitches, i.e., 340 stitches.

The hip measurement is 38 inches, therefore 38 inches × 7 stitches to the inch = 266 stitches, i.e., 270 stitches.

The waist measurement is 28 inches, therefore 28 inches

$\times$ 7 stitches to the inch $=$ 196 stitches, i.e., 200 stitches. The diagram is self-explanatory.

3. *Stitch gauge*—8 stitches to the inch.

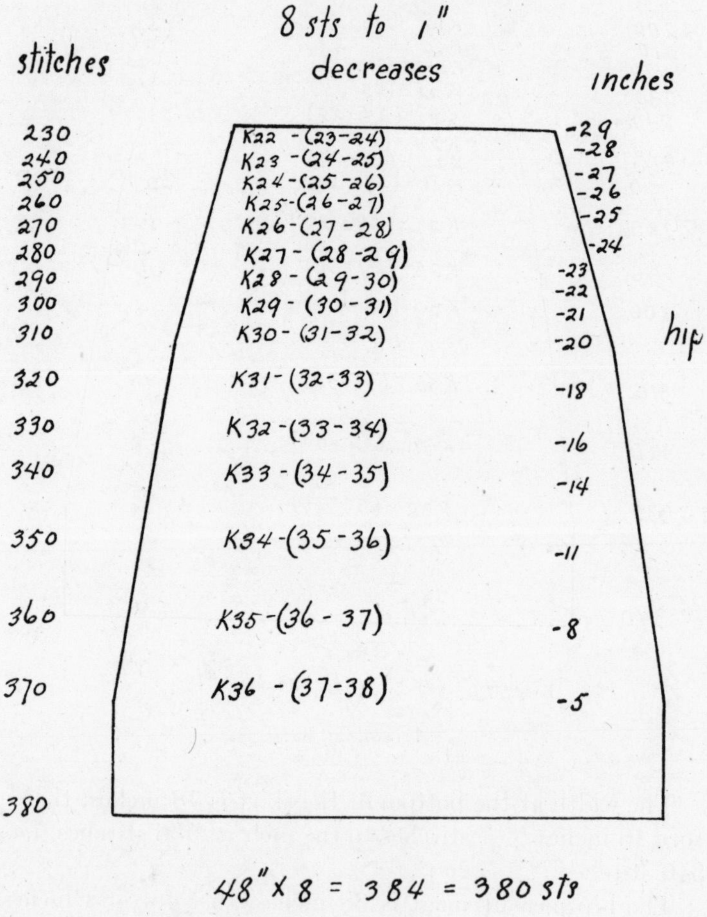

8 sts to 1"

stitches	decreases	inches
230	K22 – (23–24)	–29
240	K23 – (24–25)	–28
250	K24 – (25–26)	–27
260	K25 – (26–27)	–26
270	K26 – (27–28)	–25
280	K27 – (28–29)	–24
290	K28 – (29–30)	–23
300	K29 – (30–31)	–22
310	K30 – (31–32)	–21
320	K31 – (32–33)	–20 hip
330	K32 – (33–34)	–18
340	K33 – (34–35)	–16
350	K34 – (35–36)	–14
360	K35 – (36–37)	–11
370	K36 – (37–38)	–8
380		–5

$48'' \times 8 = 384 = 380$ sts

DIAGRAM 83.

The width at the bottom of the skirt is 48 inches, therefore 48 inches $\times$ 8 stitches to the inch = 384 stitches, i.e., 380 stitches.

The hip measurement is 38 inches, therefore 38 inches $\times$ 8 stitches to the inch = 304 stitches, i.e., 310 stitches.

The waist measurement is 28 inches, therefore 28 inches $\times$ 8 stitches to the inch = 224 stitches, i.e., 230 stitches.

The diagram is self-explanatory.

NOTE. If the number of stitches to be decreased for a skirt is great, it is sometimes necessary to decrease 20 stitches in the round instead of 10.

FLARED SKIRTS

As for a straight skirt, the width for the bottom of a flared skirt is taken from the hip measurement. The amount added varies considerably with the wearer and the type of material to be knitted. Generally speaking, when knitting a flared skirt, any amount upward from 15 inches added to the hip measurement is considered a flared skirt.

Care must be taken in choosing the width of a flared skirt. While a slight fullness at the bottom tends to hide large hips and thighs, the flare, if too great, emphasizes the weight of the wearer. It must also be remembered, that a short flared skirt makes the short stout person appear shorter and wider. A medium flared skirt is excellent for sportswear, the width taking the place of pleats, godets, etc., added when making a straight skirt.

A knitted skirt, no matter what type, should fit from the hips to the waist and should never "cup" below the hips, no matter how slender the person. On the other hand, any bulging below the hips can readily be taken care of by decreasing in the correct places.

For an average flared skirt, the general rule is to release

the added fullness near the bottom of the skirt; the decreases toward the hip and then toward the waist, should come at the same intervals as if a straight skirt were being knitted.

CHARTING A FLARED SAMPLE SKIRT

Take the same measurements as for the straight skirt:
Waist—28 inches
Hip—38 inches
Length—30 inches

Use the same stitch gauge, 6 stitches to the inch

15 inches will be added to the hip measurement for a slightly flared skirt. The width at the bottom of the skirt will now be 38 inches plus 15 inches = 53 inches. 53 inches × 6 stitches to the inch = 318 stitches, i.e., 320 stitches.

Following the diagram, it will be noticed that the same principles for decreasing are used as for the straight skirt, with the exception of the decreasing at the beginning. At the bottom of the skirt the fullness is decreased quickly. In this way the lines of the skirt are better, and, as in a straight skirt, the most important measurement, the hip, is reached gradually.

It will be noticed that the first decrease is made when 2 inches of the fabric have been knitted. After that, a decrease occurs every 2 inches until 10 inches have been knitted, measuring from the bottom of the skirt. From then on the skirt is decreased the same as the straight skirt.

FORMULA FOR FLARED SKIRTS

1. 15 inches or more added to the hip measurement for the width at the bottom of the skirt, this varying with the needs of the wearer.

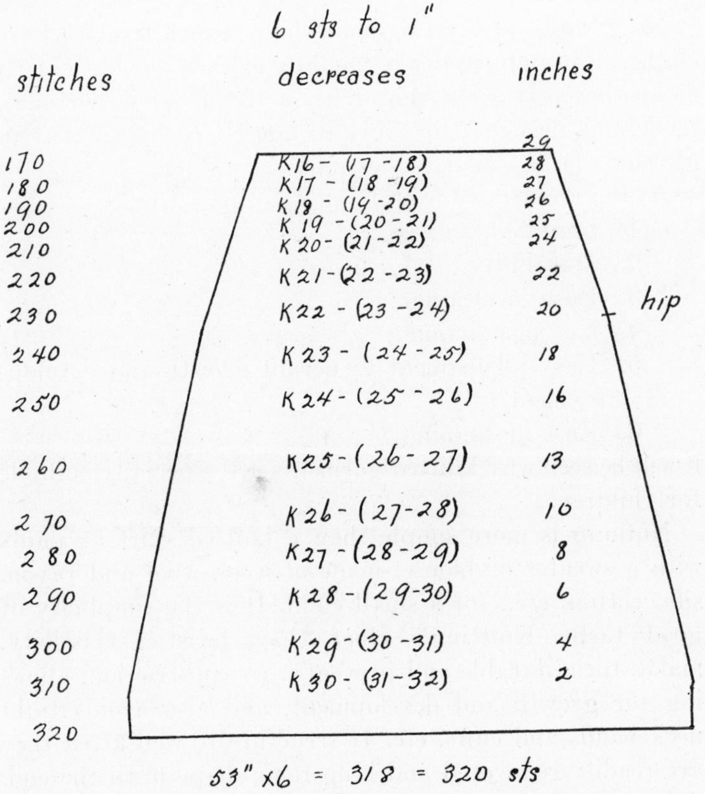

6 sts to 1"

stitches	decreases	inches
		29
170	K 16 - (17 -18)	28
180	K 17 - (18 -19)	27
190	K 18 - (19 -20)	26
200	K 19 - (20 -21)	25
210	K 20 - (21 -22)	24
220	K 21 - (22 -23)	22
230	K 22 - (23 -24)	20
240	K 23 - (24 -25)	18
250	K 24 - (25 -26)	16
260	K 25 - (26 - 27)	13
270	K 26 - (27-28)	10
280	K 27 - (28-29)	8
290	K 28 - (29-30)	6
300	K 29 - (30 -31)	4
310	K 30 - (31-32)	2
320		

hip

53" x 6 = 318 = 320 sts

DIAGRAM 84.

2. The same principles for decreasing are used as for the straight knitted skirt.

3. The fullness at the bottom of the skirt is decreased quickly in most cases. There is no hard and fast rule as to exactly when to decrease.

4. The approach to the hip and then on to the waist is charted the same as for the straight skirt.

KNITTED SKIRTS FOR CHILDREN

No greater joy can a small child receive than to have clothes, if only partially resembling mother's or big sister's or brother's. It gives him or her a feeling of importance, pride and pleasure, not only in himself or herself but in Mother who has made it possible.

As the requisites for children's clothing are:

1. Simplicity
2. Durability
3. Ease in cleaning
4. No constriction
5. Easy adjustment to permit growth and development
6. Ease in donning,

it will be seen why knitted garments are especially suitable for children.

Nothing is more simple than a knitted skirt or pants with a sweater or blouse, made of wool, wool and rayon, silk, cotton, etc., for a small child. It is the simplicity of good taste. Knitting's chief characteristic, elasticity, makes them durable and prevents any constriction, allowing for growth and development, and also avoids tight neck bands and cuffs, etc. If structurally well-fitted they are readily renovated and keep their shape until the end. As knitted garments may be easily adjusted for growth of children, it is possible to lengthen skirts, pants, sleeves and waists without much difficulty. They are also easily donned, instilling in the child the ability to help himself or herself.

Pleated skirts or flared skirts for larger girls give freedom of movement and if the fullness is decreased near the bottom it forms a ripple over the knee. Care must be taken not to knit small girls' skirts too short, always remembering that the vital organs need protection; and growing girls' skirts should cover the bend of the knee. If skirts are knitted separately and hung on underbodices, the weight is carried to the shoulders, and if they are worn without an underbodice they should not fit too tightly around the waist but rather should be worn low to have the support of the bony structure of the pelvis.

There are only two measurements necessary for a child's skirt:

1. The waist measurement
2. The length of the skirt

As before mentioned, the length depends upon whether the skirt is going to be worn with or without a bodice for support, but in either case the waist measurement should be taken loosely. The length of the skirt is at the discretion of the knitter and should, as for the grown person, be suited to the age and needs of the wearer.

Generally for a child's skirt, the width at the bottom may be made twice the waist measurement.

For a sample plain skirt the following measurements are used:

1. Waist—22 inches
2. Length—18 inches (17 inches knitted and 1 inch allowed for crocheting)
3. Width at the bottom of the skirt—44 inches

Stitch gauge—6 stitches to the inch

The same principles governing a knitted skirt for a grown person are used when charting a child's skirt.

44 inches is the width at the bottom, therefore 44 inches × 6 stitches to the inch = 264 stitches, i.e., 260 stitches for the bottom.

22 inches is the waist measurement; therefore 22 inches ×6 stitches to the inch = 132 stitches, i.e., 140 stitches for the waist.

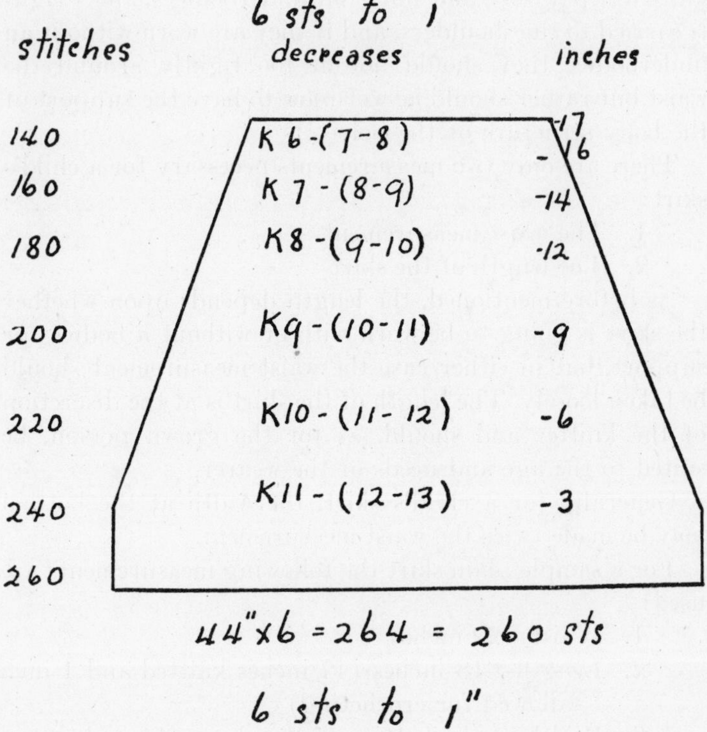

6 sts to 1"

stitches	decreases	inches
140	K 6 - (7 - 8)	-17/16
160	K 7 - (8 - 9)	-14
180	K 8 - (9 - 10)	-12
200	K 9 - (10 - 11)	-9
220	K 10 - (11 - 12)	-6
240	K 11 - (12 - 13)	-3
260		

44" x 6 = 264 = 260 sts

6 sts to 1"

DIAGRAM 85.

Follow the diagram.

As is advised when knitting a skirt for an adult, a knitted skirt for a child is started at the bottom. 260 stitches are cast on, and one must be careful not to twist the stitches. The decreases are made gradually, coming closer together as the waistline is neared.

The first decreases are made when 3 inches of the fabric have been knitted. By this time the work should be even and the correct stitch gauge ascertained. It is advisable, however, to check the gauge a little higher up the skirt, where any change may be rectified.

As a child's skirt is necessarily shorter than that of an adult, it is necessary that more stitches be decreased at one time. After spacing the decreases it is found advisable to decrease 20 stitches at one time. 20 into 260 goes 13 times, therefore in every 13 stitches, 1 stitch is to be decreased. That is, 11 stitches are knitted and every 12th and 13th stitches knitted together all around the skirt, making 20 decreases and leaving 240 stitches on the needle.

NOTE. So the decreases come at regular intervals throughout the skirt, it is advisable to mark the beginning of the first decreased row with a marker and keep this on the needle throughout the whole skirt.

The next decrease comes at 6 inches, therefore knit even until the skirt measures 6 inches from the bottom or 3 inches from the last decrease. There are, at present, 240 stitches on the needle. 20 into 240 goes 12 times; therefore in every 12 stitches, 1 stitch is to be decreased. That is, knit 10 stitches and every 11th and 12th stitch is knitted together all around the skirt, leaving 220 stitches.

Continue to decrease in this manner, following the diagram. It will be noticed that the last inch is knitted even. When the skirt measures 17 inches, bind off loosely so that the head and shoulders will easily pass through.

Finishing

Single crochet around the top and bottom as for the adult skirt, then work a beading for elastic or fasten to an underbodice as desired.

NOTE. It should not be necessary to block a child's skirt. Turn inside out and steam as for sweaters. This is all that should be required.

FORMULA FOR PLAIN SKIRT FOR A CHILD

1. Two measurements are necessary:
   Waist measurement—taken loosely
   Length—depending upon the wearer
2. The width at the bottom of the skirt is approximately twice the waist measurement.
3. Multiply the waist and the bottom of the skirt measurements by the stitch gauge to ascertain the necessary number of stitches at these points.
4. Deduct one inch from the length to allow for crocheting at the top and bottom.
5. To simplify the charting, use the next highest number divisible by 10 for the waist and the nearest number divisible by 10 for the bottom.
6. Decrease 10 or 20 stitches evenly around the skirt, the decreasing rows coming closer toward the waist.
7. Check the stitch gauge when approximately half the skirt is knitted.
8. Bind off loosely.

CHILD'S PLEATED SKIRT

The effect of a pleated skirt in knitting is achieved either by means of ribbing of knit and purl stitches, the widths of the ribbing varying with individual taste and need, or by using a special combination of stitches which form pleats. These are given at the back of the book along with the texture stitches.

For a child's pleated skirt the same measurements as for a plain skirt are necessary.

1. The waist
2. The length

The width at the bottom of the skirt may be twice the waist measurement or more as desired.

SAMPLE PLEATED SKIRT

For a sample pleated skirt the same measurements and stitch gauge are used as for the sample plain skirt. They are

1. The waist—22 inches
2. The length—18 inches

Stitch gauge—6 stitches to the inch

The first thing to decide is the approximate width at the bottom of the skirt, then the desired width of each pleat.

Approximately 48 inches, a little over twice the waist measurement is used for the width at the bottom, that is, 48 inches × 6 stitches to the inch = 288 stitches. The desired width of each pleat is 3 inches and therefore requires 18 stitches at 6 stitches to the inch. These knitted ribs are separated by narrow purl ribs of 2 stitches each, making 18 knits and 2 purls = 20 stitches for each pleat. The number of stitches at the bottom of the skirt must therefore be divisible by 20. 20 into 288 goes 14 times and 8 stitches over, therefore 280 stitches is the number to be used for the bottom of the skirt, and there are 14 pleats.

As the decreasing for a pleated skirt (where the knit ribs are much larger than the purl ribs) comes in the knitted ribs, if the decreases are made in every pleat, 14 stitches will be decreased one time around.

Following the diagram, it will be seen the same principles are employed as for charting a plain skirt. The first thing to do when charting a pleated skirt is to figure how many decreases will be necessary by decreasing in each pleat, which in this case is 14 stitches each time. It will be found that it takes 10 decreases of 14 stitches each to decrease 140 stitches and leave 140 stitches, which is the nearest number to 132 stitches, the stitches required for

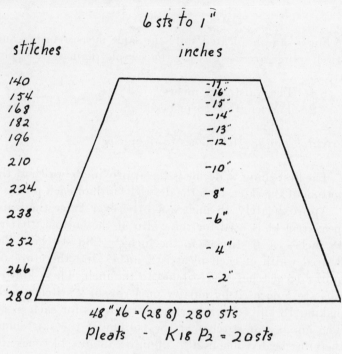

6 sts to 1"

stitches   inches

140   -17"
154   -16"
168   -15"
182   -14"
196   -13"
                            -12"
210   -10"
224   -8"
238   -6"
252   -4"
266   -2"
280

48" x 6 = (288) 280 sts
Pleats - K18 P2 = 20 sts

Diagram 86.

the waist, as 22 inches × 6 stitches to the inch = 132 stitches.

The next thing to figure is the distance between the decreases. As the length of the skirt is 17 inches, the decreases are made in each pleat at intervals of 2 inches until 12 inches is reached, and at intervals of 1 inch thereafter, the last inch between 16 and 17 inches being worked even.

Note. The decreases may be made approximately in the center of each rib, or they may come alternately first at one side then at the other side of each pleat, always knitting plain the stitch next to the purled rib. In this way, if the decreases are knitted tight they are apt to be less conspicuous.

Finishing

A pleated skirt is finished the same as a plain skirt, but as little single crochet as possible is to be worked around the bottom of the skirt and care must be taken not to frill the bottom, but to leave the purls indented, as it were, so as not to take away the effect of the pleats.

FORMULA FOR CHILD'S PLEATED SKIRT

1. Two measurements are necessary:
   The waist
   The length—depending upon the wearer
2. The width at the bottom of the skirt is to be twice the waist measurement and more if desired.
3. Multiply the waist and the bottom of the skirt measurements by the stitch gauge to ascertain the approximate number of stitches at these points.
4. Determine the width of each pleat (this includes the knit and purl stitches) and make the number of stitches for the bottom of the skirt divisible by the number of stitches for each pleat.
5. Calculate the number of pleats and hence the amount of stitches decreased in each round.
6. Figure the number of decreasing rows in order to reach the necessary length at the waist.
7. Check the stitch gauge when approximately ½ of the skirt is knitted.
8. Bind off loosely.

NOTE. When single crocheting around the bottom of the skirt, care must be taken not to frill the bottom and thus take away the pleated effect.

CHARTING OF A CHILD'S PLEATED SKIRT USING DIFFERENT MEASUREMENTS AND DIFFERENT STITCH GAUGE

Measurements

Waist—24 inches
Length—19 inches (18 inches knitted)
Width at the bottom of the skirt—48 inches

Stitch gauge—8 stitches to the inch

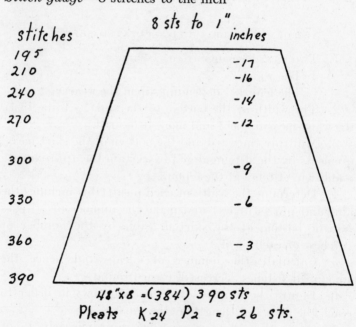

stitches   8 sts to 1″
                               inches
195   –17
210   –16
240   –14
270   –12
300   –9
330   –6
360   –3
390

48″×8 =(384) 390 sts
Pleats K 24 P 2 = 26 sts.

DIAGRAM 87.

METHOD. 48 inches, the width at the bottom × 8 stitches to the inch = 384 stitches. Pleats, 3 inches wide with 2 purl stitches between = 3 × 8 stitches to the inch = 24 stitches plus 2 stitches = 26 stitches for each pleat, therefore 390 stitches are the necessary number of stitches for the bottom of the skirt, and there are 15 pleats.

Follow the diagram.

2 decreases are made in each panel, reducing the number of stitches by 30 in each round. The first decreasing is made when the skirt measures 3 inches, and every 3 inches thereafter until the skirt measurement is 12 inches. From then on, the decreasing is made every 2 inches until the last decrease, which is only one inch from the other decrease and here it is necessary to decrease only once in each panel, thus reducing 15 stitches instead of 30 stitches.

Note. The first knit stitch before and after the purl rib is knitted before the decreases are made.

The last inch may be worked in ribbing of K.1, P.1, and the skirt either sewn to an underbodice or finished with a beading.

Measurements

Bust—26 inches
Waist to underarm—7 inches plus 3 inches for ribbing (worn below waist)
Shoulder—11 inches
Armhole—13 inches
Upperarm—8 inches
Length of Skirt—14½ inches (Sewn to bodice)

Materials

10 ounces of 2 ply wool and rayon yarn
#3 straight steel needles

Stitch gauge—6 stitches to the inch

For this child's two piece dress a block pattern which naturally forms pleats is used. This pattern requires a multiple of 10 stitches.

CHILD'S TWO PIECE DRESS
(AGE 6-8 YEARS)

ILLUSTRATION 9.

Row 1. * K.1, P.9. *	*Row 9.* * K.9, P.1. *
Row 2. * K.8, P.2. *	*Row 10.* * K.2, P.8. *
Row 3. * K.3, P.7. *	*Row 11.* * K.7, P.3. *
Row 4. * K.6, P.4. *	*Row 12.* * K.4, P.6. *
Row 5. * K.5, P.5. *	*Row 13.* * K.5, P.5. *
Row 6. * K.4, P.6. *	*Row 14.* * K.6, P.4. *
Row 7. * K.7, P.3. *	*Row 15.* * K.3, P.7. *
Row 8. * K.2, P.8. *	*Row 16.* * K.8, P.2. *

Repeat these 16 rows for pattern. (This pattern is shown with the other combinations of stitches toward the end of the book.)

1. *Skirt*

This is made on #3 straight needles working back and forth. Cast on 300 stitches which at 6 stitches to the inch gives a width of 50 inches at the bottom. As the stitches naturally form a pleated fabric and the skirt is sewn on an underbodice, no deduction in length has to be made for crocheting and no decreases are worked until the skirt measures 13½ inches or 1 inch from the waist line; therefore, work in pattern for 13½ inches, at which point decreasing is made. The pleats will be easily discernible and when you are reducing, the pleats have to remain still in position; therefore it is necessary to make a small inverted pleat at the top of each pleat to draw it in.

There are 10 stitches in each pleat; therefore if 2 stitches are used for each of 2 parts of inverted pleat (See Diagram 88) 6 stitches out of the 10 stitches still remain at the top of each pleat, which leaves $^{6}/_{10}$ of 300 stitches = 180 stitches on the needle. Now work in ribbing of K.2, P.2 for 1 inch, then bind off loosely.

Blouse

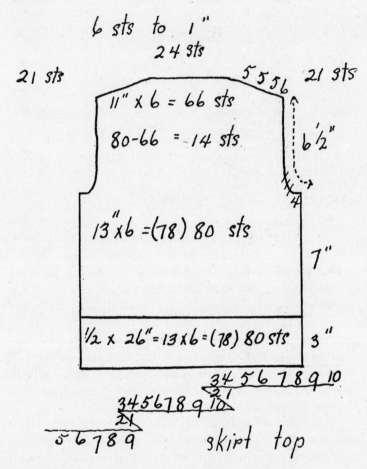

6 sts to 1"

24 sts

21 sts

5 5 5

21 sts

11" × 6 = 66 sts

80-66 = 14 sts

6½"

13" × 6 = (78) 80 sts

7"

½ × 26" = 13 × 6 = (78) 80 sts   3"

3 4 5 6 7 8 9 10
21

3 4 5 6 7 8 9 10
21

5 6 7 8 9   skirt top

DIAGRAM 88.

1. *Back*

Cast on 80 stitches and work in ribbing of K.2, P.2 for 3 inches. Next knit the block pattern for 7 inches to the underarm.

Armhole

Change to stockinette stitch. Bind off 4 stitches at the beginning of the next 2 rows, then decrease by knitting 2 together at the beginning and end of every other row, 3 times, leaving 66 stitches on the needle. Work even until the armhole measures 6½ inches around.

Bind off 6 stitches at the beginning of the next 2 rows and 5 stitches at the beginning of the next 6 rows. Then bind off the last 24 stitches loosely.

2. *Front*

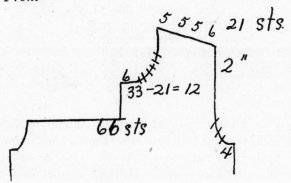

DIAGRAM 89.

The front is worked the same as the back until the binding off for the armholes has been completed and 66 stitches remain. At this point the opening is begun by making 6 stitches of garter stitch at the center for 6 rows, then working to the center, keeping 3 stitches in garter stitch and knitting one side at a time.

The round neck line is begun 2 inches below the tip of the shoulder, by binding off 6 stitches all at one time, then knitting 2 together at the beginning of every other row, 6 times. At this point, the shoulder is worked the same as the back shoulder. Then the other side is knitted to correspond.

3. Sleeves

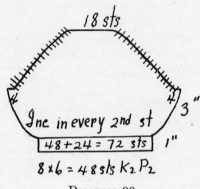

DIAGRAM 90.

Cast on 48 stitches and work in ribbing of K.2, P.2 for 1 inch. On the first row after the ribbing, increase in every 2nd stitch making 48 stitches plus 24 stitches = 72 stitches. The sleeves are knitted in stockinette stitch for 3 inches, then 4 stitches are bound off at the beginning of the next 2 rows, then 2 stitches are knitted together at the beginning and end of every knitted row until 22 stitches remain. Before binding off knit 2 together twice at the beginning and the end of the row, leaving 18 stitches, which are bound off.

4. *Collar*

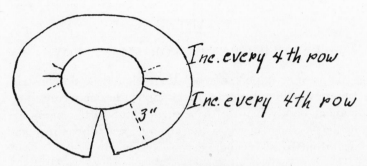

DIAGRAM 91.

With the inside of the blouse facing one, pick up the stitches around the neck. Work in stockinette stitch for 3 inches, increasing every 4th row about 1 inch before and after the shoulder seams, making 4 increases in the round. Bind off loosely.

Finishing

Join the skirt and sew to an underbodice. Sew the seams of the blouse together and put in sleeves, the same as in the directions for sewing sweaters. Single crochet on the right side of the collar. Two rows may be necessary to make the collar lie flat. Steam.

CHAPTER X

KNITTED PANTS FOR SMALL BOYS

It is very important that there should be no constriction in small boy's pants. Ill-fitting clothes may cause permanent bodily injuries to a small child. Often pants are made too short in the seat, causing great discomfort and irritation to body and nervous system.

Five measurements are necessary for a small boy's knitted pants:

1. The waist measurement, which is taken loosely to allow for growth
2. The hip measurement, the fullest part, which is also taken loosely to allow for bending, climbing and growth
3. The length measurement on the side from the waist to the desired length. This is made long enough to allow for approximately 1 inch of ribbing or other stitch for the waist band
4. Center front of waist to crotch, not tightly
5. Measurement around the thigh, or the desired length

In the charting of the sample pants, no allowances have been made for plackets, buttonholes, or fastenings of any kind, but this is easily adjusted after the general directions are understood.

The following measurements are those which are used:

1. Waist measurement—24 inches
2. Hip measurement—30 inches
3. Length—11½ inches

248

CHARTING OF SAMPLE PANTS

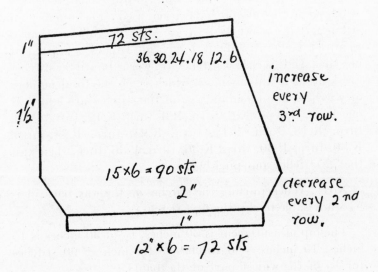

DIAGRAM 92.

4. Crotch—8½ inches
5. Thigh—12 inches

Stitch gauge—6 stitches to the inch; 8 rows to the inch

The pants are made in two pieces, the left side and the right side. The left side is the one which is charted. The right side is worked the same as the left, except that the increasing and decreasing are reversed.

METHOD. The waist measurement is 24 inches. ½ of 24 inches is 12 inches. 12 inches × 6 stitches to the inch = 72 stitches for ½ the waist measurement.

Work ribbing of either K.2, P.2 or K.1, P.1 for 1 inch.

In order to give fullness in the back of the pants, immediately after the 1 inch of ribbing, the stitches along the first row are gradually knitted until approximately ½ the stitches on the needle have been used. The number of stitches that are worked varies with the fullness that is required. Generally about 1 inch of stitches is knitted at one time. In this case 6 stitches are worked until 36 stitches are knitted in this manner, which is ½ the total number of stitches. The remaining ½ of the stitches are added at one time; that is, K.6, turn, P.6, turn, K.12, turn, P.12, turn, K.18, turn, P.18, turn, K.24, turn, P.24, turn, K.30, turn, P.30, turn, K.36, turn, P.36, turn, then knit the 72 stitches and purl back.

NOTE. When purling the stitches on the way back, it is advisable to slip the first stitch.

The hip measurement is 30 inches. ½ of 30 inches is 15 inches. 15 inches × 6 stitches to the inch = 90 stitches for ½ of the widest part of the pants.

Change to stockinette stitch. 90 stitches — 72 stitches = 18 stitches, the number of stitches to be increased until the length of the crotch is reached.

8½ inches — 1 inch of ribbing = 7½ inches in which to make 18 increases. The increases are made only on one side, therefore 7½ inches × 8 rows to the inch = 60 rows. 18 into 60 goes approximately 3 times, therefore the increases are made every 3rd row at the right side (when the right side of the work is facing toward the front) until there are 90 stitches on the needle and 8½ inches of fabric have been knitted, measuring the center.

11½ inches — 8½ inches = 3 inches for the leg, 1 inch of which is allowed for ribbing at the bottom, leaving 2 inches in which to make the necessary decreases.

12 inches is the thigh measurement, 12 inches × 6 stitches to the inch = 72 stitches necessary. There are at present 90 stitches on the needle; therefore 18 decreases have to be made, and at both sides the leg is decreased the same, that is, 9 decreases on each side; allowing 8 rows to the inch, 2 inches equals 16 rows. 9 into 16 goes approximately 2 times, therefore the decreases are made at the beginning and end of every 2nd row until 72 stitches remain and the leg measures 2 inches. Now work 1 inch of ribbing even, then bind off loosely.

Work the other side.

Finishing

Baste and sew the two parts together and if buttonholes or plackets are desired, turn to the Chapter on Details for directions. These, however, must be decided upon before the pants are begun, in order to make the necessary allowances when charting.

BOY'S KNITTED PANTS

(Using the Same Measurements as the Sample Pants but with a Different Stitch Gauge)

Measurements

1. Waist—24 inches
2. Hip—30 inches
3. Length—11½ inches
4. Center of waist in front to crotch—8½ inches
5. Thigh—12 inches

Stitch gauge—7½ stitches to the inch

10 rows to the inch

ILLUSTRATION 10.

The pants are made in two pieces, the left side and the right side. The left side is the one which is charted. The right side is worked the same as the left, only the increasing and decreasing are reversed.

METHOD. The waist measurement is 24 inches. ½ of 24 inches = 12 inches × 7½ stitches to the inch = 90 stitches for the waist measurement.

Work ribbing of K.1, P.1 for 1 inch, then change to stockinette stitch.

$$12'' \times 7\tfrac{1}{2} = 90 \text{ sts}$$

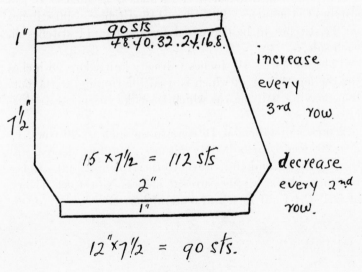

DIAGRAM 93.

In order to give fullness in the back, 8 stitches at a time are worked until 48 stitches, which are a little over ½ the total number, have been used, then the remaining stitches are knitted to make the total number of stitches, which is 90 stitches. That is, K.8, turn, P.8, turn, K.16, turn, P.16, turn, K.24, turn, P.24, turn, K.32, turn, P.32, turn, K.40, turn, P.40, turn, K.48, turn, P.48, turn, K.90, and purl back. This gives 14 extra rows at the back, a little over an inch.

The hip measurement is 30 inches. ½ of 30 inches = 15 inches × 7½ stitches to the inch = 112 stitches.

112 stitches — 90 stitches = 22 stitches to be increased at the right side. (Follow diagram 93.) At 10 rows to an inch, there are 10 rows × 7½ inches = 74 rows.

22 into 74 goes approximately 3 times, therefore increase every 3rd row until there are 112 stitches on the needle and 8½ inches of fabric have been knitted.

The thigh measurement is 12 inches. 12 inches × 7½ stitches to the inch = 90 inches. 112 stitches — 90 stitches = 22 stitches to be decreased for the leg. 11 stitches on each side.

11½ inches — 8½ inches (already knitted) = 3 inches for the leg, 1 inch of which is used for ribbing at the bottom, leaving 2 inches in which to make the necessary decreases.

2 inches of fabric at 10 rows to the inch = 20 rows. 11 into 20 goes approximately 2 times, therefore decrease at the beginning and end of every other row until 90 stitches remain and the leg measures 2 inches. Now work 1 inch of K.1, P.1 for 1 inch and bind off loosely.

CHAPTER XI

BLOUSES

BLOUSES may be joined to skirts forming full length, one piece garments, or they may be unattached, forming complete upper garments in themselves. A dressy blouse should closely follow the lines, texture and color of the skirt, while an unattached blouse should conform harmoniously with the skirt or suit with which it is to be worn.

Blouses may be knitted of wool, silk and wool, wool and rayon, rayon, linen or cotton, using texture stitches or lace patterns, depending upon their use.

The charting of sweaters was considered in much detail in a previous chapter and, as there are very few differences between the charting of knitted blouses and sweaters, it is essential that the charting of sweaters be understood.

Practically the same measurements are necessary for knitting a blouse as for knitting a sweater. They are:

1. Waist
2. Bust measurement in front
3. Across the back from underarm to underarm
4. Waist to underarm
5. Shoulder to shoulder
6. Wrist
7. Upperarm
8. Armhole
9. Sleeve underarm length

Read the directions as to the way in which these measurements should be taken when knitting a sweater. Remember the sweater measurements allow for freedom of action. While many persons desire blouses that are loose, there are others who like blouses to fit. This is a matter of individual taste and need, and should be considered when the measurements are taken.

There are two main differences between knitting a blouse and knitting a sweater. First, the back and the front are not made the same width. For a sweater, except in individual cases, ½ the bust measurement is used for the front and ½ for the back. Not so for a blouse. Across the back from underarm to underarm is used for the width of the blouse at the back, while the bust measurement from underarm to underarm is used for the front. Also, a little less than ½ the armhole measurement is used for the back armhole, and a little more than ½ is used for the front.

CHARTING OF A SAMPLE BLOUSE WITH ROUND NECK AND LONG SLEEVES

The same measurements as for the sample sweater are used for the blouse. They are:

Waist—29 inches

Across the back from underarm to underarm—16 inches

Waist to underarm—9 inches

Shoulder to shoulder—13½ inches

Wrist—6 inches

Upperarm—10 inches

Armhole—17 inches

Bust measurement in front—18 inches

Sleeve underarm length—18 inches

Stitch gauge—6 stitches to the inch

The waist measurement is 29 inches. ½ of 29 = 14½ inches × 6 stitches to the inch = 88 stitches for the ribbing. Therefore K.2, P.2 for 3½ inches.

The measurement across the back from underarm to

Back

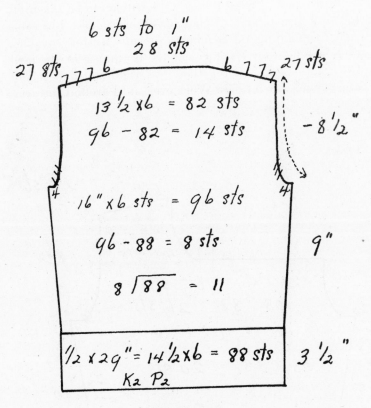

6 sts to 1"
28 sts

27 sts   7 7 6   6 7 7   27 sts

$13\frac{1}{2} \times 6 = 82$ sts

$96 - 82 = 14$ sts

$-8\frac{1}{2}$"

4   4

$16" \times 6$ sts $= 96$ sts

$96 - 88 = 8$ sts

$8\overline{)88} = 11$

9"

$\frac{1}{2} \times 29" = 14\frac{1}{2} \times 6 = 88$ sts

$3\frac{1}{2}$"

K2 P2

DIAGRAM 94.

underarm = 16 inches. 16 inches × 6 stitches to the inch
= 96 stitches.

96 stitches — 88 stitches = 8 stitches to be added across
the first row of the ribbing. 8 into 88 goes 11 times, therefore increase in every 11th stitch. Purl back and work
even for 9 inches to the underarm.

The shoulder to shoulder measurement is 13½ inches. 13½ × 6 stitches to the inch = 82 stitches.

96 stitches — 82 stitches = 14 stitches to be taken off for both armholes, 7 stitches for each armhole. The same rule for binding off armholes prevails as for sweaters, therefore bind off 4 stitches at the beginning of the next two rows and knit 2 together, the beginning and end of every other row 3 times. Work even until around the arm-

Front

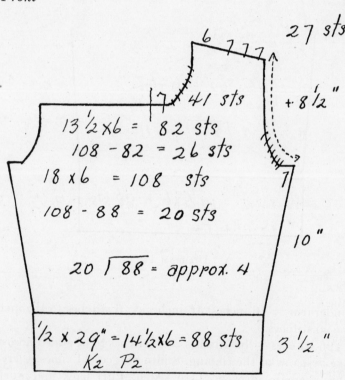

27 sts

6 7 7 7

7 41 sts

+ 8½ "

13½ × 6 = 82 sts

108 − 82 = 26 sts

18 × 6 = 108 sts

108 − 88 = 20 sts

7

10 "

20 ⟌ 88 = approx. 4

½ × 29" = 14½ × 6 = 88 sts

K2 P2

3½ "

DIAGRAM 95.

hole measures a little less than ½ the armhole measurement, i.e., a little less than 8½ inches.

The shoulders are bound off the same as for sweaters, therefore bind off 7 stitches at the beginning of the next 6 rows and 6 stitches at the beginning of the next 2 rows, then bind off the last 28 stitches loosely.

The waist measurement is 29 inches. ½ of 29 inches = 14½ inches × 6 stitches to the inch = 88 stitches for the ribbing.

The bust measurement in front = 18 inches. 18 inches × 6 stitches to the inch = 108 stitches. 108 stitches — 88 stitches = 20 stitches. 20 into 88 approximately 4 times, therefore increase in every 4th stitch to 108 stitches. Work even for 10 inches, which is one inch longer than the back, the same as for a woman's sweater, to allow for the bust.

The shoulder measurement is the same as the back, therefore 13½ inches × 6 stitches to the inch = 82 stitches for the shoulder.

108 stitches — 82 stitches = 26 stitches to be taken off for both armholes, i.e., 13 stitches for each armhole. Using the rule for binding off armholes, bind off 7 stitches at the beginning of the next 2 rows, then knit 2 stitches together at the beginning and end of every other row 6 times.

Work even to where neck line begins. This is 3 inches below the tip of the shoulder. Work ½ the stitches, which is 41 stitches and place the remaining 41 stitches on a stitch holder. 41 stitches — 27 stitches, the necessary number of stitches for each shoulder = 14 stitches for ½ of the neck line, therefore bind off 7 stitches at the beginning of the next row and then decrease by knitting 2 together at the beginning of every other row, 7 times.

The shoulder is bound off the same as the back shoulder, when around the armhole measures a little over half the armhole measurement, i.e., a little over 8½ inches.

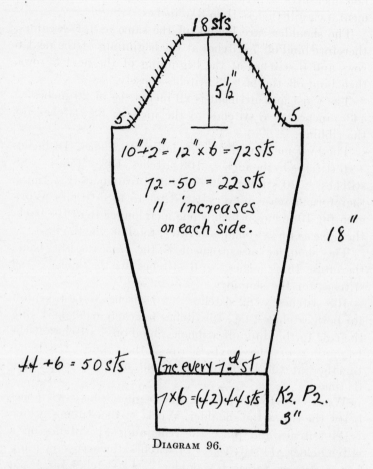

18 sts

5½"

5

5

$10" + 2" = 12" \times 6 = 72$ sts

$72 - 50 = 22$ sts

11 increases
on each side.

18"

$44 + 6 = 50$ sts

Inc. every 7th st.

$7 \times 6 = (42) + 44$ sts

K2. P2.

3"

DIAGRAM 96.

The sleeves are charted the same as for a sweater. If a tight fitting, long sleeve is desired, it is not necessary to add 2 inches to the upperarm measurement for the width of the sleeve as for the sweater with long sleeves, but at least 1 inch of stitches must be allowed, for even sleeves that fit snugly are never skin tight.

7 inches for cuff. 7 inches $\times$ 6 stitches to the inch = 42 stitches. 44 stitches of K.2, P.2 for 3 inches.

Increase one inch of stitches on the first row after the cuff. 6 into 44 goes 7 times, therefore increase in every 7th stitch to make 50 stitches.

10 inches, the upperarm measurement, plus 2 inches = 12 inches for the width of the sleeve.

12 inches $\times$ 6 stitches to the inch = 72 stitches for the width of the sleeve. 72 stitches — 50 stitches = 22 stitches to be increased on both sides, 11 stitches on each side, therefore increase every inch on both sides 11 times, making 72 stitches, and work even until the underarm sleeve measurement is 18 inches.

To find how many to take off at the beginning of the sleeve, add the number of stitches that were bound off at the beginning of the back and front underarms and divide the number by 2. In this case it is 4 plus 7 = 11 stitches, therefore divided by 2 = 5 stitches to be bound off at the beginning of the next two rows, the same as were taken off for the sample sweater sleeve, and continue by knitting 2 together at the beginning and end of every other row until the cap of the sleeve measures approximately 5½ inches.

NOTE. It is possible to knit a right sleeve and a left sleeve the same as when sewing. The stitches would be bound off to match the back and front underarms in each case. Binding off the same number of stitches at each side simplifies matters when knitting, and answers the same purpose.

Finishing

The blouse is finished exactly the same as the sweater. If a collar is desired, see the Chapter on Details for directions.

Back

1. ½ the waist measurement times the stitch gauge = the number of stitches for the ribbing.

2. Across the back from underarm to underarm × the stitch gauge = the number of stitches for the body of the blouse.

3. The difference between the number of stitches for the body of the blouse — number of stitches for ½ the waist measurement = the number of stitches to be added on the first row after the ribbing.

4. Divide the number of stitches to be added into the number of stitches for the ribbing to learn at which intervals stitches have to be added.

5. Shoulder to shoulder measurement × the stitch gauge = the number of stitches necessary for the shoulder.

6. The difference between the stitches for the shoulder and the stitches for the back underarm to underarm measurement = the number of stitches to take off for both armholes.

7. Bind off ½ the total number of stitches for each armhole at one time, the remainder to be decreased by knitting 2 together every other row.

8. The measurement around the armhole = a little less than ½ the total armhole measurement.

9. Allow approximately 1/3 of the stitches for each shoulder and the remaining 1/3 for the back of the neck.

10. Slope the shoulders in from 4 to 8 steps depending upon the weight of the yarn, and needles. The smaller the stitch gauge the fewer steps necessary.

Front

1. ½ the waist measurement times the stitch gauge = the number of stitches for the ribbing.

2. The front bust measurement from underarm to underarm = the number of stitches for the body of the blouse.

3. The difference between the number of stitches for the body of the blouse and ½ the waist measurement = the number of stitches to be added on the first row after the ribbing.

4. Divide the number of stitches to be added into the stitches for ribbing to learn at which intervals the stitches have to be added.

5. The waist to underarm measurement is 1 inch or more longer than the back waist to underarm measurement, depending upon necessity.

6. Shoulder to shoulder measurement × the stitch gauge = the number of stitches necessary for the shoulder.

7. The difference between the stitches for the shoulder and the stitches for the bust = the number of stitches to take off for both armholes.

8. Bind off ½ the total number of stitches for each armhole at one time. The remainder is to be decreased by knitting 2 together every other row.

9. Neck lines charted the same as for sweaters.

10. Measurement around the armhole a little more than ½ the armhole measurement.

11. Shoulder stitches bound off the same as the back.

NOTE. If a person has a particularly large bust, and hence the front is considerably larger than the back, extra stitches may be allowed for the neck and if necessary a dart near the shoulders.

Sleeves

1. Wrist measurement plus 1 inch of stitches = the necessary number of stitches for the cuff.

2. Add 1 inch of stitches on the first row after cuff is completed.

3. Upperarm measurement plus 1 inch for tight fitting sleeves, more added if wider sleeve is desired.

4. The difference between the stitches at the completion of the cuff and the number of stitches necessary for the width of the sleeve = the number of times to increase on both sides of the sleeve.

5. To learn where to increase, divide the number of times to increase into distance over which increases have to be made (Should be completed between 3 and 4 inches from armpit).

6. After increasing the necessary number of stitches, knit even to the desired underarm length.

7. Number of stitches first bound off for cap of sleeve = the number of stitches first bound off for back and front underarm, divided by 2.

8. Knit 2 together at the beginning and end of every other row until around the cap measures the same as the armhole. The average length of cap is 5½ inches from the first bind off.

9. Approximate number of stitches to be bound off at the top of the cap = 3 inches for adult and 2 inches for average child.

> NOTE. If the blouse is joined to the skirt to form a one piece garment, ½ inch of stockinette stitch is knitted instead of ribbing, and is included in the underarm measurement.
>
> When making a one piece garment, it is better to knit the skirt and top separately, then crochet a beading at the top of the skirt and the bottom of the blouse and weave elastic through both beadings at one time to join them together. In this way the dress hangs better, and it is much easier to wash and block when in two separate parts.

CHAPTER XII

BLOUSES MADE FROM DIFFERENT COMBINATIONS OF STITCHES

BLOUSES may be made of stockinette stitch, any of the texture stitches, or combinations of stitches to form a series of motifs that make a lace pattern.

Whether a texture stitch or lace pattern is to be used depends upon the purpose for which the blouse is intended. Lace motifs should never be used for sportswear, yet how appropriate are some of the combinations of stitches, texture stitches so named, embroidered in brilliant tints, using cross stitch, lazy daisy, stem and chain stitch and varying the effect by using different yarns and threads to contrast with the background!

The material, be it yarn or thread, should be suited to the garment and to the stitches whereof it is made. Lace motifs from their appearance and inspiration call for fairly fine and well-twisted yarns and thread. How futile to knit a garment using a lace pattern of some of the newer texture or nubby yarns, or the more loosely spun yarns, e.g., Shetland floss. All the fragile beauty and delicacy would be lost. Needless to say, it is not advisable to knit garments of very fine thread—eyes are too precious! But there are on the market exquisite yarns and threads that deservedly win a place for their delicacy for this truly artistic work. Naturally if a little coarser yarn or thread is used, the work changes in character, but it is equally elegant and serves the purpose, sometimes even better than when very fine thread or yarn is knitted.

No matter what design of stitch is used, it is from the actual combination of stitches or motifs to be used for the blouse that the stitch gauge is measured. If a lace pattern is desired, it is advisable to knit several patterns for a gauge. In the first place it will be easier to measure the stitch gauge on a larger piece, and secondly, the pattern will be learned gradually. Seemingly intricate looking patterns are generally easy to knit. Of course, it is not advisabe for a beginner to start an intricate piece of lace work. In knitting, as in every other branch of art, efficiency comes with practice.

It is a great mistake to commence a garment with a lace motif without at first knowing the pattern. Many hours are lost and much discouragement ensues, if one blindly tries to knit a lace blouse. There is usually one stitch which may be used as a guiding stitch and this is generally easily discernible.

It will readily be understood why it is necessary to know the pattern when one considers the shaping for a blouse. A straight piece of knitted lace is fairly simple if one can follow directions, but to shape the garment and keep the lace pattern correct is a different matter.

As for all stitch gauges, it is necessary, when using a lace pattern, to steam the lace before the stitch gauge is taken. Generally a lace pattern widens considerable after it is steamed and it is only then that its real beauty is disclosed.

To shape a blouse with a lace motif, it is advisable, if possible, to allow a certain number of whole motifs or patterns for each part: for example 8 whole patterns for across the back from underarm to underarm and 6 whole patterns for the shoulder to shoulder measurement. In this way the beginnings and ends of the rows are not so complicated. As mentioned previously, the shaping is the problem. If it is found difficult to shape, for example around the armholes, place a marker on the needle at the end of the first pattern and before the last, and, until the neces-

LACE BLOUSE WITH A SINGLE MOSS STITCH YOKE
LONG TIGHT-FITTING SLEEVES AND SQUARE NECK LINE

ILLUSTRATION 11.

sary number of stitches are bound off, always knit to the marker and then work the motifs in the usual way until the marker at the end is reached, when the stitches are again knitted. If more than one pattern is necessary, place the marker after the second pattern and so on, until the necessary stitches are decreased.

Measurements

Waist—26 inches
Bust—34 inches
Across the back from underarm to underarm—16 inches
Underarm to waist—8 inches
Shoulder to shoulder—13½ inches
Armhole—17 inches
Upperarm—9 inches
Wrist—6 inches
Sleeve underarm measurement—18 inches

Materials

8 ounces of 2 ply wool and rayon yarn
1 pair #2 steel needles

Stitch gauge

Stockinette stitch—8 stitches to the inch
Lace pattern—6½ stitches to the inch

LACE PATTERN

Multiple of 8 Stitches

Row 1. * K.1, Y.0, K.2, slip 1, K.2 together, pass the slip stitch over, K.2, Y.0, * ending with an increase in the last stitch instead of a Y.0.

Row 2. Purl

Row 3. * K.2, Y.0, K.1, slip 1, K.2 together, pass the slip stitch over, K.1, Y.0, K.1, *

Row 4. Purl

Row 5. * K.3, Y.0, slip 1, K.2 together, pass the slip stitch over. Y.0, K.2, *

Row 6. Purl

Repeat the 6 rows for pattern.

Note. For explanations concerning lace pattern, refer to Chapter on Stitches.

Back

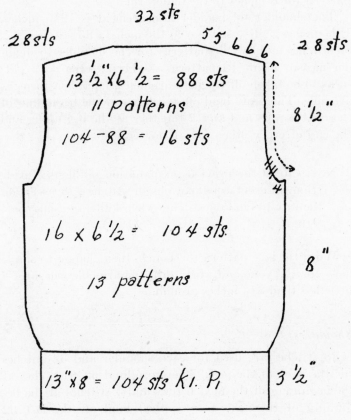

32 sts

28 sts   5 5 6 6 6   28 sts

13 ½" x 6 ½ = 88 sts

11 patterns

104 - 88 = 16 sts

8 ½"

4

16 x 6 ½ = 104 sts.

13 patterns

8"

13" x 8 = 104 sts K 1. P 1

3 ½"

Diagram 97.

The waist measurement is 26 inches. ½ the waist measurement, 13 inches, times 8 stitches to the inch = 104 stitches for the ribbing K.1, P.1 for 3½ inches.

Across the back from underarm to underarm = 16 inches. 16 inches × 6½ stitches to the inch = 104 stitches, therefore the lace pattern widens the desired amount and the number is divisible by 8, so no extra stitches are necessary and there will be 13 whole patterns. Work the lace pattern for 8 inches to the underarm.

The shoulder to shoulder measurement is 13½ inches. 13½ inches × 6½ stitches to the inch = 85 stitches, i.e., 88 stitches or 11 whole patterns for the shoulder to shoulder measurement. 13 patterns — 11 patterns = 2 patterns to be taken off for both armholes, 1 pattern for each armhole. Therefore bind off 4 stitches at the beginning of the next 2 rows and knit 2 together at the beginning and the end of every other row, 4 times.

NOTE. Read the previous explanation on blouses made from different combinations of stitches, to ascertain the way to bind off stitches when knitting a lace pattern.

Work the lace pattern for 1 inch, then change to single moss for the yoke and work until the armhole measures a little less than 8½ inches around.

Shoulders

28 stitches are used for each shoulder and 32 stitches for the back of the neck. Therefore bind off 6 stitches at the beginning of the next 6 rows and 5 stitches at the beginning of the next 4 rows, then bind off the last 32 stitches loosely.

Front

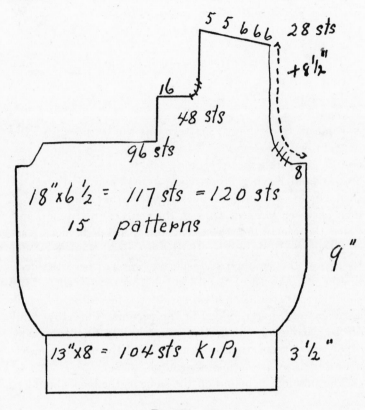

5 5 6 6 6   28 sts

+ 8½"

16

48 sts

96 sts

18" x 6½ = 117 sts = 120 sts

15   patterns

8

9"

13" x 8 = 104 sts K1 P1

3½"

DIAGRAM 98.

½ the waist measurement is 13 inches. 13 × 8 stitches to the inch = 104 stitches for the ribbing of K.1, P.1 for 3½ inches.

The bust measurement from underarm to underarm = 18 inches for the front of the bust. 18 inches × 6½ stitches to the inch = 117 stitches, therefore the number of stitches must be 120 stitches to be divisible by 8.

120 stitches — 104 stitches = 16 stitches to be added.

16 into 104 goes approximately 6 times, therefore increase in every 6th stitch until there are 120 stitches. Work in pattern for 9 inches, 1 inch more than the back from the waist to underarm.

The front has 2 patterns more than the back, therefore 1 more pattern is used for the armholes, making 3 patterns to be bound off for both armholes, 1½ patterns for each armhole.

Bind off 8 stitches (1 pattern) at the beginning of the next 2 rows and then knit 2 together at the beginning and end of every other row 4 times, making 1½ patterns decreased and leaving 96 stitches. Work 1 inch of pattern then change to single moss stitch for the yoke. After 1 inch has been knitted, work to the center, 48 stitches, and place the remaining 48 stitches on a stitch holder. Knit single moss stitch on the 48 stitches until 3 inches from the tip of the shoulder is reached. This is where the neck line begins. As 28 of the 48 stitches are required for the shoulder, 20 stitches remain for ½ the neck line, which is a square neck line rounded at the corners. Therefore bind off 16 stitches on the first row and knit 2 together every other row 4 times, then work even until the armhole measures a little over 8½ inches around.

The shoulder is bound off the same as the back shoulder.

Sleeve

7 inches × 8 stitches to the inch = 56 stitches for the cuff of K.1, P.1 for 2 inches. 56 stitches = 7 patterns.

11 patterns for the width of the sleeves = 88 stitches. 88 stitches — 56 stitches = 32 stitches, therefore 16 increases on each side. Increase every 6th row on both sides until there are 88 stitches.

NOTE. Knit the increased stitches until sufficient stitches are added on each side to form a complete pattern.

Work even until the underarm sleeve measurement is 18 inches.

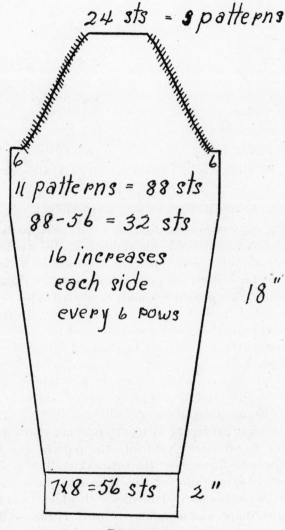

24 sts = 8 patterns

6   6

11 patterns = 88 sts

88 - 56 = 32 sts

16 increases
each side
every 6 rows

18"

7 x 8 = 56 sts   2"

DIAGRAM 99.

Cap of Sleeve

Bind off 6 stitches at the beginning of the next 2 rows, then K.2 together at the beginning and end of every other row until 3 patterns remain, that is 24 stitches, then bind off.

Finishing

Sew parts together and work a row of single crochet around the opening and neck line, then block as given in directions for blocking.

SKIRT KNITTED ENTIRELY OF A LACE PATTERN

Generally the directions for lace patterns are given for knitting on straight needles, and thus the pattern is knitted once on the right side and once on the wrong side, throughout. When a lace pattern is worked on a circular needle, as for a skirt, the work is always on the right side. Therefore, every second row must be altered. This is easily accomplished if every second row of straight knitting is purled. On the other hand if every second row is composed of fancy stitches, these must be changed to suit the right side of the work.

It is advisable to work a piece of lace fabric, using 2 straight needles and to notice any change that will be necessary when working on round needles.

A skirt knitted from a lace pattern is not charted like a plain or flared skirt. Naturally the pattern has to remain the same throughout the entire skirt. This is accomplished by having different sizes of needles, three sizes being the fewest number of needles with which to obtain a skirt with shape, and more may be used. If three different sizes are used, the skirt is knitted from the bottom to the hip with one needle, from the hip to 3 inches within the waist with the second and the last 3 inches with the third.

As has been mentioned before, the hip measurement is the important measurement for a skirt, therefore when knitting a skirt using a lace pattern, a piece of the lace material is knitted with the needle that is to be used at the hip and from this is calculated the number of patterns that are necessary at this point. Two or three sizes larger in a needle, according to the desired width for the bottom of the skirt, give the added width at the bottom, the number of patterns remaining the same.

Similarly, two sizes smaller decrease the skirt toward the waist line.

Correctly measuring the amount knitted is generally a problem when knitting a lace skirt. It must be remembered that a lace pattern increases both the length and width, some considerably more than others, when blocked. Therefore when measuring, place the skirt on a table and stretch the patterns as they will be stretched after they have been blocked.

CHAPTER XIII

MITTENS AND GLOVES

Knitted accessories are the next to be considered.

It is possible to be dressed appropriately with matching hats, gloves or mittens, scarves and hand bags, knitted of yarn, either of wool, very coarse or fine, wool and rayon, rayon or silk, cotton or linen thread, as the occasion demands.

It is in knitted mittens, caps, hoods, stockings for sportswear that striking and brilliant colors may be used to give picturesque effects, as in the case of the imported mittens one sees from Austria, Scandinavia, Estonia and other parts of the world.

Mittens and gloves are the first of the accessories to be discussed here. Although mittens and gloves are synonymous in purpose, one suggests the rigors of winter, the other, a mode. Rightly so, perhaps, for mittens are fingerless, affording much warmth, and are ideal protection for the enjoyment of winter sports or any other activity where individual fingers are not called into play. On the other hand, gloves offer freedom for individual fingers.

But do not look upon mittens as articles that will deter from the attractive appearance of the wearer. They can possess the same color and texture relationships to the rest of the costume, as their more refined sister, gloves.

Knitted mittens and gloves are washable, except when made of silver, copper, bronze or gold thread, and are therefore inexpensive to keep clean. They may also be constructed so as to be suitable for all occasions, from the simple, plain morning glove, the bright-hued mitten for sports, the angora mitten for formal wear to the more elaborate mitten or glove knitted of silver, bronze or gold thread to match evening slippers.

It was the desire for self-expression that is innate in all of us that motivated me to make formulas for knitted garments and accessories. While everyone cannot paint pictures or write stories, there is in knitting an opportunity for self-expression which requires the use of all the art principles of color, line, texture and composition. When once the simple formulas have been assimilated, then comes the opportunity for self-expression.

As the shaping of a mitten or a glove is the first important factor, it is necessary to understand how to knit a plain mitten or glove before individual tastes may be gratified.

The following diagrams and formulas for mittens and hence gloves are suited to all sizes of hands and any type of material to be knitted.

CHARTING OF MITTENS

As in all the previous shapings, measurements and stitch gauge are the only necessary factors when considering the knitting of a mitten. The wrist measurement is the first necessary measurement because it is here the mitten begins. The measurement around the knuckles of the hand is used because the hand must be able to pass through the cuff.

CHARTING OF SAMPLE MITTEN

In order that the knitter may understand the principles of charting a mitten, the simplest or easiest measurement and stitch gauge is the one explained the first. While the average knuckle measurement for a woman is 7 inches, 6 inches will be used for present purposes, with a stitch gauge of 6 stitches to the inch.

METHOD. 6 inches × 6 stitches to the inch = 36 stitches
for the cuff of the mitten, which may be either K.2, P.2 or
K.1, P.1 as desired, therefore cast on 36 stitches, 12
stitches on each of the 3 needles and work the ribbing for 3
inches. The length of the cuff is a matter of choice.

(Refer to the Chapter on Fundamentals for instructions on how to cast on stitches in this manner and also to
the Chapter on Details for how to hold a set of needles
when knitting.)

Change to stockinette stitch for the rest of the mitten.
Knit ¾ inch even, at which time the gusset for the thumb

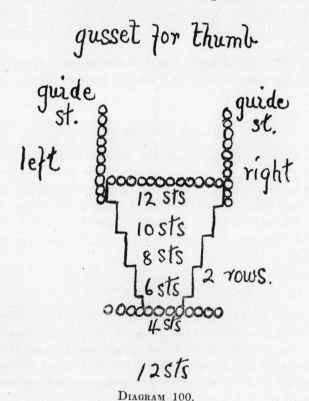

DIAGRAM 100.

is begun. This is done on one needle only and any needle will suffice because there are equal numbers of stitches on each needle, 12 stitches. These stitches are divided into 1/3, making 4, 4, 4. Again markers play an important role. Knit one round, placing a marker after the first 4 stitches and another before the last 4 stitches. That will leave 4 stitches between the markers.

Knit a round, increasing after the first marker and before the second marker—increasing by knitting first in the front of the stitch and then in the back of the same stitch—this will make 6 stitches between the markers.

Knit two rounds even and again increase after the first marker and before the second marker, making 8 stitches between the markers.

Continue in this way increasing after and before the markers, every third row, until there are 12 stitches between the markers, i.e., 12 stitches for the gusset for the thumb: in other words, until there are the same number of stitches for the increase of the thumb as there were originally on the whole needle.

NOTE. At this point be sure the depth for the separation of the thumb and hand is reached. If extra rows are required, knit them without increasing.

Knit around to the first marker, then place the 12 stitches for the thumb on a stitch holder (the thumb is worked later). Now turn the work to the wrong side and cast on 4 stitches to take the place of the 12 stitches for the thumb. In other words, the original number of stitches will now be on the needles, which is 36 stitches.

Again turn the work and knit the 4 remaining stitches on the needle. Continue to knit around and around in stockinette stitch until the center of the small fingernail is reached. Now is the time to begin decreasing for the top.

There are several ways to decrease the top of a mitten, but from experience I consider the most satisfactory way is to decrease as for the toe of a sock or stocking. In the first place, it conforms to the shape of the hand, and secondly, it helps toward understanding the position of the fingers when knitting gloves.

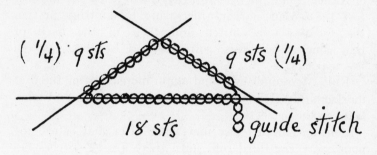

DIAGRAM 101.

One of the most important points in making either mittens or gloves is now reached—the correct position of the thumb. (Follow diagram.) It is here that the difference between the right and left hand of a mitten begins. The 12 stitches for the gusset for the thumb are on a stitch holder. Follow the next stitch that comes on the right hand side of the gusset. This stitch is the one that comes up the center of the outside of the index finger for the right hand mitten. The first stitch that comes on the left hand side of the gusset is the one that comes up the center of the outside of the index finger for the left hand mitten.

Divide the total number of stitches into ¼ and allow 18 stitches or ½ the total number, for the front needle and ¼ the total number, or 9 stitches, for each of the other 2 needles.

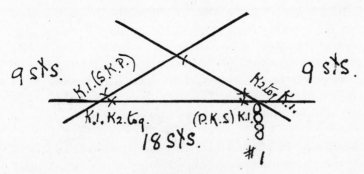

9 sts.　K.1.(S.K.P.)　9 sts.

K.2.tog. K.1.

K.1. K.2.tog.　(P.K.S) K.1.

18 STS.

#1

DIAGRAM 102.

The crosses mark the decreases which come directly at the sides. The first decrease begins at #1 on the needle with 18 stitches. Work as follows: K.1, slip 1, K.1, pass the slip stitch over the K. stitch (1 stitch decreased). Knit to the last three stitches on this needle then K.2 together, K.1 (2nd stitch decreased). The third decrease comes on a needle with 9 stitches. Work as follows: K.1, slip 1, K.1, pass the slip stitch over the knit stitch and the fourth decrease at the end of the second needle of 9 stitches is K.2 together, K.1.

Decrease in this manner every other row for ¾ of an inch. This is the same amount as was knitted before the increasing for the thumb was begun.

Then decrease every row until 12 stitches are left on the needle.

Place on one needle the 3 stitches that remain on each of the needles that had 9 stitches, that will be 6 stitches on one needle, and there will be 6 stitches on the other. Weave the stitches together as explained in Chapter on Details.

Thumb

Place on 2 needles the 12 stitches that are on the stitch holder.

Beginning at the center of where the 4 stitches were cast on, working from right to left on the right side, pick up 2 stitches that were cast on and an extra stitch at the side. This is permissible because the extra stitches can be decreased to form a gusset afterwards. Knit the 6 stitches on each of the 2 needles then pick up an extra stitch at the side and the remaining stitches that were cast on, join and knit around. The number of stitches necessary for the thumb are 12 stitches plus the 4 cast on stitches = 16 stitches, therefore any stitches above this number, 4, must be decreased by knitting 2 stitches together at each end of the needle, taking one or two rounds if necessary in which to make the decreases.

Continue to knit even on the 16 stitches until the center of the thumb nail is reached, at which time the decreasing for the top of the thumb is begun.

The decreasing is knitted as follows:

K.2 stitches, K.2 together for one round.

Knit one round even (finer yarn or thread 2 rounds).

K.1 stitch, K.2 together for one round.

Knit 1 round even.

K.2 together all the way round.

Draw the remaining stitches tightly together and darn in the ends.

Work the other mitten to correspond, placing the thumb at the left hand side.

FORMULA FOR PLAIN MITTENS

1. The measurement around the knuckles of the hand is used for the wrist measurement.

2. The wrist measurement $\times$ the stitch gauge = the number of stitches for the cuff.

The number of stitches is to be divided as evenly as possible on 3 needles. If K.2, P.2 is used, the number of stitches on each needle must be divisible by 4. If ribbing of K.1, P.1 is used, the number of stitches on each needle must be divisible by 2, and so on.

3. From ½ inch to 1 inch is knitted even in stockinette stitch before starting the gusset for the thumb, 1 inch being knitted for an adult, ¾ inch for average child and ½ inch for small child.

4. Divide the stitches into thirds, allowing as near as possible a third on each needle. If there is a difference in the number of stitches on the needles, the needle with the least number of stitches may be used to make the increases for the thumb.

5. Divide the stitches on the needle where the thumb is to be increased, into thirds. If there is a difference of a stitch either way, make these the center stitches on which the thumb is increased.

6. Place markers after the first third of the stitches and before the last third of stitches on which the thumb is to be made.

7. Increase after the first marker and before the second marker, leaving 2 rounds even, if the stitch gauge is 6 stitches to the inch, or if the stitch gauge is 7 or 8 stitches to the inch, 3 rounds even are necessary, and for finer yarns 4 rounds are necessary between the increases.

8. Increase until the number of stitches between the markers, that is the gusset for the thumb stitches = the number of stitches on the needle in the first place. Place these on a stitch holder.

9. The number of stitches cast on across the thumb = the number of stitches used for the gusset for the thumb, therefore the stitches for the hand will be the same number as the stitches for the cuff.

10. Work even until the center of the nail of the small finger is reached. The first stitch outside the stitches for the gusset for the thumb, either right or left, is the stitch

that comes at the center of the side of the index finger.

11. Divide the total number of stitches into ¼, allowing ¼ of the stitches for one needle, ¼ for another and ½ on the third, the front needle. The stitch at the center of the index finger will be the guide stitch as to position.

12. Decrease every other row for the same distance as was knitted even before the gusset for the thumb was begun.

> NOTE. The (slip 1, K.1, pass) decrease is worked on the right hand side of the needle while the knit 2 together decrease comes on the left hand side.

13. Decrease every row until from 8 to 16 stitches are left across the top, depending upon the size and type of yarn used.

Thumb

14. Place the stitches from the stitch holder on 2 needles. Pick up the stitches that were cast on across the thumb or more if necessary, then decrease to form a gusset. Knit even until the center of the thumb nail is reached. Decrease as follows:

K.2 stitches, K.2 together for one round.

Knit one round even (finer yarn or thread 2 rounds).

K.1 stitch, K.2 together for one round.

Knit one round even.

Knit 2 together all the way around.

Draw the remaining stitches tightly together and darn in the end.

> NOTE. Any variation in the number of stitches that is necessary, should be made at the discretion of the knitter. This refers especially to the number of stitches decreased for the thumb.

Mittens—Large Size

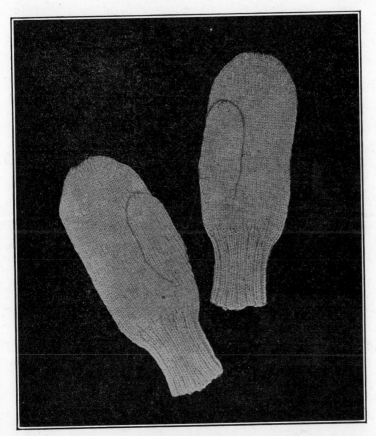

Plate XLV.

Measurements

Wrist—8 inches (knuckle measurement)
Cuff—3 inches
Total length of mitten—10½ inches
Total length of the thumb—5½ inches

1 inch before the gusset for thumb is started

6 inches of stockinette stitch before the decrease at the top is begun

1½ inches for the decrease at the top

Materials

1 set of #11 needles

3 ounces of Knitting Worsted

Stitch gauge—6 stitches to the inch

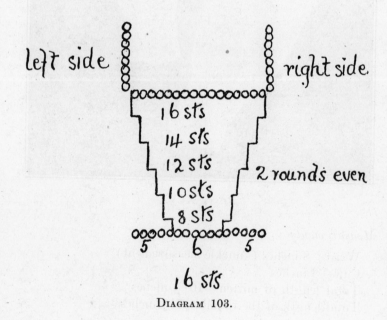

gusset for thumb

left side   right side

16 sts
14 sts
12 sts
10 sts
8 sts

2 rounds even

5   6   5

16 sts

DIAGRAM 103.

8 inches $\times$ 6 stitches to the inch $=$ 48 stitches. 16 stitches on each of the 3 needles.

Work in ribbing of K.2, P.2 for 3 inches. Knit 1 inch of stockinette stitch before the gusset for the thumb is commenced. 48 stitches divided into thirds $=$ 16 stitches. 16 stitches on the needle where the gusset is made. 16 divided by 3(5.6.5), the increases for the thumb coming after the first five and before the last five stitches and increasing every third row until there are 16 stitches between the markers, in other words, 16 stitches for the gusset for the thumb.

Place the 16 stitches on a stitch holder and cast on 6 stitches to take their place. The original number of stitches will now be on the needles, i.e., 48 stitches.

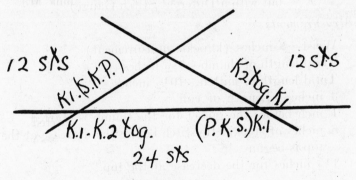

DIAGRAM 104.

Work even until there are 6 inches of stockinette stitch from the cuff. The first stitch outside the gusset, either right or left, marks the center side stitch of the index finger. Place 24 stitches (as in diagram) on the front needle, and 12 stitches on each of the other two. Decrease every other row for 1 inch, then every row until 16 stitches are left, 8 stitches on each of two needles.

Weave the stitches together as in directions for weaving.

Thumb

Place the 16 stitches from the stitch holder on 2 needles. Pick up the 6 stitches that were cast on across the thumb and 2 extra stitches on each side, these to be decreased later. This makes 16 stitches plus 8 stitches for the thumb = 24 stitches. Decrease the extra stitches that were added and work even until the length for the thumb from the cuff equals 5 inches, then decrease for the top as in the directions for decreasing the thumb in the formula.

CHARTING A MITTEN

(Using the Same Measurement as the Previous Mitten but with a Different Stitch Gauge)

Measurements

Wrist—8 inches (knuckle measurement)
Total length of thumb—5½ inches
Total length of mitten—10½ inches
3 inches—Length of cuff
1 inch before the gusset for the thumb is started
6 inches of stockinette stitch before the decrease at the top is begun
1½ inches for the decrease at the top.

Materials

1 set of #12 steel needles
3 ounces of sport yarn

Stitch gauge—7 stitches to the inch

8 inches × 7 stitches to the inch = 56 stitches. The stitches divided as follows, 20, 20, 16 stitches on each of 3 needles. Work in ribbing of K.2, P.2 for 3 inches. Knit 1

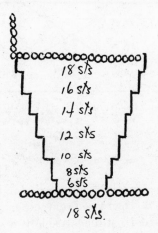

18 s/s

16 s/s

14 s/s

12 s/s

10 s/s

8 s/s

6 s/s

18 s/s.

DIAGRAM 105.

inch of stockinette stitch before the gusset for the thumb is commenced.

56 stitches divided into thirds = 19, 19, 18 stitches. The gusset for the thumb is made on the smallest number, which is 18 stitches. 18 divided into thirds = 6, 6, 6, the gusset for the thumb being increased on the middle 6 stitches, placing the markers after and before the first and last 6 stitches.

The stitch gauge is 7 stitches to the inch, therefore there are three even rows between the increases. Increase every 4th row after and before the markers until there are 18 stitches for the gusset for the thumb. Place the 18 stitches on a stitch holder and cast on 6 stitches to take their place. The original number of stitches will now be on the needle, i.e., 56 stitches. Work even until there are 6 inches of stockinette stitch from the cuff. The first stitch outside the gusset, either right or left, marks the center outside stitch of the index finger.

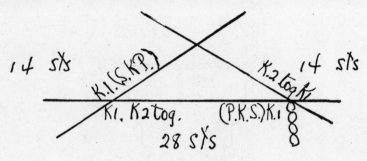

DIAGRAM 106.

Place 28 stitches on the front needle and 14 stitches on each of the other 2. Decrease every other row for 1 inch, then every row until 16 stitches are left, 8 stitches on each of 2 needles. (Follow diagram.)

Weave the stitches together as in the directions for weaving.

Thumb

Place the 18 stitches from the stitch holder on 2 needles. Pick up the 6 stitches that were cast on across the thumb (more if necessary to prevent holes, these to be decreased later); this makes 18 stitches plus 6 stitches = 24 stitches. Work even until the length of the thumb from the cuff equals 5 inches, then decrease for the tip as in the directions for decreasing.

NOTE. Decrease more stitches if necessary between the thumb and the hand.

GLOVES

If the principle by which mittens are knitted to size is understood, it will not be difficult to chart and hence knit gloves for any size hand. As before mentioned, it is simply the fingers that make the difference between mittens and

TABLE SHOWING DIVISION OF STITCHES WHEN KNITTING
MITTENS OR GLOVES

No. of Stitches for Cuff	How Stitches Are Divided on Needles for Cuff	How Stitches Are Divided on Needles When Gusset Is to Be Knitted	How Stitches on Gusset Needle Are Divided for Thumb
24	8.8.8.	8.8.8.	3.2.3.
36	12.12.12.	12.12.12.	4.4.4.
44	16.16.12.	15.15.14.	5.4.5.
48	16.16.16.	16.16.16.	5.6.5.
56	20.20.16.	19.19.18.	6.6.6.
60	20.20.20.	20.20.20.	7.6.7.
72	24.24.24.	24.24.24.	8.8.8.
80	28.28.24.	27.27.26.	9.8.9.

NOTE. The center stitches on the gusset needle are where the gusset is increased.

gloves; therefore when knitting gloves, the same directions prevail until the start of the fingers.

As you look at a hand, it will be noticed that the small finger joins the hand lower than the other fingers. When you knit gloves the fingers all start in the same place, therefore it is advisable that they begin where the first (index) finger joins the hand.

When knitting gloves, follow the same rules as when knitting mittens, until the fingers are reached. In knitting gloves the position of the thumb and fingers is an important factor. How to find the center side stitch of the index finger has already been discussed when charting mittens.

DIRECTIONS FOR SAMPLE GLOVES

The same measurements are used as for sample mittens.

Stitch gauge—6 stitches to the inch.

Directions for mittens requiring 48 stitches have already been given. As this is one of the easiest numbers to consider when charting fingers for gloves, 48 stitches are used first.

There are 48 stitches for 4 fingers. Allowing an equal number of stitches for each finger, it would be 12. 12. 12. 12 stitches respectively. As the first (index) finger, from the nature of its position and size, requires more stitches than any of the other fingers, allow 1/3 of the total number of stitches for the index finger. 1/3 of 48 stitches = 16 stitches; therefore 16 stitches of the 48 stitches are used for the index finger. The number of stitches for the second finger remains the same, while the extra 4 stitches are taken from the 3rd and 4th fingers making 10. 10. 12. 16 stitches respectively.

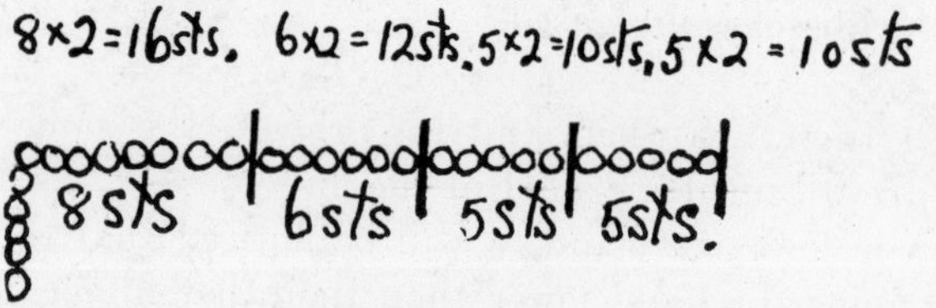

DIAGRAM 107.

The center stitch of the side of the first or index finger is the first stitch outside the gusset for the thumb, either right or left depending on the hand. From this point 8 stitches are placed on one needle and 8 stitches on another, while the remainder of the 48 stitches are put on a thread to be held for the other fingers.

Index Finger

The number of stitches added between the fingers is the difference between the number of stitches for the first and second fingers, i.e., $16 - 12 = 4$ stitches to be cast on between the fingers; therefore when knitting the first or index finger there will be 8 stitches plus 8 stitches plus 4 stitches $= 20$ stitches.

Note. If fewer stitches are necessary, decrease where the stitches were added.

Divide the 20 stitches on 3 needles and knit round and round in stockinette stitch until the center of the nail is reached. The fingers are decreased as follows:

K.2 stitches, K.2 together for one round
Knit one round even
K.1. stitch, K.2 together for one round
Knit one round even
Knit 2 together all the way around
Draw the remaining stitches tightly together and weave in the ends.

Second Finger

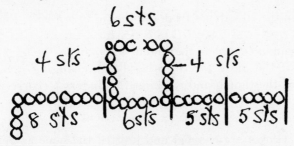

DIAGRAM 108.

Slip 6 stitches from the end of the thread on the upper side of the hand onto needle and knit the stitches. Pick up the 4 cast on stitches on the side of the first finger (more if necessary and decrease later). Slip 6 stitches from the other end of the thread (palm side of hand) onto needle and knit. Cast on 4 stitches for the other side of 2nd finger. Place the 20 stitches on 3 needles and work in stockinette stitch until the center of the nail is reached. Decrease as for the first finger.

Third Finger

Slip 5 stitches from the end of the thread on the upper side of the hand onto needle and knit. Pick up the 4 cast on stitches from the second finger (more if necessary and decrease later). Slip 5 stitches from the other end of thread onto a needle and knit. Cast on 4 stitches. On these 18 stitches work the third finger the same as the second.

Fourth or Little Finger

Slip the remaining 10 stitches from the thread onto 2 needles and knit. Pick up 4 stitches on the 4 cast on stitches from the third finger, making 14 stitches. Work the fourth finger, the same as the third finger.

Thumb

Slip the 16 stitches from the thread to a needle. Pick up the 6 cast on stitches. 16 plus 6 stitches = 22 stitches for the thumb. Complete the thumb the same as the fingers.

Knit the glove for the other hand, changing the position of the thumb and working the fingers to correspond.

FORMULA FOR GLOVES

1. Gloves are charted and knitted the same as mittens until the fingers are reached.

2. Divide the total number of stitches for the hand into ¼ths.

3. The number of stitches for the first (index) finger = 1/3 of the total number of stitches.

4. The extra stitches added to the first finger are subtracted from the stitches for the 3rd and 4th fingers.

5. The difference between the stitches for the first and second fingers = the number of stitches to be cast on between the fingers.

6. The thumb and fingers, after the center of the nail is reached, are decreased as follows:

> K.2 stitches, K.2 together for 1 round
> Knit one round even (finer yarn or thread 2 rounds even)
> K.1 stitch, K.2 together for one round
> Knit 1 round even
> Knit 2 together all the way around
> Draw the remaining stitches tightly together and weave in the ends.

> Note. If fewer stitches are necessary for the fingers, decrease the necessary number of stitches between the fingers to form a gusset.

STRING GLOVES WITH SINGLE MOSS STITCH CUFF

Measurements

Wrist—7 inches (knuckle)

Materials

1 Set of steel needles #13
1 Ball of string 800 yards

Stitch gauge—8 stitches to the inch

Method. The cuff which is 9 inches wide at the bottom, is made of single moss stitch. 9 inches × 8 stitches to the inch = 72 stitches. 73 stitches for single moss stitch (see

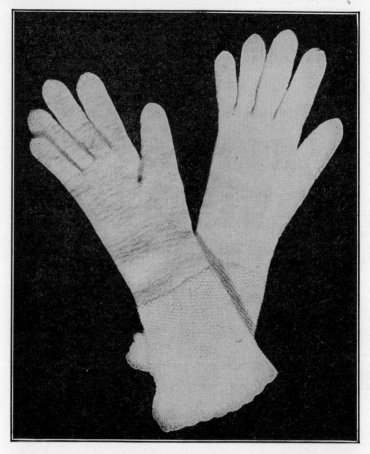

PLATE XLVI.

texture stitches at the back of the book). The first inch is knitted on straight needles, then the cuff is joined and the stitches placed on three needles.

The knuckle measurement is 7 inches. 7 inches × 8 stitches to the inch = 56 stitches for the wrist. Therefore, after the cuff is joined, decrease every 4th row before and after the joining, working the remainder of the stitches in single moss stitch, until 56 stitches remain and the cuff is 4 inches long.

Work 1 inch even in stockinette stitch.

Gusset for Thumb

Total number of stitches, 56 stitches—divided into thirds, 19. 19. 18 stitches on each needle. The gusset for the thumb is made on the needle with 18 stitches. 18 stitches divided into 1/3rds is 6. 6. 6. stitches respectively. The gusset for the thumb is increased on the middle 6 stitches.

The stitch gauge is 8 stitches to the inch, therefore there are three even rows between the increases, so the increases are made after and before the first and last 6 stitches, (which should be marked with markers) every 4th row until there are 18 stitches for the gusset for the thumb.

Place these 18 stitches on a stitch holder or thread and cast on 6 stitches to take their place, making 56 stitches again on the needle. Work in stockinette stitch until the fingers are reached.

Fingers

Divide the 56 stitches into ¼ths, i.e., 14. 14. 14. 14. stitches respectively. Allow 1/3 of the total figures for the index finger (first) 1/3 of 56 stitches = 18 stitches for the first finger, 14 stitches for the second finger and 12 stitches for each of the other two fingers.

The difference between the number of stitches for the 1st and 2nd fingers, 18 stitches minus 14 stitches = 4 stitches, therefore 4 stitches are cast on between the fingers making a total of:

18 stitches plus 4 = 22 stitches for the first finger
14 stitches plus 4 plus 4 = 22 stitches for the second finger

12 stitches plus 4 plus 4 = 20 stitches for the third finger

12 stitches plus 4 = 16 stitches for the fourth finger

and 18 stitches plus 6 stitches = 24 stitches for the thumb

Work in stockinette stitch until the center of the nail is reached in each case, decreasing the top of the fingers as follows:

K.2 stitches, K.2 together for one round

Knit 2 rounds even

K.1 stitch, K.2 together for one round

Knit 1 round even

K.2 together all the way around

Draw the remaining stitches tightly together and weave in the ends.

Thumb

Place the 18 stitches from the stitch holder on 2 needles. Pick up the 6 stitches that were cast on across the thumb (more if necessary to prevent holes, these to be decreased later). This makes 18 stitches plus 6 stitches = 24 stitches.

Finish the same as the fingers.

Work the glove for the other hand, changing the opening for the cuff and the position of the thumb, then work the fingers to correspond.

Finishing

Around the cuff is crocheted a shell stitch comprising of 3 double crochets made in one stitch * skip a stitch, a single crochet in the next stitch, skip a stitch and 3 double crochets in the next stitch * repeat around.

GLOVES WITH LACE CUFF
(Size for Average Woman's Hand)

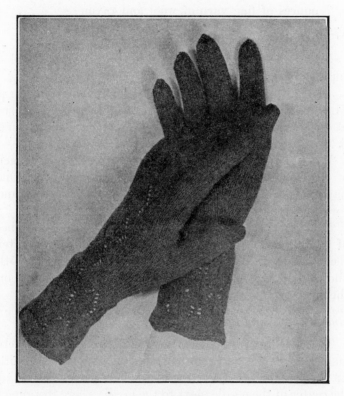

PLATE XLVII.

Measurements

Around the knuckles—7 inches
Length of 1st finger—3 inches
Length of 2nd finger—3½ inches
Length of 3rd finger—3 inches
Length of 4th finger—2½ inches
Length of thumb from gusset—2¾ inches

Materials

    1 set of steel needles—#13
    2 ounces of fine yarn of wool and rayon

Stitch gauge—8 stitches to the inch

METHOD. 7 inches × 8 stitches to the inch = 56 stitches for the wrist.

The multiple of stitches required for the leaf pattern is 11 (directions for which are given with other lace patterns at the back of the book); therefore 6 patterns require 6 × 11 = 66 stitches.

Work 6 patterns, i.e., 66 stitches = 22 stitches on each of three needles until 2 whole patterns are knitted. One pattern is continued up the center of the back of the hand for 3 patterns.

56 stitches are needed at the wrist, therefore 10 stitches of the 66 stitches have to be reduced on the first row after the cuff has been knitted, i.e., approximately every 5th and 6th stitch are knitted together, making 56 stitches on the needles for the wrist.

Gusset for Thumb

The stitches are divided 19. 19. 18 stitches respectively on the needles. The thumb is increased on the needle with 18 stitches. The center stitch of the lace pattern comes at the center of the needle, next to the needle where the gusset for the thumb is made, therefore the 10th stitch of the next needle is the center stitch of the lace pattern, going up the back of the hand. Work 1 inch before the gusset for the thumb is commenced.

The 18 stitches are divided 6. 6. 6, the middle 6 stitches being increased for the gusset every 4th row until there are 18 stitches for the thumb. These are placed on a thread and 6 stitches cast on to take their place, making 56 stitches, the original number of stitches.

Work the one pattern and stockinette stitch until the fingers are reached. Allow 18 stitches for 1st finger, 14 stitches for 2nd finger, and 12 stitches for 3rd and 4th fingers respectively, with 4 stitches cast on between the fingers.

Work in stockinette stitch until the center of the nail is reached in each case, which is approximately ½ inch shorter than the entire finger.

Decrease the tip of the fingers and thumb as follows:

K.2 stitches, K.2 together for one round
Knit 2 rounds even
K.1 stitch, K.2 together for one round
Knit 1 round even
K.2 together all the way around
Draw the remaining stitches tightly together and weave in the ends.

Thumb

Place the 18 stitches from the stitch holder on 2 needles. Pick up the 6 stitches that were cast on across the thumb (more if necessary to prevent holes, these to be decreased later). This makes 24 stitches for the thumb. Finish the same as the fingers.

Work the glove for the other hand, changing the position of the thumb, then work the fingers to correspond.

Finishing

Work one row of single crochet around the bottom of the cuff to prevent the lace pattern from curling.

CHAPTER XIV

SOCKS AND STOCKINGS
FOR MEN, WOMEN AND CHILDREN

When buying socks and stockings do we stop to consider the importance hosiery plays in regulating our well-being, or do we purchase hose mainly for their appearance? One should remember that the feet carry the weight of the entire body, therefore, when they are not in good condition, through being cold, damp or badly formed, the whole body is handicapped. It is therefore very important that hose be knitted of the correct fiber, long enough so that they do not crowd the toes and wide enough so that the breadth of the foot and toes are able to keep their normal position.

It is a fallacy for women to consider only silk hose, chiffon or service chiffon correct for all occasions. How out of place is a pair of chiffon hose topped with a fur coat! All clothing should protect the sensitive parts of the body, hence the ankles and knees require their share. On the other hand, wearing a pair of silk hose (for the sake of appearances) for sportswear, and wearing woolen socks over them defeats the purpose of the woolen socks, as they should come next to the feet.

Wool is the warmest fiber. On account of its structure, which permits it to be spun into yarn containing many air spaces, it holds air more than other fibers, and so maintains the temperature of the body. It is also absorbent, being capable of holding as much as 30% of its own weight of moisture without feeling wet to the touch, therefore it does not feel cold and clammy even when very damp.

Silk stockings are out of place for sportswear during

any season of the year. For sports, as for any other occasion, hose should be in harmony with the rest of the costume, and thus hose should be sturdy and simple, befitting their use and providing warmth and protection from the elements.

Many imagine wool to be itchy and prickly when worn. This is a notion of the inexperienced, because there are on the market wools as smooth and soft as the finest silk, besides the many varieties of wool and silk and wool and rayon. There are many weights of wool and wool mixtures from sturdy 4 ply worsted, suitable for hard wear, Spanish stocking yarn, which is a little tighter spun but which stands wear and tear with fortitude, soft yarns of the finest Australian and Cashmere stock, and soft Saxony baby yarn, to the tightly spun French zephyr (2 ply), all suitable for socks and stockings for different occasions and purposes.

Persons with cold, clammy or perspiring feet should try wearing fine woolen hose for winter. They are a boon to the factory worker and adolescent boy who suffers from excessive perspiration. They can be knitted to look as attractive—probably not so sheer, which is not desired—as the finest hosiery made from any other fiber. If worn by the business woman or high school girl, except for evening wear, it will be found that 2 pairs of hose of neutral shade will last throughout the winter, thus making a great saving and in keeping with many family budgets. Most office and high school girls spend too much to keep up appearances, and one of the greatest problems in dress for a high school student is the amount of money expended on silk or rayon stockings. On the other hand what looks worse than a stocking full of runs or plastered with nail polish to prevent long runs? Surely, these are neither beautiful nor necessary, if only a little common sense is used in developing the correct attitude when considering the type of hose that is suitable for the occasion on which it is worn! What could be more practical, suitable and attractive than a tailored suit with blouses or sweaters of varying shades and worn with fine knitted hose in harmony with the general color scheme of the costume?

Kinds of Hose

Women's hand knitted hose are either full or anklet length.

Men's hose may be either:

1. Three quarter hose for golf and general sportwear.

2. Half socks for general wear and sportswear, knitted according to taste and season—about 14 inches long.

3. Sweat socks or short sports socks, generally knitted about 1 inch longer than the ribbing before the heel begins.

4. Work socks, which are generally around 9 inches to 11 inches long and are made heavier and sturdier than men's regular half hose.

Children's stockings vary as to length:

1. Full length stockings
2. Knee length
3. Half hose
4. Anklets

These can be knitted of plain, ribbed or fancy stitches.

Women's stockings vary in length, an average length being from 20 to 22 inches from the top of the heel. The elastic character of knitting makes it unnecessary to add more stitches for the top of the stocking than for the fullest part of the calf, hence this is the measurement used for the top of the stocking.

For plain socks use a ribbing varying from K.1, P.1 for 1 inch for baby socks, to 4 inches of K.2, P.2 for a man's or boy's heavier sock.

For three quarter hose and short socks to wear for

skating or for outdoor winter wear, the ribbing is usually covered with a cuff either of a fancy pattern or using bright colored yarns in quaint designs to match the cuff of mittens and bands on hats.

The legs of stockings or socks are knitted either plain or in ribs depending upon individual desires. If knitted of ribbing, the stitch gauge may be taken from stockinette stitch. As ribbing is knitted looser than stockinette stitch, this allows for the drawing-in character of ribbing.

The measurements necessary when knitting socks or stockings are:

1. Calf—at the desired height of sock, or the fullest part, if knitting stockings.

2. Ankle measurement, which is generally the same width as the foot.

3. Length of the foot (the size in a bought stocking). This is the length of the foot from the center back of the heel to the longest point at the toes. In order to give greater comfort and better service, this should never be measured too short.

4. The length of the sock or stocking is the distance from the bottom of the heel over the curve of the ankle up to the stocking or sock top.

Stockings and socks for men, women and children are all knitted on the same principle, therefore to understand how to chart one, means to understand the principles by which the others are charted; therefore the charting of a man's half sock for general wear will be given for a sample.

CHARTING A MAN'S SOCK FOR GENERAL WEAR

Measurements

Calf 13 inches—measurement at the desired height
Length of sock to bottom of heel—12 inches

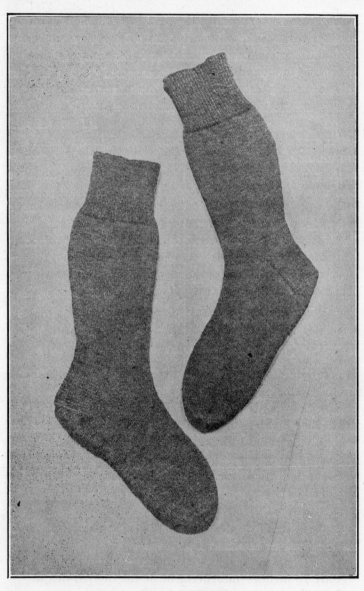

PLATE XLVIII.

Ankle measurement—10 inches
Length of foot—10½ inches

Materials

4 ounces of sport yarn
1 set of #12 steel needles

Stitch gauge

6 stitches to the inch
8 rows to the inch

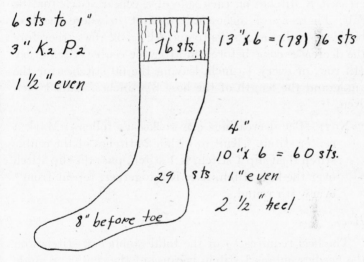

6 sts to 1"

3". K.2 P.2

1½" even

76 sts.

13" x 6 = (78) 76 sts

4"

10" x 6 = 60 sts.

29 sts 1" even

2½" heel

8" before toe

DIAGRAM 109.

The measurement of the calf is 13 inches. 13 inches ✕ 6 stitches to the inch = 78 stitches for the ribbing of K.2, P.2; this must be divisible by 4, and therefore 76 stitches are cast on the three needles, 24 stitches on the first needle, 24 stitches on the second needle and 28 stitches on the third; work in ribbing of K.2, P.2 for 3 inches.

Four double pointed steel needles are used for knitting socks and stockings and the knitting is worked in continuous rounds without turning, except at the heel, which is worked back and forth with 2 needles, the other stitches remaining on the 2 needles.

Work in stockinette stitch for 1½ inches making the length of leg 4½ inches from the beginning.

Decreasing the Leg

The ankle measurement is 10 inches. 10 inches $\times$ 6 stitches to the inch = 60 stitches for the ankle measurement. 76 stitches — 60 stitches = 16 stitches to be decreased, 8 stitches on each side of a center stitch for the calf. There are 5 inches still to knit to where the heel begins. 4 inches at 8 rows to an inch = 32 rows; therefore the decreases come before and after the center stitch every 4th row, or every ½ inch, leaving the 60 stitches for the ankle and the length of the hose 8½ inches. Knit 1 inch even.

> NOTE. The decreasings are worked as follows: Mark a center stitch. * Knit to within 2 stitches of the center stitch then slip 1 stitch, K.1 stitch, pass the slip stitch over the knit stitch, K.1, K.2 together, repeat from * every 4th round.

Heel

The heel requires ½ of the total number of stitches on the needles, minus 1 stitch, because of the center or guide stitch. 60 stitches, the total number of stitches on the needles, ½ of 60 = 30 stitches — 1 stitch = 29 stitches for the heel, which are placed on 1 needle with the guide stitch marking the center stitch. The remaining 31 stitches form the instep stitches and remain on the other two needles.

Knit one row, purl one row on the heel needle, not slipping the first stitch as generally advised. From experience, it has been found that if the first stitch is slipped often a small hole is made when the stitches are picked up at the side. Work the heel until it measures 2½ inches. Finish on a purl row.

Turning the Heel

1. Knit to 2 stitches past the center stitch. Slip 1 stitch, K.1 stitch, pass the slip stitch over the knit stitch, K.1, turn.

2. Slip a stitch, purl to 2 stitches past the center stitch, P.2 together, P.1, turn.

3. Slip a stitch, knit 3 stitches past the guide stitch, slip a stitch, K.1 stitch, pass the slip stitch over the knit stitch, K.1 stitch, turn.

4. Slip a stitch, purl to 3 stitches past the center stitch, P.2 together, P.1, turn.

   Note. The last stitch of the decreased row becomes the first stitch of the next decrease.

5. Continue in this way, adding one extra stitch until all the stitches have been used.

With the right side of work toward you, knit to the center of the heel.

Instep Shaping

With the right side of the work toward you, and with a needle that will be named the first needle, knit the remaining stitches on the heel needle then pick up the stitches at the side of the heel—2½ inches of sts. = 15 sts. With a second needle, knit across the two needles left for the instep. With a third needle, pick up the stitches on the other side of the heel (should have the same number of stitches on each side) and knit to the middle of the heel.

The stitches are now on three needles ready for the shaping at the instep.

The instep shaping is done at the end of the first needle

Instep

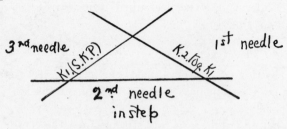

DIAGRAM 110.

and the beginning of the third needle. Knit to within 3 stitches of the instep on the first needle, then K.2 together (decrease), K.1, knit across the instep. (Second needle.) Then K.1, slip 1, K.1, pass the slip stitch over the knit stitch for the decrease on the third needle, then knit without decreasing to the end of the round. Continue decreasing every other round until the total stitches that remain are equal to the number of stitches at the ankle, which was 60 stitches.

Foot

The foot is knitted without any shaping from the instep to the place where the decreasing for the toe begins. Any pattern or ribbing is carried on the second (instep) needle until the shaping for the toe is reached.

Decreasing for Toes (same as decreasing for mittens)

Allow the same number of inches for decreasing the toes as was knitted for the length of the heel, which was 2½ inches.

The length of the foot is 10½ inches, therefore knit even until the length of the foot from the center stitch at the back of the heel measures 8 inches.

The stitches are already divided correctly on the needles, 30 stitches on the instep needle and 15 stitches on each

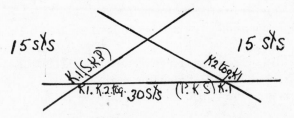

DIAGRAM 111.

side of the other 2 needles. Decrease starting at the right side of the instep needle. K.1 stitch, decrease by slipping 1 stitch, K.1 stitch, pass the slip stitch over the knit stitch, then knit to the last three stitches of the instep, which are decreased by K.2 together, K.1. On the next needle (third needle) K.1 stitch, decrease by slipping 1 stitch, K.1 stitch, pass the slip stitch over the knit stitch, then knit to the end of the needle. On the last needle, knit to the last three stitches then K.2 together, K.1 (follow the diagram).

Continue decreasing in this manner every other row for 2 inches, then every row for about ½ inch, at which time there will remain a little over one inch of stitches at the toe, which in this case is 8 stitches for the instep needle and 4 stitches on each of the other 2 needles. The 4 stitches on the last 2 needles are placed on one needle, making 8 stitches, which leaves the 2 needles with 8 stitches each.

Break the yarn, leaving about 12 inches. Hold the two needles side by side, and weave the stitches together then fasten the yarn on the inside. (See Chapter on Details for Weaving.)

FORMULA FOR SOCKS AND STOCKINGS

1. Measurement of the calf of the leg at the desired height or the fullest part if knitting stockings, multiplied by the stitch gauge = the number of stitches to cast on.

2. Ankle measurement multiplied by the stitch gauge = necessary number of stitches at the ankle.

3. Number of stitches for calf — number of stitches for ankle = the number of stitches to be decreased toward the ankle.

4. The decreasings made before and after the center stitch, about every ½ inch for medium weight yarn and oftener for finer yarn. Leave 1 inch to be knitted even before the heel.

5. No decreasings and therefore no center stitch is necessary for short sport socks.

6. The heel requires ½ the total number of stitches minus 1 stitch. The guide stitch to be the center stitch of the heel.

7. The heel. Purl a row, knit a row on the heel stitches, until the heel measures 2½ inches for a man, 2 inches for a woman and varying accordingly for a child.

8. Turning the heel.

1. Knit to 2 stitches past the center stitch. Slip 1 stitch, K.1, pass the slip stitch over the knit stitch, K.1, turn.
2. Slip a stitch, purl to 2 stitches past the center stitch, purl 2 together, P.1, turn.
3. Slip a stitch, knit to 3 stitches past the guide stitch, slip a stitch, K.1 stitch, pass the slip stitch over the knit stitch, K.1 stitch, turn.
4. Slip 1 stitch, purl to 3 stitches past the center stitch, P.2 together, P.1, turn.
5. Continue in this way, adding a stitch, until all the stitches have been used.

NOTE. The last stitch of the decreased row becomes the first stitch of the next decrease.

6. Knit to the center of the heel on the right side.

9. Knit the remaining stitches on the heel needle, then pick up the stitches on the right side of the heel. With a

second needle, knit across the next 2 needles for the instep. With a third needle, pick up the stitches on the other side of the heel and knit to the middle of the heel.

NOTE. The number of stitches picked up to equal the length of the heel, e.g., 2 inches or 2½ inches of stitches, etc.

10. Instep Shaping

The instep shaping is worked at the end of the first needle and the beginning of the third, as follows: Knit to within 3 stitches of the instep on the first needle, then K.2 together, K.1, knit across the instep (on the second needle) then K.1, slip 1, K.1, pass the slip stitch over the knit stitch, for the decrease on the third needle, then knit without decreasing to the end of the round. Continue decreasing every other round until the total number of stitches equal the number of stitches at the ankle.

11. The foot is knitted without any shaping until the decreasing for the toe begins.

12. Allow the same number of inches for decreasing the toe as was knitted for the length of the heel.

13. Decrease the same as mittens, which is as follows: Starting at the right side of the instep, K.1, stitch, slip 1 stitch, K.1 stitch, pass the slip stitch over the knit stitch, then knit to the last 3 stitches of the instep which are decreased by K.2 together, K.1 (see diagram 111). On the next needle K.1 stitch, slip 1 stitch, K.1 stitch, pass the slip stitch over the knit stitch, then knit to the end of the needle. On the last needle knit to the last three stitches then K.2 together, K.1.

Continue decreasing in this manner every other round for almost the entire length of the toe, then decrease every round until a little over 1 inch of stitches remain for men, varying to ½ inch for children.

14. Weave the remaining stitches together.

GOLF HOSE

PLATE XLIX.

Measurements

1. Top—15 inches (large to be worn outside pants)
2. Ankle—10 inches
3. Length of sock—17 inches plus 3 inches for cuff
4. Length of foot—11½ inches.

Materials

1 set of #12 stocking needles
9 ounces of knitting worsted

Stitches

Double moss stitch for cuff
Ribbing of K.2, P.2 throughout

Stitch gauge

6 stitches to the inch
8 rows to the inch

15 inches for the calf = 15 inches × 6 stitches to the inch = 90 stitches, therefore, 92 stitches for double moss cuff of K.2, P.2 for 3 inches.

Change to ribbing of K.2 and P.2 and work even for 5½ inches.

Decreasing Toward Ankle

Ankle measurement—10 inches × 6 stitches to the inch = 60 stitches to the ankle. 92 stitches — 60 stitches = 32 stitches, 16 decreases on each side. 8 inches to decrease 16 stitches, therefore decrease every ½ inch or every 4th row before and after the center knit rib, so a knit rib comes straight down the center of the leg, until 60 stitches remain.

Work 1 inch even.

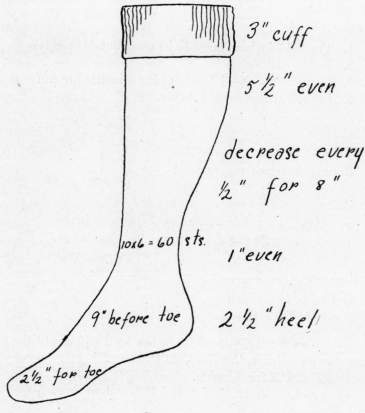

3" cuff

5½" even

decrease every ½" for 8"

10x6 = 60 sts.

1" even

9" before toe

2½" heel

2½" for toe

DIAGRAM 112.

Heel

Allow 30 stitches for the heel and follow the directions as in formula using two stitches for the center stitches.

Shaping the Instep

Follow the directions as in formula.

Foot

The length of the foot is 11½ inches, therefore knit even on the 60 stitches until the foot measurement equals 9 inches, then decrease the toe as in the formula.

BOY'S SPORT SOCKS

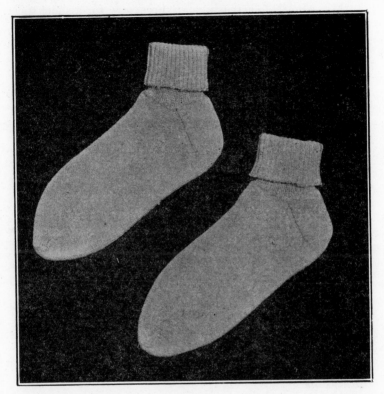

PLATE L.

Measurements

Ankle—8 inches
Length of foot—9½ inches
Cuff—2 inches

Materials

1 set of #13 needles
2 ounces of cashmere sport yarn

Stitch gauge—7 stitches to the inch

METHOD. No decreasings are necessary for a short sock.

8 inches, the ankle measurement = 8 inches × 7 stitches to the inch = 56 stitches for the ribbing of K.1, P.1 for 4 inches.

Heel

½ the total stitches for the heel — 1 stitch = ½ of 56 stitches or 28 stitches — 1 stitch = 27 stitches for heel which is 2 inches long.

Follow the formula for each part.

Foot

After decreasing for instep, work even in stockinette stitch until the foot measures 7½ inches, allowing 2 inches for the decreasing at the toe.

BABY STOCKINGS

Lace Pattern (Refer to Lace Patterns) requires multiple of 11 stitches.

Materials

1 ounce of 2 ply Saxony
1 set of #13 needles

Lace Pattern

Row 1. K.2 together, K.2 together, Y.O., K.1, Y.O., K.1, Y.O., K.1, Y.O., K.2 together, K.2 together.
Row 2. Knit.
Row 3. Knit.
Row 4. Knit.
Repeat the four rows.

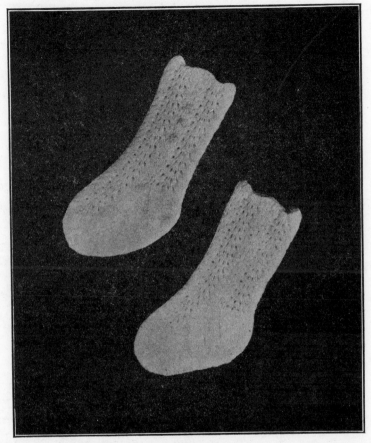

Plate LI.

Method. 44 stitches are used for the leg, this making 4 complete patterns. The stitches are divided on 3 needles as follows: 16. 16. 12.

Work ribbing at the top of K.2, P.2, for 4 rows. Then the pattern is commenced and worked until the leg measures 3½ inches.

The principles by which the heel, the turning of the heel and the instep are knitted, are exactly the same as for any other sock or stocking. Therefore, 21 stitches are required for the heel, which is 1 inch in depth. (See formula for heel, turning of heel and reducing for instep.) Carry the pattern down the instep and knit until the length of the foot is 2½ inches.

Decrease the toe as directed in formula, until 6 stitches on each of 2 needles remain, then weave the stitches and fasten off the yarn on the outside.

BABY BOOTEES

Materials

½ ounce of 2 ply baby yarn of silk and wool
1 set of #10 needles
The same lace pattern used as for the stockings

METHOD. Larger needles are used than for the stockings, therefore only three patterns are required, that is, 33 stitches, 11 stitches on each of 3 needles. Work the pattern for 2½ inches before commencing the heel, then use 16 stitches for the turn of the heel.

As one pattern is continued down the instep, this must come in the center of the instep needle, therefore there will be 3 stitches knitted before and after the pattern on the instep needle.

Follow the directions for baby stockings for completing, then thread ribbon through the holes of pattern at the ankle and fasten in a bow at the front. Other bows may be added if desired.

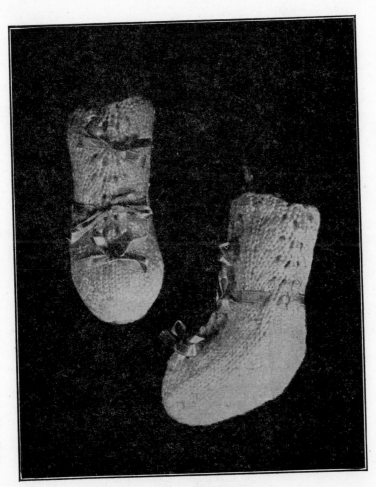

PLATE LII. Baby Bootees.

CHAPTER XV

HATS

Have you ever considered how important a hat is, compared with the rest of the costume? It is, in reality, the most important single item of the wardrobe, as it forms a framework for the face. It can do more to alter the contours of one's face (the most distinguishing part of one's anatomy) than any other part of one's apparel. Besides, it is the only article that is entirely visible when one is in a crowd.

While it is not the intention of the author to discuss different types of hats for different individuals, the more salient points should be noted.

1. The headdress should form a becoming background for the face.
2. It should be appropriate for the height, weight and age of the wearer.
3. It should be suitable for the occasion on which it is worn.
4. In harmony with the rest of the costume in color, design and texture.
5. It should keep the head in proportion and shape to the whole figure of the wearer.

The first hat to be discussed is a simple beret. The construction of a French beret and Scotch tam-o-shanter is identical. The difference is in size and the tassel which is generally placed in the center of a tam-o-shanter.

It is possible, after understanding the making of a simple beret, to adjust the directions and vary the shape so a beret may be suitable for many types of persons and even becoming to persons who wear glasses.

As previously stated, mathematics have an important part in knitting garments and accessories. As a matter of fact, it should have been apparent up to this point that one is as important as the other, for without correct calculations, measurements and reasoning, the garment or accessory would not fit and hence would be useless.

As we have progressed throughout the book, mathematics have become a little more complex and in making berets a new phase is reached.

BERET

The stitch gauge and measurements are again important.

The necessary measurements are:

1. The head size
2. The diameter of the beret. (This naturally depends upon the suitability of the size to the wearer.)

NOTE. When taking the head size with the tape, care must be taken that the fullest part of the head is measured; that is, measure any protrusion at the back of the head, but do not hold the tape too low across the forehead.

Owing to the nature of knitted fabric, elasticity being its chief characteristic, it is advisable to subtract 2 inches for an adult, varying to 1½ inches for a small child, from the actual head size. This prevents the beret from slipping down over the face.

A beret is knitted with a set of 4 needles, the same as used for mittens and socks. (See Chapter on Details on how to use a set of needles.)

To expedite instructions for the charting of a sample beret, the simplest measurement and stitch gauge are chosen, therefore, a head size of 22 inches is used and a stitch gauge of 6 stitches to the inch.

Plate LIII.

The head size is 22 inches. 22 inches — 2 inches = 20 inches multiplied by 6 stitches to the inch = 120 stitches, 40 stitches on each of the three needles.

Head band

For a beret the head band is generally narrow unless one wishes to wear the beret off the face with a wide band for a ribbon. For this beret the head band is ½ inch wide and may be knitted of ribbing of K.1, P.1, or K.2, P.2, or may be simply stockinette stitch, the same as the rest of the beret.

Increasing

6 increases are necessary in a complete round, increasing every other row. There are 120 stitches on the needles. 6 into 120 goes 20 times. Before the first round of the shaping is begun, it is advisable to knit one row marking with markers every 20 stitches.

NOTE. Arrange the markers so any increases do not have to be made at the ends of rows, keeping the markers on the needles throughout the knitting of the entire beret.

Now increase before the 6 markers every other row until the desired width of beret is reached. (Increase by knitting first in the front of the stitch and then in the back of the same stitch.)

How to Know When the Beret is Wide Enough

The size of the beret depends, of course, upon the needs of the wearer. This is where simple geometry is resorted to. The circumference of a circle is 3.1416 times the diameter, or, for our purpose, the circumference is approximately 3 times the diameter. Reversing the process, the diameter is approximately 1/3 of the circumference and it is the diameter of a beret which is measured for size.

The knitted head size in this case is 20 inches. That is 20 inches in circumference. Dividing this by 3, gives approximately 6½ inches in diameter. If a 10-inch beret is

$$20'' \div 3 = approx \ 6\frac{1}{2}''$$

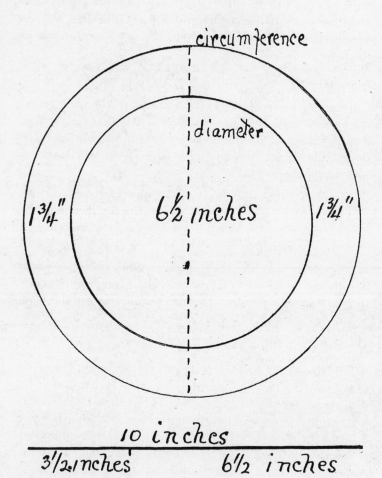

Diagram 113.

desired, as in this case, (see diagram) that means the increasing has to be continued until 10 inches — 6½ inches = 3½ inches, or 1¾ inches has to be increased on the outside of the head band. (Do not include the amount knitted for the head band when measuring and do not measure on the increases but on a row.)

Decreasing

First knit one inch even to give form to the beret. If this is not done, the beret will be 6 sided instead of round.

The decreasing is made before the markers every other row, by knitting 2 together, until it is 2 inches from the center of the beret (or until the diameter is 4 inches), at which time decrease every row until 2 stitches remain on each needle. These may either be woven together or drawn together with the yarn then the end may be fastened inside the beret.

FORMULA FOR BERETS

1. 2 inches for adult varying to 1½ inches for very small children, deducted from the head size for head band of beret to prevent slipping.

2. Size of head band × the stitch gauge = the number of stitches for the head band.

NOTE. The number of stitches must be divisible by 6.

3. Knit the band the desired width, then increase 6 times in the round, every other row.

4. Place markers where increases are to be made, and increase before them.

5. (a) The head size divided by 3 gives the approximate diameter of the head size.

   (b) The diameter of the finished beret — the diameter of the head size, divided by 2 = the amount to be increased. (See diagram 113.)

6. After increasing to the desired size of beret, knit 1 inch even, varying to ½ inch for small child, to give form to the beret.

7. Decrease before markers every other row until 2 inches from the center, at which time decrease every row until approximately 2 stitches remain on each of the three needles.

8. Weave together the remaining stitches or draw them together with yarn.

BOY'S CAP

Measurements

Head Size—20 inches

Materials

Knitting Worsted—3 ounces
1 set of #11 needles

Stitch gauge—6 stitches to the inch

NOTE. When knitting a cap with a turned back cuff, the actual head size is taken for measurement.

METHOD. Cast on 120 stitches, 40 stitches on each of the three needles. Work in ribbing of K.2, P.2, for 6 inches.

Decreasing

1. K.2 stitches, P.2 stitches together for one round, leaving a ribbing of K.2, P.1 which is worked for ½ inch.

2. K.2 stitches together, P.1 for 1 round, leaving a ribbing of K.1, P.1, which is worked for ½ inch.

3. K.1, P.3 stitches together for 1 round, leaving a ribbing of K.1, P.1, which is worked for ½ inch.

4. K.2 together all the way around.

5. Draw remaining stitches together and fasten off.

PLATE LIV. Boy's Cap.

SPORTS CAP

Plate LV.

Materials

Knitting worsted
1 set of #11 needles

METHOD. 120 stitches are necessary, 40 stitches on each of 3 needles. The cap is knitted of K.2, P.2 throughout, and is 10 inches long. The colors are arranged as follows: Blue stripe, 5 inches wide and each of the following in the order named are ½ inch wide. Orange, green, red, yellow, blue, orange, red, brown, yellow and blue.

Finishing

The top is arranged in 3 points, then overcast, and a huge pompom about 4 inches in diameter fastened in the center.

Variations in the completion of similarly knitted sports caps may be made:

1. Joined across the top and pompoms or tassels attached to the ends.
2. Left open at the top, a portion turned down and tassels for decoration.
3. A round piece knitted to fit inside the top (Made on the same principle as decreasing for a beret).

BABUSHKA OR BONNET

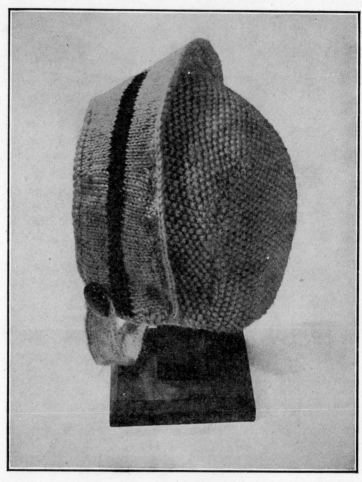

PLATE LVI.

These sports bonnets had their origin in Russia, from where the name originated. They make an ideal head covering for winter sports as they provide ample protection from the elements, and at the same time look very attractive, especially if worn with mittens and scarf to match.

An attractive one could be knitted of bright crimson with a black stripe, and mittens and a scarf to match would complete the ensemble.

Materials

    1 pair of #4 steel needles
    4 ply knitting worsted—almost 4 ounces

Stitch

    Single Moss for bonnet
    Stockinette stitch for poke

Stitch gauge—6 stitches to the inch

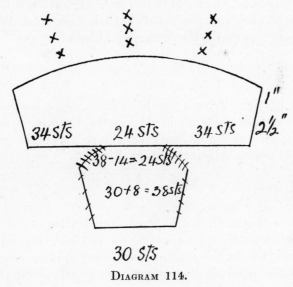

DIAGRAM 114.

Commence at the back allowing 5 inches of stitches for across the back of the neck. Cast on 30 stitches and work in single moss stitch, increasing at both ends every inch until 4 inches are knitted and 30 plus 8 stitches = 38 stitches are on the needle. Continue working in single moss stitch and decrease at both ends every 2nd row, 7 times, making 38 — 14 stitches = 24 stitches left. (Follow diagram.) Cast on 34 stitches on each side, making a total of 92 stitches and knit even for 2½ inches in single moss stitch.

Shaping of the Top of the Bonnet

Work in single moss stitch until 6 stitches from the end of the row. Turn, slip the first stitch, and knit until 6 stitches from the other end. Turn, slip the first stitch and again leave 6 more stitches not knitted at the end of the row. Turn, slip the first stitch and leave 6 more stitches at the other end. Continue in this manner, leaving 6 fewer stitches at each end until all the stitches are used. Work 1 inch even on all the 92 stitches and bind off.

Poke

Pick up the stitches around the front of the bonnet on the wrong side and work in stockinette stitch for 5 rows. Continue, increasing 3 times every 6th row, as in diagram, until the poke is 2½ inches wide. Bind off.

Finishing

Knit a strip 6 stitches wide and 5 inches long of stockinette stitch with a buttonhole at the end for strap under the chin. Sew to the side of the bonnet. Single crochet around the front of the bonnet, around the strap and across the back and also over the millinery wire around the poke to make it stand up. Sew on a button.

KERCHIEFS

One more use has been added to the triangular kerchief or scarf. Formerly they were arranged in many different ways around the throat to take the place of collars and add a softening effect or a touch of color. Today they are used in every conceivable manner as headdress. It is probable their origin was conceived from their use by the peasant women of Europe (just as the dirndl from Scandinavia has inspired a new vogue in dress) who at first knotted huge kerchiefs under their chins to prevent their hair from whipping their faces while they went about their many chores. Today these same kerchiefs have assumed a new elegance and are worn on every occasion from sports to evening wear. Often they are worn in the original peasant fashion, knotted under the chin.

Let me here give a word of warning about these kerchiefs. Before deciding to wear one, take a square of fabric about 21 inches square and fold from one corner to another to form a triangle. Arrange it on your head and look from all angles, in your mirror, to see if it is becoming to your particular type. Satisfied that one would be suitable, a knitted kerchief of brilliant colors for sportswear, or a dainty one of fine angora or silver or gold thread would add charm to your evening attire.

They are very simple to make.

METHOD. Use any combination of stitches that is suitable for the occasion on which the kerchief is to be worn. With the material, make a sample of the stitches to be used and take a stitch gauge. The base of the triangle, which is the longest side, is generally about 30 inches;

therefore multiply 30 inches by the stitch gauge, which will give you the number of stitches to cast on the needles and reduce at both ends by knitting two together at the beginning and end of every other row until the triangle, which is an isosceles, is knitted.

CHAPTER XVI

BABY CLOTHES

What one should consider when selecting baby clothes:

1. Lightness of weight
2. Large enough size to provide for rapid growth
3. Ease in dressing and undressing
4. Softness and smoothness, no irritating seams and fastenings
5. Simplicity in design and decoration
6. Suitability to the climate
7. Color, which should change with the baby's growth and interests

Let us here stop to consider what baby clothes may be knitted. There are bootees, stockings, soakers, bonnets, mittens, sweaters, sacques, wraps, blankets, spreads and even fine dresses.

The nature of knitted fabrics and the properties of wool, which were discussed in an earlier chapter, make soft woolen knitted garments ideally suited for baby clothes and there are, on the market, special baby yarns whose softness is surpassed by no other material.

SAMPLE BABY SWEATER

(Slip-On, Round Neck and Front Opening)

Materials

2 ounces of 3 ply Saxony
1 set of #3 bone needles

Stitch gauge—7 stitches to the inch

The measurements for the following sweater will fit an average sized baby up to six months old. As babies grow so rapidly, it seems a waste of time to knit garments so small they can be worn only a few weeks.

A few comparisons are noted at this point:

1. The width of the sweater is the same as the length of the sweater from the underarm.
2. The sleeve underarm length is a little over ½ the width of the sweater.
3. The back of the neck is a little less than ½ the width of the sweater.
4. It will also be noticed that the sweater is made in one piece and the shaping of the neck line follows the same principles by which children and adult neck lines are shaped.

Starting at the bottom of the back, the width is 8 inches, 8 inches × the stitch gauge = 8 × 7 stitches to the inch = 56 stitches. A short ribbing of 1½ inches of K.1, P.1 or single moss stitch, or popcorn stitch as a border is suitable, then knit even in stockinette stitch until 8 inches to the underarm is reached.

Sleeves

The underarm sleeve measurement is 5 inches, 1 inch of which is used for a cuff. If K.1, P.1 is used for the cuff, only 4 inches are added for the sleeve, the cuff of 1 inch of ribbing to be added later. If single moss or popcorn stitch is used, 5 inches of stitches are added at one time, 4 inches worked in stockinette stitch and 1 inch to match bottom of sweater, the cuff being knitted at the same time as the rest of the sleeve. 5 inches × 7 stitches to the inch = 35 stitches, 34 stitches, even number, cast on at each

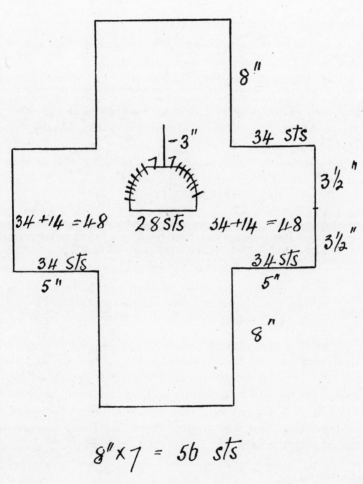

8″

34 sts

−3″

34 +14 =48   28 sts   34 +14 =48

3½ ″

3½ ″

34 sts   34 sts
5 ″   5 ″

8 ″

8″ × 7 = 56 sts

Diagram 115.

side for the sleeves, then knit even for 3½ inches, at which time the stitches for the back of the neck are cast off.

Neck—Round with Opening

4 inches of stitches allowed for the back of the neck. 4 inches × 7 stitches to the inch = 28 stitches.

Knit the 34 stitches for the sleeve plus 14 stitches. Place these on a stitch holder then bind off 28 stitches loosely for the back of the nec and knit to the bottom of the other sleeve. Work ½ inch even, at which time the shaping for the neck is begun.

28 stitches were bound off for the neck, i.e., 14 stitches at each side. Following the rule, add 1 stitch every other row 7 times, then 7 stitches all at once.

> NOTE. When making a slip-over sweater for a baby it must be remembered that a baby's head is large in proportion to the rest of his body, therefore sufficient room must be allowed for the head to pass through. It is advisable to make an opening in the front or across the shoulder, these being preferable to an opening at the back.

Start the opening for the front and at the same time continue knitting the sleeve until 3½ inches are knitted from the bind off for the neck, then bind off the 34 stitches added for the sleeve. Continue knitting the front until the opening is 3 inches long, then work the other side to correspond, and join the fronts. Work the front to correspond with the back.

Finishing

Sew the sides and sleeves together, being careful that the seams do not bind and there are no irritating joinings. The stitches may be picked up around the neck for a band, or one made of crochet.

NOTE. A coat sweater may be knitted on the same principle. Continue down one side of the front without joining, knitting a border to match the cuffs, then complete the second front to match.

A baby sacque may be knitted on the same principle, using a simple lace pattern if desired.

BABY COAT, BONNET AND BOOTEES
(6 MONTHS TO 1 YEAR)

PLATE LVII.

Materials

3 ounces of 2 ply baby yarn, either zephyr or saxony
2 ounces required for the coat
1 ounce for the bonnet and bootees
1 set of #3 needles

Pattern

Multiple of 13 stitches

1. * K.2 together, K.4, Y.0, K.1, Y.0, K.4, K.2 together repeat from *.
2. Purl.
3. Same as the first row.
4. Knit.

Pattern for the Yoke

Row 1. Knit.
   2. Purl.
   3. Knit.
   4. K.1, P.1.

NOTE. Stitches shown in the Chapter on Patterns.

METHOD. Cast on 91 stitches (7 patterns). Work 4 ridges (8 rows) in garter stitch, then change to lace pattern and work until the back measures 7 inches.

Shaping of Armhole

Bind off 4 stitches at the beginning of the next 2 rows, then knit 2 together at the beginning and end of every other row, 3 times, leaving 77 stitches.

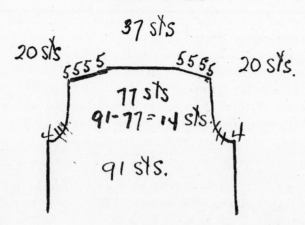

DIAGRAM 116.

Work the yoke in second pattern and continue until the armhole measures 4½ inches around.

Shaping of Shoulders

Bind off 5 stitches at the beginning of the next 8 rows, i.e., 20 stitches bound off for each shoulder, leaving 37 stitches for the back of the neck, which are bound off loosely.

Fronts

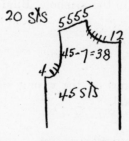

DIAGRAM 117.

Cast on 45 stitches (3 patterns and 6 stitches for the border of garter stitch).

Work the same as the back to the underarm, keeping 6 stitches at the front edge in garter stitch for border. Bind off 4 stitches for the underarm, then knit 2 together every other row 3 times. Change to second pattern and work until the armhole measures 3 inches around.

Neck

Bind off 12 stitches at the neck edge, then knit 2 together every other row, 6 times, and 20 stitches remain for the shoulder. Then bind off 5 stitches at the beginning of every other row at the armhole edge until all the stitches are bound off.

Work the other front to correspond making the border stitches and the shapings on the opposite side.

Sleeves

Cast on 36 stitches. Work ribbing of K.1, P.1 for 2 inches. Increase in every stitch making 72 stitches.

Work the sleeve in the second pattern until the underarm measures 6 inches.

Bind off 4 stitches at the beginning of the next 2 rows, then 2 stitches at the beginning of every row until the cap of the sleeve fits into the armhole. Bind off the remaining stitches.

Finishing

Overcast the seams on the wrong side, being sure the armholes do not bind.

BONNET

Cast on 91 stitches (7 patterns). Work 4 ridges in garter stitch. Knit 10 patterns. Cast off 31 stitches, knit 29 stitches, cast off the remaining 31 stitches. Join the yarn at the right hand side of the 29 stitches and work in garter stitch until the center piece measures the same as the bound off stitches on the sides. Sew the sides together, pick up the stitches along the back of the bonnet on the right side. Knit 2 together on the center 12 stitches, 6 times, then work ribbing of K.1, P.1 for 1½ inches. Bind off.

BOOTEES

Cast on 39 stitches. Work 2 ridges in garter stitch. Knit 5 patterns. Knit 2 rows in stockinette stitch. Make the beading for cord as follows:

K.1, * Y.O., K.2 together repeat from * for one row, then purl back, Knit 2 rows in stockinette stitch.

Divide the stitches into thirds, 13.13.13. Work 12 ridges (24 rows) of garter stitch on the center 13 stitches. Break the yarn and begin again on the 13 stitches at the left hand side. Pick up 12 stitches along the other side of the instep, knit across the 13 instep stitches, pick up 12 stitches along the other side and knit the remaining 13 stitches, making 63 stitches altogether.

Knit 8 ridges, then decrease to shape the bottom as follows: K.1, K.2 together then knit to the center 4 stitches of instep, K.2 together twice on these 4 stitches, knit to the last 3 stitches, then K.2 together, K.1, knit the second row. Repeat these 2 rows twice, then bind off and sew the sides and bottom together.

SOAKERS

(MEDIUM SIZE)

PLATE LVIII.

Soakers are a boon both to mothers and babies. As wool is absorbent, being capable of holding as much as 30% of its own weight of moisture without feeling wet to the touch, it does not feel cold and clammy even when very damp. How different from the rubber pants of former days, which afforded outer protection but often caused great discomfort and irritation!

It is not advisable to use yarn that is too coarse for soakers. The delicacy of a baby's skin warrants a fairly soft yarn even for this purpose, and besides, the soakers should not be too cumbersome. Because of constant washings, they should not be knitted too tight or they will become hard and matted, and if knitted too loose they won't serve their purpose. White is the only color to use for this purpose. There is no chance of the dye having any harmful effect upon the baby's skin.

Materials

   2 ounces of medium weight white yarn
   1 pair of #3 needles

Stitch gauge—6 stitches to the inch

These soakers are knitted in the form of a triangle, not shaped like small boys' pants. The position in which a small baby holds his legs makes this shape more desirable.

METHOD. Cast on 120 stitches, K.2, P.2 for ¾ of an inch, or 6 rows, then work a row for the beading as follows: * K.2, P.2, K.2, Y.O., P.2 together, repeat from * to the end of the row. Work 6 more rows of ribbing.

Change to garter stitch and decrease by knitting 2 together every other row at both ends. That is K.2, K.2 together, then continue knitting to the last 4 stitches of the row, then K.2 together, K.2 stitches. Continue decreasing every other row until all stitches are used.

Finishing

Sew the ends of the ribbing together. Fold so the point meets the seam of the ribbing, then sew the edges so almost half the space is left for the leg openings.

With a double strand of yarn crochet a chain about 30 inches long and draw this through the beading, then complete each end with a small tassel.

SHOULDERETTE

PLATE LIX.

Material

> 1 ounce of either 2 ply Saxony or some other fine baby yarn
> 1 set of #3 needles for cuff
> 1 set of #5 needles for pattern

Pattern

Multiple of 17 stitches

Row 1. K.2 together, K.2 together, K.2 together, Y.O., K.1, Y.O., K.1, Y.O., K.1, Y.O., K.1, Y.O., K.1, Y.O., K.2 together, K.2 together, K.2 together.

Row 2. Knit.

Row 3. Knit.

Row 4. Purl.

Repeat the 4 rows.

NOTE. Refer to Chapter on Stitches.

METHOD. With #3 needle, cast on 48 stitches and work in ribbing of K.2, P.2 for 2 inches. Increase to 59 stitches by increasing in every 4th stitch. Purl back. Change to larger needles and work in pattern, making a garter stitch border of 4 stitches at both ends. Knit in pattern until the length of work measures 15 inches. Knit every 4th and 5th stitch together, making 48 stitches for the cuff. Work the cuff to correspond with the other, that is K.2, P.2, for 2 inches, making the total length 17 inches.

Finishing

Sew the seams at the cuffs. Turn back a portion across the center to represent a collar and crochet a shell stitch border of * 5 double crochets in one stitch, skip 2 stitches, a single crochet in the next stitch, skip 2 stitches, repeat from * around the collar.

CHAPTER XVII

PATTERNS OR STITCHES

TEXTURE PATTERNS

For the following combinations of stitches the name of texture patterns has been suggested because of the differences in the surface quality made by the re-arranging of knit and purl stitches.

It will be noticed that these patterns have been graded so the understanding of different combinations of stitches will be simplified. It is advisable to knit as many of these as possible even if one does not intend to use the design immediately, as it will afford excellent practice.

A different number of stitches are required for the different combinations. This is generally referred to in the following manner: The pattern requires a multiple of so many stitches and possibly so many more for the beginning and end of the rows.

For example, a multiple of 5 plus 4 means that 5 stitches are necessary for each pattern and 4 extra stitches are required for the beginning and end of the rows; therefore if 8 patterns are desired, $8 \times 5 = 40$ stitches plus $4 = 44$ stitches. The actual pattern is designated by asterisks (*) at the beginning and the end of the pattern. Not all texture patterns have names; the more common are given:

1. *Moss or Seed Stitch*

PLATE LX.

A Multiple of 2 plus 1

* K.1, P.1, repeat from * to the last stitch, which is K.1.
Repeat this row for the desired number of rows.

2. *Double Moss*

Plate LXI.

A Multiple of 4

Row 1. * K.2, P.2, repeat from *.
Row 2. Repeat row 1.
Row 3. * P.2, K.2, repeat from *
Row 4. Repeat row 3.

Repeat the 4 rows for pattern.

3.

PLATE LXII.

A Multiple of 2

Row 1. All knit.

Row 2. All purl.

Row 3. All knit.

Row 4. * K.1, P.1, repeat from *.

Repeat the 4 rows for pattern.

4.

PLATE LXIII.

A Multiple of 4

Row 1. All knit.
Row 2. All purl.
Row 3. All knit.
Row 4. * K.3, P.1, repeat from *.

Repeat the 4 rows for pattern.

5.

PLATE LXIV.

A Multiple of 8 Plus 8

Row 1. All knit.

Row 2. All purl.

Row 3. * P.2, K.6, repeat from *.

Row 4. * P.6, K.2, repeat from *.

Row 5. All knit.

Row 6. All purl.

Row 7. K.4. * P. 2, K.6. * P.2, K.2.

Row 8. P.2, K.2. * P.6, K.2. * P.4.

Repeat the 8 rows for pattern.

6.

Plate LXV.

A Multiple of 6

Row 1. All knit.
Row 2. * P.4, K.2, repeat from *.

Repeat these 2 rows for pattern.

7. *Basket Weave*

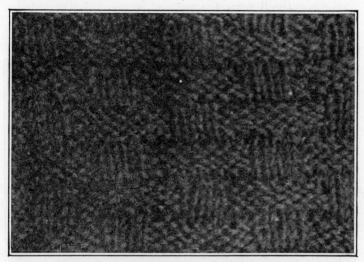

PLATE LXVI.

A Multiple of 10 Plus 3

Row 1. * K.3, P.7, repeat from * K.3.
Row 2. * P.3, K.7, repeat from * P.3.
Row 3. The same as row 1.
Row 4. Purl.
Row 5. P.5. * K.3, P.7, repeat from *. The last 8 stitches are K.3, P.5.

Row 6. K.5. * P.3, K.7, repeat from *. The last 8 stitches are P.3, K.5.

Row 7. Same as row 5.

Row 8. Purl.

Repeat the 8 rows for pattern.

8. *Diagonal Rib*

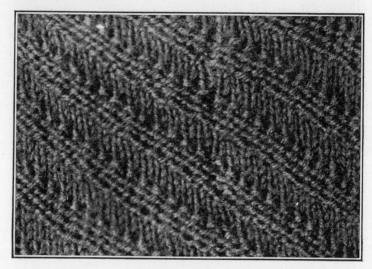

PLATE LXVII.

A Multiple of 8

Row 1. * K.4, P.4, repeat from *.

Row 2. P.1, * K.4, P.4, repeat from * K.4, P.3.

Row 3. K.2, * P.4, K.4, repeat from * P.4, K.2.

Row 4. P.3, * K.4, P.4, repeat from * K.4, P.1.

Row 5. * P.4, K.4, repeat from *.

Row 6. K.1, * P.4, K.4, repeat from * P.4, K.3.

Row 7. P.2, * K.4, P.4, repeat from * K. 4, P.2.

Row 8. K.3, * P.4, K.4, repeat from * P.4, K.1.

Repeat the 8 rows for pattern.

9. *A Block Pattern Which Naturally Forms Pleats*

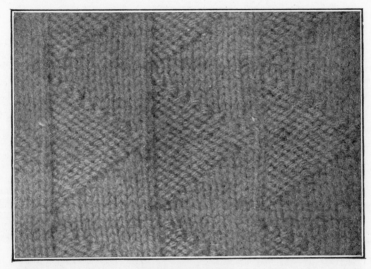

PLATE LXVIII.

A Multiple of 10

Row	*1.*	* K.1, P.9, *.	*Row*	*9.*	* K.9, P.1, *.
Row	*2.*	* K.8, P.2, *.	*Row*	*10.*	* K.2, P.8, *.
Row	*3.*	* K.3, P.7, *.	*Row*	*11.*	* K.7, P.3, *.
Row	*4.*	* K.6, P.4, *.	*Row*	*12.*	* K.4, P.6, *.
Row	*5.*	* K.5, P.5, *.	*Row*	*13.*	* K.5, P.5, *.
Row	*6.*	* K.4, P.6, *	*Row*	*14.*	* K.6, P.4, *.
Row	*7.*	* K.7, P.3, *.	*Row*	*15.*	* K.3, P.7, *.
Row	*8.*	* K.2, P.8, *.	*Row*	*16.*	* K.8, P.2, *.

Repeat these 16 rows for pattern.

10. *Different Forms of Cable Patterns*

a.

PLATE LXIX.

A Multiple of 5

Row 1. * K.1, P.1, K.2, P.1, repeat from *.

Row 2. * K.1, P.2, K.1, P.1, repeat from *.

Row 3. K.1, P.1, knit in the back of the second stitch on the left hand needle, leave the stitch on the needle, knit the first stitch on the left hand needle, take off both stitches, P.1, repeat from *.

Row 4. Same as row 2.

Repeat the 4 rows for pattern.

b.

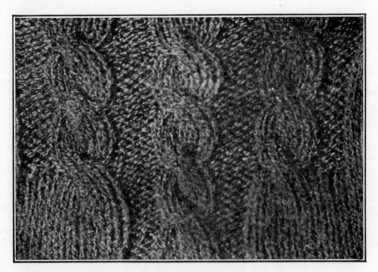

PLATE LXX.

A Multiple of 10 Plus 2

Row 1. K.1, * P.2, K.6, P.2, repeat from * K.1.

Row 2. P.1, * K.2, P.6, K.2, repeat from * P.1.

Repeat these 2 rows twice, making 6 rows.

Row 7. K.1, * P.2, with a double pointed needle slip the next 3 stitches onto it, from the back, knit the next 3 stitches, then knit the 3 stitches on the double pointed needle, P.2, repeat from * K.1.

Row 8. Same as the second.

Repeat the 8 rows for pattern.

c.

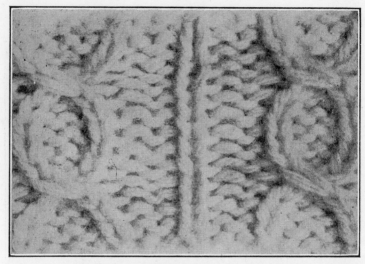

PLATE LXXI.

A Multiple of 10 Plus 1

Row 1. * K.1, P.2, K.1, P.3, K.1, P.2, repeat from * K.1.

Row 2. * P.1, K.2, P.1, K.3, P.1, K.2, repeat from * P.1.

Rows 3 and 4. Repeat first and second rows.

Row 5. K.1, * P.2, slip the next 4 stitches onto a double pointed needle, from the back, knit the next stitch, then slip 3 of the 4 stitches from the double pointed needle back to the left hand needle, place the double pointed needle in the front of the work, and purl the next 3 stitches, then knit the stitch on the double pointed needle. P. 2, K.1, repeat from *.

Row 6. * P.1, K.2, P.1, K.3, P.1, K.2, repeat from * P.1.

Repeat the 6 rows for the pattern.

d.

PLATE LXXII.

A Multiple of 21 Plus 5

Row 1. * K.5, P.2, K.12, P.2, repeat from * K.5.
Row 2. * P.5, K.2, P.12, K.2, repeat from * P.5.
Row 3. * K.5, P.2, slip the next 4 stitches onto a double pointed needle, keep at the back of the work, knit the next 4 stitches, then bring the first 4 stitches on the double pointed needle in front of the work, and knit the

next 4 stitches, then knit the 4 stitches from the double pointed needle, P.2, repeat from * K.5.

Row 4. Same as *Row 2.*

Row 5. Same as *Row 1.*

Repeat *Rows 4 and 5,* 2 more times, then repeat *Row 2* once.

Repeat the pattern from *Row 3.*

LACE PATTERNS OR STITCHES

As was explained in the chapter on lace blouses, yarn over is the foundation of all lace patterns. When knitting, this is made by bringing the yarn from the back of the work as though one were going to purl the next stitch, then knit the next stitch as usual. A yarn over when purling is made by taking the yarn over the needle to the back of the work and then to the front again. Y.O. is the abbreviation for yarn over.

1. *Fagoting Stitch*

PLATE LXXIII.

A Multiple of 2 Plus 2

K.1, * Y.O., K.2 together * K.1.

Repeat this row for the desired number of rows.

2. *Popcorn Stitch*

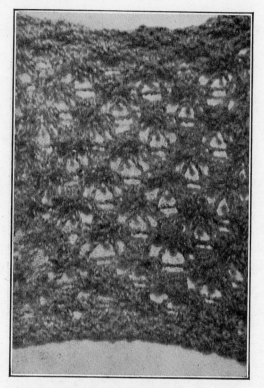

PLATE LXXIV.

A Multiple of 6

Row 1. All purl.

Row 2. * K.1, P.1, K.1 (all in one stitch) P.3 together, *.

Row 3. All purl.

Row 4. * P.3 together, K.1, P.1, K.1 (all in one stitch) *.

Repeat the 4 rows for pattern.

NOTE. The purl side is the right side of the work.

3. *Fern Stitch—Different Versions*

a.

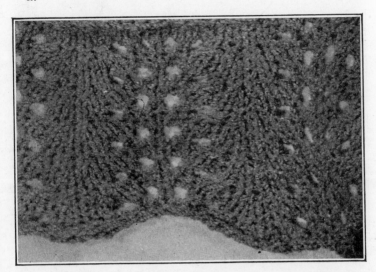

PLATE LXXV.

A Multiple of 11

Row 1. * K.2 tog., K.2 tog., Y.O., K.1, Y.O., K.1, Y.O., K.1, Y.O., K.2 tog., K.2 tog. *.
Row 2. All purl.
Row 3. All knit.
Row 4. All purl.

Repeat the 4 rows for pattern.

b.

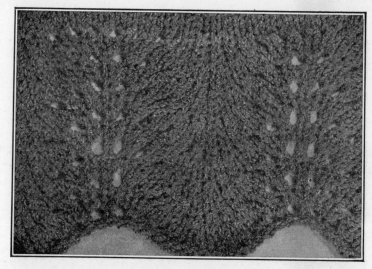

Plate LXXVI.

A Multiple of 17

Row 1. * K.2 tog., K.2 tog., K.2 tog., Y.O., K.1, Y.O., K.1, Y.O., K.1, Y.O., K.1, Y.O., K.1, Y.O., K.2 tog., K.2 tog., K.2 tog. *.

Row 2. All purl.

Row 3. All knit.

Row 4. All purl.

Repeat the 4 rows for pattern.

c.

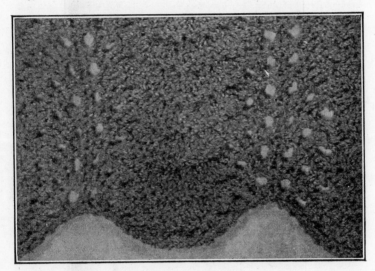

PLATE LXXVII.

This is the same as "b" (Plate LXXVI) with the exception of the *second row*, which is all knitted.

4. *Diamond Pattern*

PLATE LXXVIII.

A Multiple of 8 Plus 1

Row 1. K.2, * K.2 tog., Y.O., K.1, Y.O., K.2 tog., K.3, repeat from *, ending K.2 instead of K.3.

Row 2. All purl and all even rows.

Row 3. K.1, * K.2 tog., Y.O., K.3, Y.O., K.2 tog., K.1, repeat from *.

Row 5. K.2 tog., * Y.O., K.5, Y.O., slip 1, K.2 tog., P.S.S.O., repeat from * Y.O., K.2 tog., instead of slip 1, K.2 tog., P.S.S.O.

Row 7. K.1, * Y.O., K.2 tog., K.3, K.2 tog., Y.O., K.1, repeat from *.

Row 9. K.2, * Y.O., K.2 tog., K.1, K.2 tog., Y.O., K.3, repeat from * ending Y.O., K.2, instead of Y.O., K.3.

Row 11. K.3, * Y.O., slip 1, K.2 tog., P.S.S.O., Y.O., K.5, repeat from * ending Y.O., K.3, instead of Y.O., K.5.

Row 12. All purl.

Repeat the 12 rows for pattern.

5. *Leaf Pattern*

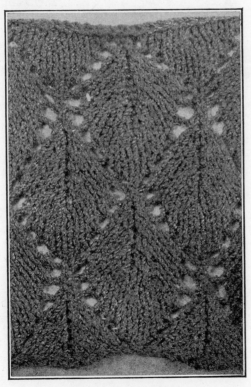

PLATE LXXIX.

A Multiple of 11 Plus 4

Row 1. K.2, * K.2 tog., K.3, Y.O., K.1, Y.O., K.3, slip 1, K.1, P.S.S.O., repeat from * K.2.

Row 2. All purl and all even rows.

Row 3. K.2, * K.2 tog., K.2, Y.O., K.3, Y.O., K.2, slip 1, K.1, P.S.S.O., repeat from * K.2.

Row 5. K.2, * K.2 tog., K.1, Y.O., K.5, Y.O., K.1, slip 1, K.1, P.S.S.O., repeat from * K.2.

Row 7. K.2, * K.2 tog., Y.O., K.7, Y.O., slip 1, K.1, P.S.S.O., * repeat from * K.2.

Row 9. K.1, K.2 tog., * Y.O., K.4, K.2 tog., K.3, Y.O., slip 1, K.1, P.S.S.O., repeat from * K.1 (*rows 9 to 18* have one stitch fewer across the row).

Row 11. K.2, * Y.O., K.3, slip 1, K.1, P.S.S.O., K.2 tog., K.3, Y.O., K.1, repeat from * Y.O, K.2.

Row 13. K.3, * Y.O., K.2, slip 1, K.1, P.S.S.O., K.2 tog., K.2, Y.O., K.3, repeat from *.

Row 15. K.4, * Y.O., K.1, slip 1, K.1, P.S.S.O., K.2 tog., K.1, Y.O., K.5, repeat from * Y.O., K.4.

Row 17. K.5, * Y.O., slip 1, K.1, P.S.S.O., K.2 tog., Y.O., K.7, repeat from * Y.O., K.5.

Row 19. K.6, * Y.O., slip 1, K.1, P.S.S.O., Y.O., K.4, K.2 tog., K.3, repeat from * Y.O., K.6.

Row 20. All purl.

Repeat the 20 rows for pattern.

6.

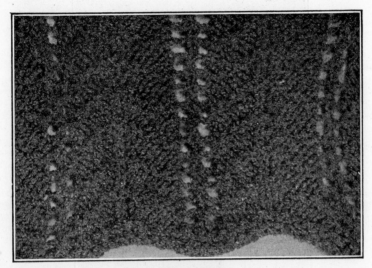

PLATE LXXX.

A Multiple of 13

Row 1. * K.2 tog., K.4, Y.O., K.1, Y.O., K.4, K.2 tog., repeat from *.

Row 2. All purl.

Row 3. The same as *row 1*.

Row 4. All knit.

Repeat the 4 rows for pattern.

7. *Marquise Pattern*

PLATE LXXXI.

A Multiple of 8

Row 1. * K.1, Y.O., K.2, slip 1, K.2 tog., P.S.S.O., K.2, Y.O., repeat from * increasing in the last stitch instead of Y.O.

Row 2. All purl.

Row 3. * K.2, Y.O., K.1, slip 1, K.2 tog., P.S.S.O., K.1, Y.O., K.1, repeat from *.

Row 4. All purl.

Row 5. * K.3, Y.O., slip 1, K.2 tog., P.S.S.O., Y.O., K.2, repeat from *.

Row 6. All purl.

Repeat the 6 rows for pattern.

8.

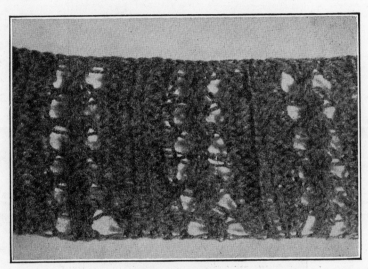

PLATE LXXXII.

A Multiple of 8

Row 1. * K.1, P.2, Y.O., K.3 tog., Y.O., P.2, repeat from *.

Row 2. * K.2, P.3, K.2, P.1, repeat from *.

Row 3. * K.1, P.2, K.3, P.2, repeat from *.

Row 4. * K.2, P.3, K.2, P.1, repeat from *.

Repeat the 4 rows for pattern.

9.

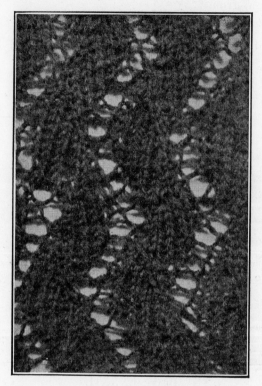

PLATE LXXXIII.

A Multiple of 6 Plus 2

Row 1. K.1, * K.4, K.2 tog., Y.O., repeat from * K.1.

Row 2. All purl and all even rows.

Row 3. K.1, * K.3, K.2 tog., K.1, Y.O., repeat from * K.1.

Row 5. K.1, * K.2, K.2 tog., K.2, Y.O., repeat from * K.1.

Row 7. K.1, * K.1, K.2 tog., K.3, Y.O., repeat from * K.1.

Row 9. K.1, * Y.O., K.2 tog., K.4, repeat from * K.1.

Row 11. K.1, * Y.O., slip 1, K.1, P.S.S.O., K.4, repeat from * K.1.

Row 13. K.1, * Y.O., K.1, slip 1, K.1, P.S.S.O., K.3, repeat from * K.1.

Row 15. K.1, * Y.O., K.2, slip 1, K.1, P.S.S.O., K.2, repeat from * K.1.

Row 17. K.1, * Y.O., K.3, slip 1, K.1, P.S.S.O., K.1, repeat from * K.1.

Row 19. K.1, * Y.O., slip 1, K.1, P.S.S.O., K.4, repeat from * K.1.

Row 20. All purl.

Repeat 20 rows for pattern.

CHAPTER XVIII

WHAT VOCATIONS ARE AVAILABLE IN THE KNITTING FIELD

THE greatest service one can render to one's community or to the country at large is to create some form of industry which will help to absorb those who are dependent upon it for a livelihood.

Let us follow along the trail in an explanatory way to discover, if possible, the opportunities in the field of knitting.

SPECIALIZED SALES PEOPLE

The sales person, to be successful, must know the product he or she is offering for sale. In the case of knitting appurtenances, such as yarns, needles, etc., it is not sufficient for the salesgirl waiting behind the counter to be an agreeable "yes" girl. "Yes, Madam, I think it is a beautiful color. Note how soft it is! It should knit up beautifully in a blouse or skirt," is not enough.

The successful salesgirl should have a knowledge of color and know why one shade is more suitable than another. She should know the different types and textures of yarns and which yarns are best suited for different purposes. Saxony, for instance, makes beautiful baby garments but one would scarcely suggest it for a child's sweater that is going to receive hard wear. Neither should one suggest worsted for a baby shoulderette. Fool's gold is attractive, but it makes for poor coinage.

A practical knowledge of knitting is a valuable asset

for any salesgirl in a large department store where art needlework is sold. She should also make herself acquainted with the workability of the yarns she is selling, what their average stitch gauges are, the different sizes of needles for obtaining the best results for the particular purpose for which the garment is being knitted.

Persons with creative and artistic ability might hope to graduate in time from a $15 a week sales job to the position of head buyer at $5,000 a year.

OWNING AND OPERATING ONE'S OWN BUSINESS

Not every one has the business acumen to establish successfully a business for oneself. But in the knitting field there is abundant opportunity for anyone who has. A knit shop is a sound venture providing one has the essential requisites to make it so. It is a clean business with that added touch of pride continually popping up through comprehensive effort.

Besides the knowledge required of the salesgirl, the operator of such a business should be able to give minute instructions, correct customer's mistakes, and chart any knitted garment or accessory from beginning to end. One should know how to buy yarns and needles intelligently. An adequate stock of each should be kept on hand but one should be careful not to overstock with slow moving numbers which are apt to tie up too much capital. Lack of attention to this important factor has brought many small stores into financial difficulties. The amount of stock to be carried depends largely upon the shopkeeper's proximity to her source of supply. Another essential point is knowing the correct amount of yarn to sell a customer for her requirements. One should not undersell unless she is able to supply more of the same dye lot and quality if needed. To oversell may mean taking back small amounts of unused yarn to litter shelves, or the inevitable alternative, having a dissatisfied customer.

The first commandment for the person launching into business by way of a knit shop should be, "Know Your Yarns." Do not be afraid to stock a staple brand because a large department store stocks that same brand. Your personality and courtesy to customers will soon overcome your difference in size. And the type of service you give will break down that "We will have to get it downtown," complex that you believe exists in your community.

KNITTING FOR A LIVELIHOOD OR PROFESSIONAL KNITTERS

There are countless numbers of women who are partial to hand-knitted garments and accessories, but either do not know how, or have not the time to knit them. Here is a field for the experienced knitter. But do not be misled, it is not so easy as all that. That Grandma, in her spare time and for her love and anxiety for your future economic welfare, taught you how to turn the heel of a sock, does not necessarily classify you as an experienced knitter.

Knitting has emerged from Grandma's heel-turning stage. It has taken on new style until today it is associated with modern art. The professional knitter must not only be a fast and expert knitter, she must be abreast of fashion, be alert to design and color. She must also be able to assume a reasonable responsibility for her work and be able to conform to the requirements of her clients. Professional knitting does not simply mean the following of directions as prescribed in some manual. An added touch of individuality or originality is a necessary adjunct.

THIS LEADS TO ANOTHER PHASE OF OPPORTUNITY FOR AN
EXPERIENCED KNITTER

There is the question of executing orders taken through large department stores for hand-knitted dresses, sweaters and sundry articles that they cannot supply through regular channels. There are many such orders. This, then, paves the way for the alert and capable experienced knitter to form a connection with such stores in a sort of interdepartmental way, in charge of her own staff. Such a connection offers opportunity for expression of personality to a clientèle already established by the store's reputation.

NEWSPAPER AND MAGAZINE ARTICLES

Articles dealing with hand-knitted garments and accessories are always welcomed by women's periodicals and the women's pages of the press.

True, there are many such articles written today, but many of them are from manufacturers or dealers in yarn, whose main objective is the sale of their product. This is deplorable, because inadequate or misinterpreted instructions often mislead the knitter. It is generally after one has progressed to a considerable degree that trouble manifests itself. What is the result? Complete discouragement from having to undo hours of labor, and the breaking down of morale and confidence in one's own creative ability.

Such articles should be written by persons who can comprehendingly answer all questions pertaining to knitting as an art. This field could easily develop into a sort of service press which would be highly beneficial to knitter, periodical or newspaper alike.

WRITING INSTRUCTIONS

Yarn manufacturers are always receptive to women who are capable of writing instructions for their manuals.

CREATING AND DESIGNING HAND-KNITTED GARMENTS AND ACCESSORIES

This field offers unlimited possibilities. It is simple enough, after someone has created, to sit down and copy. And that is precisely what we women of America have been doing. To substantiate this statement, look at the advertising columns of our daily newspapers, or at the pages of the many fashion periodicals. "By So and So, Paris." "Copied from the original by So and So, London." "Imported from England," from Scotland, Sweden, Norway, Czecho-Slovakia and a hundred other places.

Are we to sit back and proclaim these people of the old world superior in creative ability? The era of allowing others to guide us through the hallways of chic and smartness should be over. What we must do is supplant the words, "Imported from," with "Accepted by." Let our star of creative ability shine in the salons of Paris, London and other smart centers of the world. No women the world over wear clothes with more ease and grace than do the women of America. Then why not create and design the clothes and accessories we wear? The demand for such home creation is here, standing like an open door waiting to receive countless numbers of women with initiative and creative ability in the knitting field.

Nor is this field limited to women's apparel. It comprises every line of hand-knitted article from milady's wardrobe to infant's wear, shawls, spreads, afghans and every knitted accessory such as mittens, gloves, socks, caps and hats of all descriptions.

DESIGNING MACHINE-KNITTED GARMENTS

There has existed until this last year or two, an urgent need for improvement in design of machine-knitted garments. Serviceability is not enough. Warmth is not the only factor. There must be style, comfort and conformity of shape. It is simple to knit two straight pieces of fabric, sew them together, knit two more straight pieces for sleeves and call it a sweater. Until the perfection of the modern knitting machine was reached, that is substantially what the wearer of machine-knitted garments was made to endure. The fit of the garment was left to the elasticity of the yarn. Once these garments had been washed, they either hung like gunnysacks from the shoulders or shrank to the tightness of a straight-jacket.

This is no longer a necessary fault with the machine-made product. The machines are scientifically engineered to produce the finished article with design and form. However, design and form must first originate by hand. Machines are not supposed to know the amount of suffering a child must endure or the irritation caused by a pair of panties drawn tightly up into the crotch with only the stretch of the wool to offer surcease from strangulation. Nor can they know about the too-tight armhole, the uncomfortable neckband.

Knitting to form, so that the garment sits easily and comfortably at all times, is essential; therefore one must realize the necessity for design of such articles before the machine can produce them. The correctly designed article will hold its shape at all times—whether it be hand or machine-knitted—if the material itself is of such quality to make this possible.

Designers of machine-knitted garments are in demand, but they should be able to offer a touch of originality to make their efforts outstanding.

BLOCKING AND REPAIRING HAND-KNITTED GARMENTS

Blocking and repairing hand-knitted garments is an art in itself. It is a branch of garment care that the average dry cleaner has not thoroughly mastered. With the ever-mounting volume of hand-knitted garments, this offers an opportunity for one to build a clean, comfortable business of one's own.

TEACHERS

Lastly, we have the extreme necessity for trained teachers who are thoroughly skilled and who understand the many possibilities of knitting as it should be taught today, its educational advantages and its opportunities in the field of vocations.

These include instructresses in stores, teachers for recreation departments, for schools, for community colleges, for universities and for occupational therapy.

INDEX